Get the eBook FREE!

(PDF, ePub, Kindle, and liveBook all included)

We believe that once you buy a book from us, you should be
able to read it in any format we have available. To get electronic
versions of this book at no additional cost to you, purchase and
then register this book at the Manning website.

Go to https://www.manning.com/freebook and follow the
instructions to complete your pBook registration.

That's it!
Thanks from Manning!

ASP.NET Core Security

ASP.NET Core
Security

CHRISTIAN WENZ

MANNING
SHELTER ISLAND

For online information and ordering of this and other Manning books, please visit
www.manning.com. The publisher offers discounts on this book when ordered in quantity.
For more information, please contact

    Special Sales Department
    Manning Publications Co.
    20 Baldwin Road
    PO Box 761
    Shelter Island, NY 11964
    Email: orders@manning.com

Manning Publications Co.
20 Baldwin Road
PO Box 761
Shelter Island, NY 11964

Development editor:	Doug Rudder
Technical development editor:	Ben McNamara
Review editor:	Adriana Sabo
Production editor:	Andy Marinkovich
Copy editor:	Carrie Andrews
Proofreader:	Melody Dolab
Technical proofreader:	Srihari Sridharan
Typesetter and cover designer:	Marija Tudor

ISBN 9781633439986
Printed in the United States of America

To HMS.

brief contents

contents

I still remember the first time I was exposed to the topic of web application security, although I did not realize the impact at that time. Back around 1997, I was creating web applications (or, rather, websites, back then), but hosting services were really expensive. For one of my projects, the only option I could afford was one where I was allowed to create just one page (!), and I had to use the hosting provider's tooling for that—no custom HTML or CSS was possible. I had plenty of free space available on a free hosting service but could not use my own domain there; rather, I used something like http://home.someprovider.com/mysite.

One of the very few features available to me was to set the keywords of the page (back in the day, search engines actually parsed that information). If I was using "web application security, hacking," for instance, this would be turned into the following HTML markup:

```
<meta name="keywords" content="web application security, hacking">
```

After some experimenting, I found that I could try the following "keyword":

```
"><meta http-equiv="refresh" content="0;
    url=http://home.someprovider.com/mysite"><"
```

It turned out that the provider was putting this data verbatim into the <meta> tag, leading to this result (formatted for legibility, with my input in bold):

```
<meta name="keywords" content="">
<meta http-equiv="refresh" content="0;
    url=http://home.someprovider.com/mysite">
<"">
```

So I injected another <meta> tag that redirected the browser to my actual site, hosted for free somewhere else.

It took a while until I understood the implications of what I had found—it was possible to inject arbitrary content on that page. My "attack" was harmless, but it would also have been possible to add other, more malicious markup. This sparked my interest in web application security, and I haven't looked back since. I have audited countless web applications, worked with customers before or after an audit, taught developers to write secure web applications, spoken at conferences on three continents about web application security, and tried my best to make the applications I was responsible for as safe as possible. In 2004, I was awarded a Microsoft MVP (Most Valuable Professional) award for ASP.NET for the first time, and I've followed security APIs, gotchas, and concerns in that framework very closely over the years.

I had considered writing a book on the experience and knowledge I have gained over the last 25 years, but the timing was never right. In mid-2021, it suddenly was, and I started a monthslong journey to condense everything I know and consider important into the book you are about to read.

In my experience, just knowing countermeasures against certain threats is not good enough. Developers need to understand how attacks work—it's easier to defend against things you have already seen. That's why many of the chapters will first show the attack and then explain how to prevent it. Apart from making the content more accessible that way, it's also fun—we see how things can be broken and call this work!

As the title suggests, *ASP.NET Core Security* is based on ASP.NET Core, which includes both Razor Pages and ASP.NET Core MVC. The book also covers Microsoft's third web application framework, Blazor, where it's feasible. All the examples in the book use C# and are based on .NET 6 (and are expected to still be valid for many versions to come).

acknowledgments

Many people who were involved in getting this book ready for you to enjoy are mentioned on the copyright page (rightfully so!), and there are many others who helped and contributed along the way.

I am indebted to the roster of reviewers who provided useful comments at various stages of the book's development, as did the readers of the Manning Early Access Program (MEAP) edition. To all the reviewers, Al Pezewski, Billy Miguel Vanegas, Daniel Vásquez, Darren Gillis, David Paccoud, Dennis Hayes Djordje, Dorogoy Dmitry Sergevich, Doyle Turner, Emmanouil Chardalas, Guy Langston, Harry Polder, Jedidja Bourgeois, Joe Cuevas, Jose Luis Perez, Marcin Sęk, Marek Petak, Markus Wolff, Matthew Harvell, Michael Holmes, Milos Todorovic, Nick McGinness, Nik Rimington, Onofrei George, Paul Brown, Richard Vaughan, Ron Lease, Samuel Bosch, Stanley Anozie, Sumit K. Singh, Tom Gueth, Viorel-Marian Moisei, and Wayne Mather, thank you for your input and for helping to improve this book.

Several trusted colleagues and friends also gave invaluable feedback and made the book so much better. Thank you all for your insights and support!

Special thanks to Doug Rudder, my developmental editor, who not only kept the project on track, but also caught me every time I cut corners, further improving the book.

about this book

The title of the book says it all: it covers security for ASP.NET Core applications, so it details various threats and risks for web applications based on Microsoft's .NET technology. I believe in the "show, don't tell" principle, so you will see not only APIs and countermeasures, but also how an attack takes place. Real-world incidents will serve as the basis for many of the chapters.

Who should read this book?

You should understand the basics of .NET and be proficient with at least one of the web application options of ASP.NET Core (Razor Pages or MVC/Web API). If you are comfortable with HTML and CSS, as in "I understand it when I see it," even better. At least some shallow experience with JavaScript is helpful in some of the chapters. The book will use C# as the language of choice, so this is another prerequisite for you to get the most out of *ASP.NET Core Security*.

How this book is organized: a roadmap

The book is split into 5 parts with a total of 16 chapters. Part 1 of the book sets the stage for the content to come:

- Chapter 1 discusses why web application security is important and which ASP.NET Core options exist, as well as how they may be affected. You will also receive a quick refresher on the project options ASP.NET Core provides.

Part 2 shows the most common attacks against web applications and how to defend against them:

- Chapter 2 covers cross-site scripting (XSS), a very widespread attack that is usually based on injecting malicious JavaScript code. The example from the preface, where HTML was injected, also falls into this category.

- Chapter 3 discusses several ways to attack session management and how to make sessions more secure. This includes features introduced in modern web browsers.
- Chapter 4 covers cross-site request forgery (CSRF), a very dangerous attack that can be mitigated both with built-in ASP.NET Core features and with security mechanisms in recent browsers.
- Chapter 5 describes the potential effects of unvalidated data and what ASP.NET Core brings to the table. This includes model validation, which is both convenient and powerful.
- Chapter 6 covers SQL injection, a really old attack that is rare in the ASP.NET Core world due to easy-to-use countermeasures and the rise of OR mappers such as Entity Framework Core.

Part 3 deals with secure data storage:

- Chapter 7 covers storing secrets such as tokens. One option is to use encryption; another is to use select cloud offerings.
- Chapter 8 discusses handling passwords and how to securely store them. Actually, passwords should not be stored at all, but their hashes should.

Part 4 covers various security-related configuration options:

- Chapter 9 details several HTTP headers supported in modern web browsers that add an extra layer of security to an application. The chapter also discusses how to prevent revealing HTTP headers from being sent to the client.
- Chapter 10 provides an introduction to error handling for an ASP.NET Core application, including best practices.
- Chapter 11 covers two topics that are different but somewhat related: logging can make sure that diagnostic information about a site is stored for later retrieval, and health checks provide a mechanism for surveillance of the availability of a site and its services.

Part 5 covers authentication and authorization for ASP.NET Core applications:

- Chapter 12 provides an introduction to ASP.NET Core Identity, making it easy to add user management and authentication to a site.
- Chapter 13 describes securing APIs and single-page applications (SPAs) using a token-based solution. The chapter also covers OAuth and OpenID Connect from an ASP.NET Core perspective.

Part 6 covers several aspects that are part of a security process:

- Chapter 14 discusses how to make sure dependencies are secure, including various auditing tools.
- Chapter 15 focuses on audit tools that can help find vulnerabilities in web applications.

- Chapter 16 covers the OWASP Top 10, a regularly updated list of the top ten security risks for web applications, and how they are covered in this book.

Most of the chapters are independent of each other, but there are several cross-references where applicable.

About the code

This book contains many examples of source code, both in numbered listings and inline with normal text. In both cases, source code is formatted in a `fixed-width font like this` to separate it from ordinary text. In some cases, the original source code has been reformatted. I've added line breaks and reworked indentation to accommodate the available page space in the book. In rare cases, even this wasn't enough, and listings include line-continuation markers (➥). Additionally, comments in the source code have often been removed from the listings when the code is described in the text. Code annotations accompany many of the listings, highlighting important concepts.

Source code is available for chapters 1 through 13 of this book. A .NET solution called `AspNetCoreSecurity` will contain several ASP.NET Core projects (in chapter 13, there's a second solution). Depending on the chapter, the code shown will be in one or several of those projects. All source code was tested with ASP.NET Core and .NET 6. The IDE of choice was Visual Studio 2022, but the code, of course, also works with other options such as Visual Studio Code and Rider. Please always make sure you read the full chapter before trying or using the code. In several instances, code is intentionally vulnerable to demonstrate an attack. You can download the source code from the publisher's website at www.manning.com/books/asp-net-core-security.

liveBook discussion forum

Purchase of *ASP.NET Core Security* includes free access to liveBook, Manning's online reading platform. Using liveBook's exclusive discussion features, you can attach comments to the book globally or to specific sections or paragraphs. It's a snap to make notes for yourself, ask and answer technical questions, and receive help from the author and other users. To access the forum, go to https://livebook.manning.com/book/asp-net-core-security/discussion. You can also learn more about Manning's forums and the rules of conduct at https://livebook.manning.com/discussion.

Manning's commitment to our readers is to provide a venue where a meaningful dialogue between individual readers and between readers and the author can take place. It is not a commitment to any specific amount of participation on the part of the author, whose contribution to the forum remains voluntary (and unpaid). We suggest you try asking the author some challenging questions lest his interest stray! The forum and the archives of previous discussions will be accessible from the publisher's website for as long as the book is in print.

about the author

 **CHRISTIAN WENZ** is a web pioneer, technology specialist, and entrepreneur. Since 1999, he has written close to 150 books on web technologies and related topics, which have been translated into ten languages. At his day job, he consults for enterprises on digitization and Industry 4.0. A fixture at international developer conferences, he has presented on three continents. Christian has been an MVP for ASP.NET since 2004, is the lead author of the official PHP certification, and sporadically contributes to OSS projects. He holds university degrees in computer science and business informatics and is a two-time recipient of a Knuth reward check.

about the cover illustration

The figure on the cover of *ASP.NET Core Security* is "Venitienne," or "Venetian (woman)," taken from a collection by Jacques Grasset de Saint-Sauveur, published in 1797. Each illustration is finely drawn and colored by hand.

In those days, it was easy to identify where people lived and what their trade or station in life was just by their dress. Manning celebrates the inventiveness and initiative of the computer business with book covers based on the rich diversity of regional culture centuries ago, brought back to life by pictures from collections such as this one.

Part 1

First steps

No week passes without some high-profile internet security incident—data leaking to the public, popular code libraries receiving updates with malware, a new ransomware being passed around, and websites being exposed to security vulnerabilities. Many of the happenings you read about in IT news were made possible by bugs in code. Since this book is based on ASP.NET Core, chapter 1 will unveil web application options that technology provides and will analyze where attacks may happen. We will build the "mental model" for the remainder of the book.

On web application security

1

This chapter covers

- Learning why web application security is important
- Using ASP.NET Core to create web applications and APIs
- Identifying why certain parts of an application are at risk
- Exploring what to expect from this book

Nine out of ten web applications have security vulnerabilities. This is the rather frightening conclusion of a study released in 2020 by Positive Technologies (http://mng.bz/mOj2), a provider of various security solutions. Obviously, such studies can often be biased toward the business model of those who conduct them, but several other studies from previous years yielded similar outcomes. Here's a report about one study from as far back as 2009: http://mng.bz/5Qo1.

The authors of the study also found that about four out of five web application vulnerabilities are part of the code, instead of, say, the server configuration. From this, we can deduce two trends:

- The major security risk for web applications lies in their code.
- The problem is industry-wide, and the situation does not seem to be getting better.

Often, a lack of security does not immediately show—until it's too late and a web application has been successfully hacked. It is therefore mandatory to make web application security a top priority and to use security best practices from the very beginning of a project.

Most security risks for web applications lie in the way web browsers, HTTP, database servers, and other "web aspects" work; therefore, these risks are technology-agnostic. Here's one example of this: in theory, injecting JavaScript into a website works independently of the server language or framework being used. In practice, there are the following differences:

1 Some languages and frameworks have built-in countermeasures that help prevent common attacks without any extra effort during development.
2 The functions, methods, and APIs used to defend against certain attacks and risks are naturally named differently in technologies and frameworks.

Therefore, a book on web application security will need to present and describe common attacks, in a more or less general fashion, and will then need to introduce countermeasures that are tied to a certain technology. The stack we will be using in this book is Microsoft's .NET; since we are talking about web applications, its web framework, ASP.NET Core, will be the focus. The book was written with .NET 6 and ASP.NET Core 6 but is expected to be upward-compatible with newer versions.

1.1 ASP.NET Core: History and options

ASP.NET has a long history that is tied to that of .NET, which was first released as a beta in 2001 and as a final version 1.0 in early 2002. Back then, the software package was called ".NET Framework" and contained a server web application framework called ASP.NET (the first three letters were carried over from the previous Microsoft web technology ASP, which was short for "Active Server Pages"). Along with .NET Framework came a new programming language, C#, which will be used throughout this book, although other options exist (Visual Basic for .NET, or F#, a functional language).

1.1.1 ASP.NET Core version history

ASP.NET and .NET evolved over the years but are not specifically covered in this book. That may come as a surprise, especially given the book title, but in the 2010s, Microsoft worked on a new evolution of .NET that culminated in the release of .NET Core 1.0 in mid-2016. This new version of .NET was open source, was more or less platform-agnostic, and was not tied to Windows any longer. The word *Core* was used to avoid confusion with .NET, especially with version numbers. Whether that worked is a different discussion, but to add to the confusion, Microsoft dropped *Core* when .NET reached version 5.0. The reason: the latest, and probably final, version of the .NET Framework and of ASP.NET is 4.8, so there won't be .NET Framework 5; thus, ".NET 5" clearly means the new evolution of .NET.

It is a bit more complicated with ASP.NET, though. The MVC (model-view-controller) framework, ASP.NET MVC, has its own version numbers. The latest release of the ASP.NET MVC NuGet package for the .NET Framework is 5.2.8 (http://mng.bz/2nE0), so "ASP.NET 5" could actually mean three things:

- ASP.NET MVC 5 (based on the .NET Framework)
- ASP.NET Core 5 (based on .NET 5, formerly known as .NET Core)
- ASP.NET as part of .NET 5, which was the previous project name of what later became .NET Core 1.0

I think we can agree that it did make sense to leave the *Core* suffix to make the product name explicit, so *ASP.NET Core* it is—for now. You don't have to be a prophet to predict that *Core* will likely be dropped at some point in the future. But for now, if there's *Core* in the name, we are talking about a current version of Microsoft's web framework, not a legacy one. This book is based on .NET 6, where *Core* is still present.

1.1.2   *MVC*

The architectural pattern "model-view-controller" (MVC) was invented in the 1970s and originated in GUI applications, yet became very popular for web applications. Creating HTML and CSS for a web page's looks is an entirely different skill than implementing a server backend. Therefore, splitting up the UI from the logic makes sense, and MVC is one of the options available. Tailored to a web application, MVC basically works like this (figure 1.1):

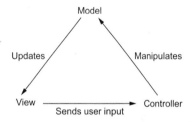

Figure 1.1   How model-view-controller works

- A controller accepts user input (in the case of a web application, data in an HTTP request).
- The controller receives and manipulates a model (often, data from a database) and then assigns this model to a view (usually an HTML page).
- The client receives the view and may use it to create a new request.

In ASP.NET MVC, these components are commonly represented as follows (since ASP.NET MVC is highly configurable, many details may be changed, but we describe the default out-of-the-box behavior):

- The controller is a C# class. Requests are mapped to "action methods," essentially public C# methods.
- The model is typically a C# object or class, often filled with database content (but not necessarily a 1:1 mapping). Microsoft samples routinely rely on Entity Framework Core, Microsoft's object-relational mapper (OR mapper, or ORM),

but this is certainly not mandatory. The controller accesses this model, may manipulate it, and then provides it to the view, if applicable.

- The view is essentially an HTML page with some extra markup to bind values from the model, or to execute code. Since we are using C#, those HTML pages have the *.cshtml* extension. The Razor view engine allows inclusion of C# code in these files, using the @ special character. The files are compiled so that the C# code may be run; the browser, of course, receives the resulting HTML.

When creating a new project in Visual Studio, the framework option you pick will set the technological standard for the app. Figure 1.2 shows some of the available project templates. Note that the fourth option, ASP.NET Core Web App (Model-View-Controller), also offers to include Web API, since they are so similar from a code point of view.

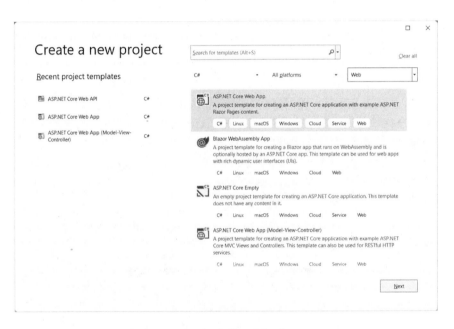

Figure 1.2   Creating a new web application in Visual Studio

Let's look at the main elements of a simple sample application. The following listing shows the controller.

Listing 1.1   The controller of a simple MVC application

```
using Microsoft.AspNetCore.Mvc;

namespace AspNetCoreSecurity.MvcSamples.Controllers
{
```

```
public class HomeController : Controller
{
    public IActionResult Index()                    ◁─┐ Shows the action
    {                                                  │ method within
        var outcome = new Random().Next(1, 7);

        var roll = new DiceRoll(outcome);

        return View(roll);        ◁─┐ Sends the dice roll result to the
    }                               │ view, which is returned to the client
}

public record DiceRoll(int outcome);
}
```

The HomeController class implements the Index() action method, which returns a
view with the result of a dice roll. The DiceRoll type is defined in the same file,
purely for simplicity. This view is shown in the next listing.

Listing 1.2   The view of a simple MVC application

```
@model AspNetCoreSecurity.MvcSamples.Controllers.DiceRoll   ◁─┐ Defines the type of
@{                                                             │ the page's model
    Layout = null;
}

<!DOCTYPE html>
<html lang="en">
<head>
    <meta charset="utf-8" />
    <meta name="viewport" content="width=device-width, initial-scale=1.0" />
    <title>Dice Roll - MVC</title>
</head>
<body>
    <h1>Dice Roll: @Model?.outcome</h1>   ◁─┐ Outputs the dice roll
</body>                                      │ outcome from the model
</html>
```

In the view, the outcome of the dice roll, a property named outcome, is shown in an
<h1> element.

1.1.3   Razor Pages

Remember the Razor view engine from the previous section? The simple yet effective
syntax was elevated to have its own approach to web development under the ASP.NET
Core umbrella.

Razor Pages are essentially HTML pages with the *.cshtml* file extension that support
the Razor syntax. In contrast to the MVC framework, there is no need for a controller.
All the code responsible for retrieving the view and handling user input is now part of
the page. For simpler scenarios, this works really well and removes some complexity
that is inherent to MVC. The following listing shows the page model of a simple sample application.

Listing 1.3   The page model of a simple application

```
using Microsoft.AspNetCore.Mvc.RazorPages;

namespace AspNetCoreSecurity.RazorSamples
{
    public class IndexModel : PageModel
    {
        public void OnGet()                           ◁─┐  Method is called whenever a page
        {                                                  is requested via HTTP GET
            var outcome = new Random().Next(1, 7);

            Roll = new DiceRoll(outcome);
        }                                                  This is the property that will
        public DiceRoll? Roll { get; set; }    ◁─┘        be used by the Razor Page.

        public record DiceRoll(int outcome);
    }
}
```

This time, we do not have a controller but rather a model class that (digitally) rolls the dice upon page load. The model, in turn, is tied to a view, which is shown in the next listing.

Listing 1.4   The Razor Page of a simple application

```
@page
@model IndexModel        ◁─┐  References the page
                             model class
<!DOCTYPE html>
<html lang="en">
<head>
    <meta charset="utf-8" />
    <meta name="viewport"
    content="width=device-width, initial-scale=1.0" />
    <title>Dice Roll - MVC</title>
</head>
<body>
    <h1>Dice Roll: @Model?.Roll?.outcome</h1>    ◁─┐  Outputs the property
</body>                                               from the model
</html>
```

The Razor view looks almost identical to the one from the MVC sample application (listing 1.2). The outcome is shown in the heading of the page.

1.1.4   Web API

With ASP.NET Web API, Microsoft provides a framework to, well, implement RESTful APIs. It is rather trivial to do a custom implementation of API endpoints—just pull data from a database, and then convert it into JSON or XML and return it. However, with the Web API framework, some of the heavy lifting is done for you:

- Depending on the value of the Accept HTTP request header, the correct format (e.g., JSON or XML) is used.

- Correct formatting of error messages and exceptions.
- An easy way to return the correct HTTP status code.
- API versioning based on HTTP headers, path components, or query strings.

From a development perspective, Web API works similarly to ASP.NET MVC; only a few base classes are different (and it's usually faster, since no Razor Pages are involved). But essentially you are working with a class that looks just like a controller and methods that behave—and look—like MVC action methods. The following listing shows the Web API controller of a trivial sample application.

Listing 1.5 The controller of a simple Web API application

```
using Microsoft.AspNetCore.Mvc;

namespace AspNetCoreSecurity.WebApiSamples.Controllers
{
    [ApiController]
    [Route("[controller]")]
    public class DiceRollController : ControllerBase
    {
        [HttpGet]
        public DiceRoll Get()                          ⊲──────  Depending on the configuration,
        {                                                        method is called when a GET
            var outcome = new Random().Next(1, 7);               request to /DiceRoll is used

            var roll = new DiceRoll(outcome);

            return roll;     ⊲──  Return value is automatically
        }                        converted to (for instance) JSON
    }

    public record DiceRoll(int outcome);
}
```

The controller is a class with a method that is called `Get()` and will be executed when a GET request is sent to the associated endpoint. The return data is automatically converted to JSON.

NOTE .NET 6 introduced "minimal APIs," where less code is used—there's not even a controller class necessary. There is no functional difference, though, and no additional (or omitted) security implications.

SignalR

The most commonly used approach to call APIs from the client is to use JavaScript as the programming language and HTTP as the application protocol. However, from a performance point of view, HTTP is not really optimized for speed. All modern browsers do support a technology called WebSocket, a protocol standardized as far back as 2011 (https://tools.ietf.org/html/rfc6455). It can work over HTTP (and

> **(continued)**
>
> is therefore compatible with existing setups and firewall rules), but does support binary data and works in a bidirectional fashion.
>
> With ASP.NET SignalR (https://signalr.net/), Microsoft offers an open source library that provides a server API to provide an endpoint and a JavaScript component to communicate with those endpoints. WebSockets are used as the protocol of choice, but if, say, an older browser does not support it, there is an automatic fallback to alternate means such as HTTP requests.

1.1.5   *Blazor*

Remember ASP.NET Web Forms, Microsoft's attempt to motivate developers who dislike web technologies to still be able to create web applications? That ship has more or less sailed, but with Blazor, Microsoft tries a different approach, this time especially catering to developers who are not very fond of JavaScript. All modern browsers support the WebAssembly standard, which defines a binary format for code that runs in the browser. With Blazor, Microsoft compiles C# code down to WebAssembly, which the browser can then execute. Consequently, it is possible to write applications in C# (or other .NET languages), and the browser can run them.

Blazor currently supports two approaches (and more are coming!), which are sketched in figure 1.3:

- *Blazor Server*—Only the UI is sent to the browser, whereas all the C# code resides on the web server. Generated JavaScript code automatically calls the server (using SignalR), which then runs the C# code and sends any changes to the DOM (Document Object Model—essentially, the contents) of the page back to the client. Here, the application loads faster but does not really work offline.

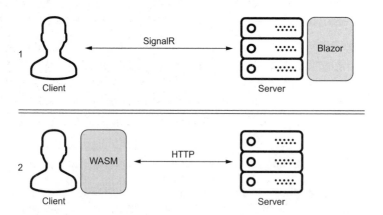

Figure 1.3   The two Blazor architecture modes

- *Blazor WebAssembly*—Everything is compiled down to WebAssembly, including those parts of .NET that are used by the application. In this case, it may take a few extra seconds to download the application, but it then runs into the browser without any server interaction except for eventual API calls. The application code may be reverse engineered as a consequence.

The following listing shows a Blazor page as part of a trivial sample application.

Listing 1.6   A Blazor page of a simple application

```
@page "/"                                          ◁──────────┐  Shows the URL associated
                                                              │  with this page
<PageTitle>Dice Roll - Blazor</PageTitle>

@{
    var outcome = new Random().Next(1, 7);
}

<h1>Dice Roll: @outcome</h1>
```

This time, both the dice roll and the output of the outcome reside in the same file, once again using the Razor syntax featuring the @ character.

1.2   Identifying and mitigating threats

As you saw in the previous sections, ASP.NET Core provides many options for creating websites: different server frameworks and approaches, and different techniques and formats for client-side aspects. Many components essentially lead to a large attack surface area, so there are many places where things may go wrong security-wise.

1.2.1   Web application components

In a modern web application, there will also be other components, such as

- Databases
- Other, external services
- Filesystem resources
- CDNs (content delivery networks) holding libraries and other, mostly static, assets

Figure 1.4 shows a typical application architecture. From a security point of view, most of the components may be at risk, including the connection between them.

Here are some of the things that web applications need to provide safeguards against, which will be covered in this book:

- User data sent to the database might contain malicious commands that are then run on the database. A typical attack is called *SQL injection*.
- User data sent to the server and later sent to a client may contain unwanted content such as malicious JavaScript code. This is commonly referred to as *cross-site scripting*.

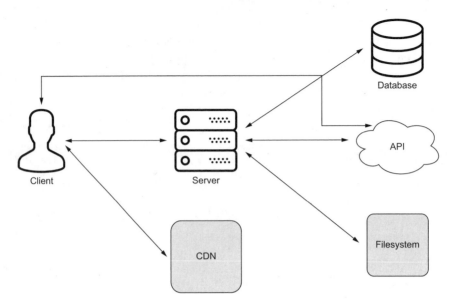

Figure 1.4   Components of a typical web application

- Data exchanged between the client and the server may be intercepted or stolen, putting parts of the application at risk. Using a secure transport mechanism can help.
- Insufficient authorization might grant users access to server resources they should not be allowed to see.
- The way authentication works in the web might be abused by crafting HTTP requests, leading to users causing the application to take undesired actions. Cross-site request forgery is a typical attack in this space.
- Unexpected user input—such as too much data, too little data, or incorrect data— leads to unwanted behavior of a web application, or provokes error messages.
- Error messages may reveal internal information about the server, which could be useful for an attacker. On the other hand, internal errors need to be properly handled and logged.
- Assets hosted on a third-party site (think CDNs) may have been manipulated.

1.2.2   *Defense in depth*

In web application security, the rule of thumb is this: if something can go wrong, it will go wrong, so we need to anticipate all of the aforementioned risks, and more, by defensively programming our application, expecting the worst, and implementing as many safeguards as possible. The second part of this book will show all the most common currently known attacks, and then it will implement countermeasures.

Sometimes, redundancy can be helpful when it comes to security measures. Better to use two safeguards than one (or none at all). Also, use security measures in various layers of the application. When talking about performance, redundancy is often considered something bad. Why do two things if one thing is good enough? On the other hand, when it comes to availability, redundancy helps to keep an application working: if one system fails, there's a backup. Web application security is more closely related to availability, so redundant measures are not a problem; in fact, they are usually welcome. We commonly talk about defense-in-depth mechanisms when we implement multiple layers of security. Even if one of those layers proves to be insufficient, there are hopefully more to keep our application from failing.

If you work in an office with a receptionist, it's likely that the door to the office or to the building is locked. You might argue that this is unnecessary since there is a receptionist who is blocking unwanted individuals from entering the premises, but this receptionist might be on a break or distracted. Therefore, defense in depth applies here. Every security measure might be prone to failing, so having another one in place can be extremely helpful. In this book, we encounter several security mechanisms that provide an extra layer of safety, without completely mitigating a risk on their own. In combination with other measures, though, a web application can be a stronghold against attacks.

1.3   Security-related APIs

Arguably the most important aspect of web application security is the mitigation of risks by anticipating attacks and implementing suitable countermeasures. However, ASP.NET Core and associated technologies come with several security-related APIs that cannot always be directly mapped to a specific attack. Here are a few examples:

- ASP.NET Core Identity provides an API for handling authentication and authorization in a web application, including login/logout, profile data, roles, and more.
- Secure communication may be enforced by a variety of options and approaches, including redirecting to HTTPS, securing cookies, and even disabling HTTP.
- Security-related HTTP headers may be explicitly set in `web.config` and controllers, and implicitly set by defining settings in the `Program` class (in .NET versions prior to 6, the `Startup` class was the go-to place for this).
- Passwords should not be stored in clear text, but they should be encrypted, or better yet, hashed. ASP.NET Core supports relevant formats and algorithms.
- Cloud providers like Microsoft Azure or AWS (Amazon Web Services) have their own APIs for storing secrets such as connection strings or passwords.

It is vital to know these APIs and ASP.NET's security philosophy and mechanisms. In the third part of this book, you will learn exactly how they work and when to use them.

In practice, however, actual security vulnerabilities in code are the main culprit, and this author's security audits confirm this over and over again.

1.4   *Security is important*

I can't stress this enough: web application security is an extremely important topic for everyone involved. Here are the motivations for several typical roles in a web project:

- Developers need to write secure applications. You cannot easily apply a patch on something that is fundamentally broken. They need to understand existing risks and how ASP.NET Core can help mitigate them.
- Project and/or engineering managers need to have an understanding of attacks, have to prioritize security efforts, and may orchestrate security testing as early as during development.
- CTOs (chief technology officers) need to be aware of the consequences of insufficient security and must understand that security does not come for free; it's an effort that must be budgeted.

Apart from that, isn't it fun to try to break applications and get paid for it? But believe me, the less I find after an audit, the happier I am.

Summary

Let's review what we have learned so far:

- The vast majority of web applications have some kind of security vulnerabilities, and most of them are caused by the website's code.
- Most attacks do not rely on the specific server technology being used, but use the common denominator of all web applications: HTML/CSS/JavaScript and HTTP.
- Many parts of a web application may be at risk: the client side, the server, the database, external resources, and the communication paths between them.
- This book will use ASP.NET Core, the web framework of .NET.
- ASP.NET comes with built-in security features, some of them enabled by default, others ready to be configured and activated. For the rest, we need to write custom code.

With the foundation laid out for us, it's time to dive deep into web application security, starting with common (and dangerous!) attacks and how to anticipate and defend against them. Better to be paranoid than offline!

Part 2

Mitigating common attacks

Web application security is a topic that's over 20 years old. Over time, there have been several novel ways to assail a web application, and new twists to decades-old attacks have been invented. This part of the book will discuss the most common specific attacks against websites and how to mitigate them with ASP.NET Core.

Chapter 2 will focus on cross-site scripting (XSS), an attack that basically consists of JavaScript injection. Chapter 3 will feature several attacks against state management; sessions are especially at risk.

In Chapter 4, cross-site request forgery (CSRF) will be explained in detail, including the built-in safeguards of ASP.NET Core and features in modern browsers that make this attack hard to pull off. Chapter 5 covers data validation with ASP.NET Core (and what can go wrong if you don't do it correctly). Many attacks are enabled by not properly handling incoming data, and this chapter shows effective countermeasures.

Finally, chapter 6 talks about SQL injection, probably one of the oldest attacks around, yet still dangerous. As usual, ASP.NET Core comes prepared and provides solid mechanisms to protect the application.

Cross-site scripting (XSS)

2

This chapter covers

- Understanding how cross-site scripting (XSS) works
- Learning about different types of XSS
- Preventing XSS by escaping output
- Using Content Security Policy (CSP) against XSS
- Judging other browser features against XSS

In 2014, the BBC reported (https://www.bbc.com/news/technology-29241563) that clicking on certain links on eBay would redirect users to a phishing site: it looked similar to eBay, but, of course, wasn't legitimate. The security researcher who found the vulnerability supposedly contacted the firm to no avail. An official inquiry by the BBC then sped things up, and the issue was resolved.

About 10 years earlier, a security researcher managed to pull a similar stunt, redirecting eBay users to phishing sites where they were prompted for their credentials—and this happened live on German television! eBay obtained an injunction against one researcher who announced he would demonstrate the exploit.

However, the TV show had already contracted a second researcher who was not covered by the injunction.

In both cases, the researchers (or, more generally, the attackers) managed to inject JavaScript code into the website, which then took care of the redirection to the phishing site. Let's have a look at how such an attack—which usually consists of injecting JavaScript code (and other content) into a website—works.

> **NOTE** This attack should probably be called "JavaScript injection"; in early 2000, a group of Microsoft security engineers came up with cross-site scripting (XSS) instead, and that name stuck. In case you are wondering, the acronym CSS was already used for Cascading Style Sheets, so XSS it was.

2.1 *Anatomy of a cross-site scripting attack*

The most common flavor of XSS is injecting JavaScript code into a page, although there are also attack vectors that use HTML or CSS. A great example to demonstrate this—and a typical place to find a security vulnerability in many websites—is the search feature. It shows a typical pattern: the user sends data (a search term), and that data is shown on the output page. This might offer an opening for an attack.

> **NOTE** When explaining the attack, we will first hack ourselves—it's just easier to get accustomed to XSS that way. But don't worry; later on we will discuss how an attacker will actually pull this off.

Let's look at a simple search page using Razor Pages. The *.cshtml* page is shown in the following listing.

Listing 2.1   A Razor Page with a search UI

```
@page
@model AspNetCoreSecurity.RazorSamples.Pages.SearchPageModel

<h1>Search</h1>

<div class="row">
    <div class="col-md-12">
        <form method="get" action="">
            <div class="form-group">
                <label class="control-label" for="searchTerm"></label>
                <input id="searchTerm" name="searchTerm" class="form-control"
                ➥/>
            </div>
            <div class="form-group">
                <input type="submit" id="btn" value="Search" class="btn
                ➥btn-primary" />
            </div>
        </form>
    </div>
</div>
<div class="row">
    <div class="col-md-12">
```

```
        @Html.Raw(Model.Result)          ◄──┐  Outputs the Result
    </div>                                   │  property of the model
</div>
```

The associated C# file containing the model and the logic can be seen in the next listing.

Listing 2.2 The page model for the search page

```
using Microsoft.AspNetCore.Mvc.RazorPages;

namespace AspNetCoreSecurity.RazorSamples.Pages
{
    public class SearchPageModel : PageModel
    {
        public string Result { get; set; } = string.Empty;

        public void OnGet(string searchTerm)
        {
            this.Result = string.IsNullOrEmpty(searchTerm) ?
                "" :
                $"Your search for <i>{searchTerm}</i> did not yield any
                ➡results.";
        }
    }
}
```

Not much happens here—the code takes the search term from the page and then constructs an HTML-formatted output containing the search term, and because no actual searching takes place in this demo, zero matches are found.

> **NOTE** For the sake of argument, this is good enough. Even if there was a database backend and matches were found, the output would probably still contain the search term, which will become relevant shortly.

If you load the page in the browser and issue a search, you will get the expected result (figure 2.1).

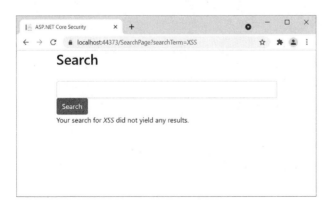

Figure 2.1 The search works (except for the lack of results).

The search term (which can be seen in the URL) appears on the page. However, what happens if the search term is a `<script>` tag with some code? An easy way to verify whether that works is to try some JavaScript that shows a modal window:

```
<script>alert('Hacked!')</script>
```

Figure 2.2 shows what happens if you use this as a search term.

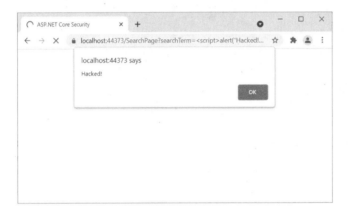

Figure 2.2   Where does this modal window come from?

The browser does not show the search term, but rather, a modal window. If you look at the generated HTML markup in the browser, you will see the following fragment within the page:

```
<div class="row">
    <div class="col-md-12">
        Your search for <i><script>alert('Hacked!')</script></i> did not
        ➥yield any results.
    </div>
</div>
```

Here is what happened: the user sent a search term to the server, and the server replied with HTML that contained `You searched for <search term>`. But in the case of this attack, the search term contained angle brackets, `< >`. The browser did (correctly, but probably undesirably) interpret the search term as HTML markup. The attacker successfully injected JavaScript code, and thus we have cross-site scripting.

This example was rather obvious, but XSS may also happen when things get a little bit more complicated. Let's look at the following listing, where—as part of an ASP.NET Core MVC project—a JSON endpoint is implemented.

Listing 2.3   A (too) naïve JSON endpoint

```
using AspNetCoreSecurity.MvcSamples.Models;
using Microsoft.AspNetCore.Mvc;
```

```
namespace AspNetCoreSecurity.MvcSamples.Controllers
{
    public class HomeController : Controller
    {
        public IActionResult Search()
        {
            return View();                        ◄── Returns the search
        }                                              HTML page/view

        public ContentResult SearchAPI(string searchTerm)
        {
            var results = new List<string>() {
                searchTerm + " 1",
                searchTerm + " 2",                     Generates search results
                searchTerm + " 3"                      (simplified implementation)
            };

            return new ContentResult
            {
                ContentType = "text/html",
                Content = $"[\"{string.Join("\", \"", results)}\"]"   ◄── Creates
            };                                                            JSON
        }
    }
}
```

The `SearchAPI` endpoint takes a search term, generates some dummy search results, and is then essentially using string concatenation to create a JSON representation of those search terms. The following listing shows the frontend side of things.

Listing 2.4 Calling the search API

```html
<h1>Search</h1>

<div class="row">
    <div class="col-md-4">
        <form>
            <div class="form-group">
                <label class="control-label" for="searchTerm"></label>
                <input id="searchTerm" class="form-control" />
            </div>
            <div class="form-group">
                <input type="button" id="btn" value="Search" class="btn
                ➥btn-primary" />
            </div>
        </form>
    </div>
</div>
<div class="row">
    <div class="col-md-4">
        <ul class="list-group" id="results">
        </ul>
    </div>
</div>
```

```
<script>
    document.getElementById("btn").onclick = () => {
        let list = document.getElementById("results");
        list.innerHTML = "";
        let searchTerm = document.getElementById("searchTerm").value;
        fetch("/Home/SearchAPI?searchTerm=" + encodeURIComponent(searchTerm))
            .then(response => response.json())
            .then(data => data.forEach(item => {
                let li = document.createElement("li");
                li.className = "list-group-item";
                li.innerHTML = item;
                list.appendChild(li);
            }));
    }
</script>
```

Retrieves the search term from the form

Calls the endpoint

Iterates over results

Creates one list item per result and adds it to the page

Figure 2.3 shows what happens if you enter `<script>alert('Hacked!')</script>` into the field: not only does the search work, but it also seems to prevent the attack we looked at before.

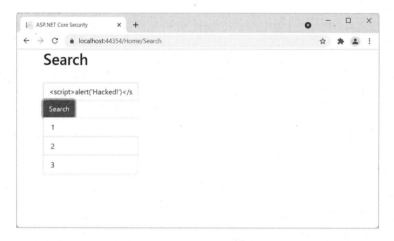

Figure 2.3   The search now returns results (of questionable quality).

Even though the search term contains a `<script>` tag, the browser does not execute it after it is dynamically added to the page. But does that mean that we are protected from XSS here? Unfortunately, no. The search API can also be directly called in the browser by using a URL like this (you need to replace `12345` with the port on your system):

```
http://localhost:12345/Home/SearchAPI?searchTerm=XSS
```

And if we use a `<script>` tag again?

```
http://localhost:12345/Home/SearchAPI?searchTerm=<script>alert('Hacked!')</
    script>
```

Figure 2.4 has an answer to this question.

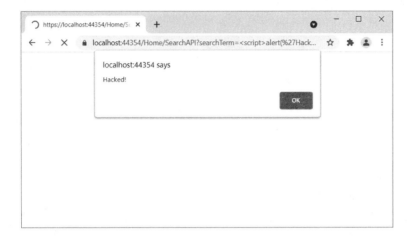

Figure 2.4   The search API is vulnerable to cross-site scripting.

The JavaScript code is once again executed. Here is the (lightly formatted) output of the search API:

```
[
  "<script>alert('Hacked!')</script> 1",
  "<script>alert('Hacked!')</script> 2",
  "<script>alert('Hacked!')</script> 3"
]
```

This is valid JSON code and unproblematic in a JSON context, but when interpreted as HTML, it's some gibberish and three `<script>` tags with code.

You may now interpose that, so far, we have attacked ourselves. That is correct, but if you look back at figures 2.2 and 2.4, you will notice that both attacks used HTTP GET requests. That means that whoever called the URL would be attacked. In the real world, the following would now happen: a real attacker would craft a URL where the malicious JavaScript code would be successfully injected and then distribute that URL

- To a specific target (e.g., via email)
- To random targets, via email or public posts on social media, or in a forum

As experience will tell us, there are enough people who just click on links without thinking twice. But what if there is a POST request involved? We could change listing 2.1 to use `method="post"` in the `<form>` tag and replace `OnGet()` with `OnPost()` in the page model class. Now the attack does not work with just the URL anymore. But the following listing can change that.

Listing 2.5   Exploiting XSS with HTTP POST

```
<form method="post" action="https://localhost:12345/SearchPagePost">
    <input type="hidden"
        name="searchTerm"
        value="&lt;script&gt;alert('Hacked!')&lt;/script&gt;">
</form>

<script>
    document.forms[0].submit();
</script>
```

◁──┐

Shows an HTML-encoded
<script> tag

The page contains an HTML form with exactly the form field name that the original search form was using. The only difference is that this time, it's a hidden form field. A <script> block then contains code to submit this form and post the XSS payload to the target page.

   In the end, the browser sends a POST request to our page, with XSS payload, and the attack is successful. This time, the villain needs to distribute a link to the HTML page (which may be hosted anywhere). Now that we have seen cross-site scripting, it's time to find out what can be done to protect against this attack.

NOTE   As we will see in chapter 4, there is a built-in security mechanism in ASP.NET Core that makes these POST requests less predictable and can prevent this specific attack vector. However, for our discussion of XSS, this feature is not relevant.

Types of cross-site scripting

The Open Web Application Security Project (OWASP), a nonprofit organization for everything web security, defines several types of cross-site scripting (https://owasp.org/www-community/Types_of_Cross-Site_Scripting). The two main ones are as follows:

- *Stored cross-site scripting (type 1)*—Also called *persistent XSS*, where the web application stores the malicious JavaScript code. Every user is now a potential victim, with no actions required of them. Just loading a page in the application where JavaScript has been injected leads to code execution.
- *Reflected cross-site scripting (type 2)*—Also called *nonpersistent XSS*, where the malicious JavaScript code is part of the HTTP request and then appears in the HTTP response. This is the type of XSS that we have seen so far, and it at least requires that the user click on a specially crafted link.

There is a third type of XSS, called *DOM-based XSS*, which we will cover later in this chapter. You can find more on OWASP in chapter 16.

2.2   *Preventing cross-site scripting*

Of course, no one is afraid of a modal window with some text injected on a page—it's embarrassing, yes, but is this really a major threat? In my opinion, the best way to understand the dangers of getting someone else's JavaScript code injected in your page is to look at the (some say only) security feature that JavaScript has: the same-origin policy (SOP).

2.2.1 Understanding the same-origin policy

Simply put, the SOP dictates that JavaScript code has access only to elements that have the same *origin* as the code. The term *origin* is defined by the Internet Engineering Task Force (IETF) as the following three values:

- *Scheme*—http: or https:
- *Fully qualified domain name*—www.example.com
- *Port*—By default, 80 for HTTP and 443 for HTTPS (when a default port is used, it is commonly not part of the "origin" value)

If all three pieces of information are identical, the origin is the same. For instance, www.example.com and example.com are *not* the same origin, since the domain names do not exactly match. The IETF's "Web Origin Concept" (https://datatracker.ietf .org/doc/html/rfc6454), which defines the same-origin policy, specifies "trust by URI." Depending on the URI (uniform resource identifier), the browser will trust content.

The term *origin* is not always intuitive in a web context, though. Imagine a web page residing on https://example.com that contains three <script> tags (figure 2.5):

- One with inline JavaScript code
- One referencing a JavaScript file on the same server as the current HTML page
- One referencing a JavaScript library from a CDN; for instance, the one from Google (https://ajax.googleapis.com)

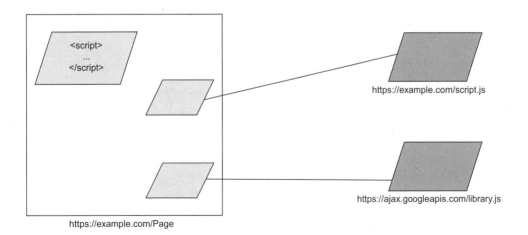

https://example.com/Page

Figure 2.5   One page, three times JavaScript

The origins of the code from the first two `<script>` tags are obviously https://example .com. But what about the third one? The intuitive answer would be https://ajax .googleapis.com, but if that was the case, the JavaScript library would have a different origin than the current HTML page. Consequently, the code could not access any of the elements on the page. Yet, the library features that access the page's DOM would be the main reasons to use the library in the first place.

Therefore, the origin of the file from the CDN is https://example.com as well! Or, to put it more generally, the origin of JavaScript code is the origin of the HTML page that contains or loads it. I personally prefer the term *security context* instead of *origin*.

And this is exactly the reason why cross-site scripting is so dangerous. The injected JavaScript code is considered a part of the attacked page and runs with the same privileges as our own code—it is using the same security context.

Here are a few ideas about what JavaScript is capable of doing, some of them general, some of them very specific:

- Redirecting the user to another site (phishing)
- Altering the HTML to make a login form send the data to a third-party site (phishing)
- Adding new HTML elements; for instance, a look-alike login form (phishing, again)
- Stealing cookies (which we will cover in chapter 3)
- Tapping into keyboard events (keylogging)
- Adding many new HTML elements, putting the browser under heavy load (denial of service)
- Mining crypto currencies using the victim's CPU
- Exploiting security vulnerabilities in web browsers or plugins (as long as they are still in use)

The list is not exhaustive but should give you a good understanding of why we should avoid XSS like the plague. Fortunately, we just need to get rid of a few special characters, and ASP.NET Core supports us out of the box.

2.2.2   *Escaping HTML*

It is easy to see why the XSS attack worked against the two sample applications: the malicious input was sent back to the client verbatim. To be a bit more precise, the attacker managed to change the context of their input. The code of our application assumed that the user input consisted of regular plain text to be shown on the web page. However, the search term was crafted in such a way that the context changed from "text" to "HTML tag." And this HTML tag happened to be `<script>`, which in turn allows the usage (and execution!) of JavaScript.

Defense against this attack is surprisingly simple. There is a finite—and short!—list of special characters that can change the context within HTML. Table 2.1 has all the details.

Table 2.1 Special characters in HTML and associated entities

Special character	Description	HTML entity
<	Beginning of tag	&lt;
>	End of tag	&gt;
"	Delimits attribute values	" or " or "
'	Delimits attribute values	' or ' or '
&	Beginning of entities	&amp;

Each of these five characters needs to be replaced with the associated HTML entities. For instance, an opening angle bracket (<) opens a new tag, whereas the HTML entity < is a representation of the opening angle bracket in text. Getting rid of these five characters can get rid of XSS in an HTML context. Just make sure that you replace the & character first—otherwise, you would escape some characters twice: < would be turned into < (which is correct) and then into &lt; (which is incorrect).

Conveniently, ASP.NET Core is already prepared to do that. In other words, the examples at the beginning of the chapter were carefully crafted to be insecure. We will analyze how we managed to sneak the vulnerabilities into the code and how you can avoid doing that.

When using the Razor view engine (i.e., if you are using ASP.NET Core MVC or Razor Pages), the @ character outputs a value and HTML encodes it, so it is doing the replacements from the list in table 2.1. This works both when outputting values as text and when setting attribute values. Take this example:

```
<input type="text" name="searchTerm" value="@Model.SearchTerm">
```

Now, consider the following value for the search term:

```
" onfocus="alert('Hacked!')
```

The Razor view engine automatically escapes this value, which leads to the following markup being sent to the server:

```
<input type="text" name="searchTerm"
➡value="&quot; onfocus=&quot;alert(&#x27;Hacked!&#x27;)">
```

In listing 2.1, we did not just use @ to output the user-supplied value; instead, we used @Html.Raw(). This helper method does exactly what the name suggests and outputs the value without any escaping. This would lead to the following markup:

```
<input type="text" name="searchTerm"
➡value="" onfocus="alert('Hacked!')">
```

The user-supplied input is marked with bold in the preceding code snippet. Notice how the end result is valid markup, but the double quotes change the context from "attribute value" to "new attribute," allowing the injection of a JavaScript event handler. As soon as the text field receives the focus, the code gets executed.

So, whenever you are using `Html.Raw()`, be absolutely certain that the data you are outputting could not have been supplied or manipulated by the user; otherwise you will be prone to cross-site scripting. Listing 2.1 uses `Html.Raw()`, and this is the very (and only) reason why the attack works there.

> **NOTE**   When you explicitly want to access the HTML-escaping functionality in your code, you can call the `HttpUtility.HtmlEncode()` method, which is defined in the `System.Web` namespace.

In listing 2.3, we also had to try hard to add a vulnerability, because the ASP.NET Core default behavior is pretty secure. We created JSON manually, using string concatenation, which is a bad idea by itself. Here is an excerpt from the code:

```
return new ContentResult                          The results variable is a list of
{                                                 (hypothetical) search results.
    ContentType = "text/html",
    Content = Content = $"[\"{string.Join("\", \"", results)}\"]"    ⟵────
};
```

Surprisingly, the main problem is not the string interpolation. It's bad practice (as string concatenation would be) and will lead to undesired results (e.g., when one of the search results contains double quotes). But the main culprit is setting the content type of the returned data to `"text/html"`. This prompts the browser to handle the data returned from the server as HTML, not as JSON. So, if the API endpoint is loaded in the browser, the HTML parser comes into play, not the JSON parser. If the JSON string happens to include an HTML tag, such as `<script>`, this tag will be parsed, and in the case of `<script>`, the JavaScript code will be executed.

But what would happen if we just removed the `ContentType` setting? Loading the same URL that triggered XSS in the browser leads to the result shown in figure 2.6.

Figure 2.6   The attack does not work with the default content type.

This time, the `Content-Type` HTTP header is automatically set to `text/plain` (due to `ContentResult` being used, which just returns plain text), and the browser is not inclined to start the HTML parser.

Let's assume we are replacing the hand-assembled API endpoint with a proper Web API controller in the following fashion:

```
using Microsoft.AspNetCore.Mvc;

namespace AspNetCoreSecurity.MvcSamples.Controllers
{
    [Route("api/[controller]")]
    [ApiController]
    public class DataController : ControllerBase
    {
        public List<string> GetData(string searchTerm)
        {
            return new List<string>() {
                searchTerm + " 1",
                searchTerm + " 2",
                searchTerm + " 3"
            };
        }
    }
}
```

ASP.NET Core Web API automatically converts the list of strings to a JSON string and sets the `Content-Type` HTTP header to `application/json`. The same thing would happen if we used an ASP.NET Core MVC controller and `JsonResult`.

That's fantastic news, actually. The built-in functionality that everyone is working with when starting with ASP.NET Core is XSS-protected out of the box. So why are we still talking about cross-site scripting, and why is it so widespread? Because not all frameworks come with sound XSS protection, and because even the built-in features do not work in certain edge cases, including, by design, when `@Html.Raw()` is used.

So far, we have been talking about HTML-escaping and handling characters that have a special meaning in an HTML context. This stops working once we are within a different context.

2.2.3 Escaping in a different context

The next listing uses the same Razor Page model as listing 2.1 but uses JavaScript to display the search results that are generated on the server.

Listing 2.6   XSS in a JavaScript context

```
@page
@model AspNetCoreSecurity.RazorSamples.Pages.SearchPageModel

<h1>Search</h1>

<div class="row">
```

```
    <div class="col-md-12">
        <form method="get" action="">
            <div class="form-group">
                <label class="control-label" for="searchTerm"></label>
                <input id="searchTerm" name="searchTerm" class="form-control"
    />
            </div>
            <div class="form-group">
                <input type="submit" id="btn" value="Search" class="btn btn-
    primary" />
            </div>
        </form>
    </div>
</div>

<div class="row">
    <div class="col-md-12" id="output">
    </div>
</div>
```

Loads the jQuery
JavaScript library

```
@section Scripts {
    <script src="https://code.jquery.com/jquery-3.6.0.min.js"
    ➥integrity="sha256-/xUj+3OJU5yExlq6GSYGSHk7tPXikynS7ogEvDej/m4="
    ➥crossorigin="anonymous"></script>
    <script>
    let result = "@Model.Result";
    $("#output").html(result);
    </script>
}
```

Uses jQuery to output the
search results on the page

The jQuery JavaScript library is used to write the search results to the page. The .html() method JavaScript provides essentially sets the HTML content of a DOM element to the desired value.

At first glance, it looks like this code sample is secure. We are properly HTML-escaping the search result when writing it to the page by using the @ character as part of the Razor syntax:

```
let result = "@Model.Result";
```

The problem is the *HTML* in HTML-escaping. The output of Model.Result does not take place in an HTML context, but rather, in a JavaScript context. To be precise, it takes place in the "within a JavaScript string" context.

Strings in JavaScript have several special characters. Some of them, like single or double quotes, are also special characters in HTML and will therefore be handled (not properly, but we will take care of that later). But what about the backslash character (\)? This will be left alone by @ and by HttpUtility.HtmlEncode(), which will cause problems.

For starters, assume that the value of Model.Result is a sole backslash. This would lead to the following output:

```
let result = "\";
```

Obviously, there is now a syntax error in the JavaScript code. But an attacker can go one step further. Injecting `<script>` will not work since angle brackets are properly escaped. But the backslash may be used to create representations of those angular brackets:

- Within a JavaScript string, `\x3c` is an opening angle bracket.
- Within a JavaScript string, `\x3e` is a closing angle bracket.

Similarly, `\x27` represents a single quote within a JavaScript string. Now look at the following search string for the application in listings 2.3 and 2.4:

```
\x3cscript\x3ealert(\x27Hacked!\x27)\x3c/script\x3e
```

The `@` character—or `HttpUtility.HtmlEscape()`—will escape none of these characters since none of them appears in table 2.1. In the JavaScript part of the page, it will lead to this output:

```
let result = "\x3cscript\x3ealert(\x27Hacked!\x27)\x3c/script\x3e";
```

The string now actually contains this value:

```
<script>alert('Hacked!')</script>
```

Figure 2.7 shows what will happen when this value is written into the output element with jQuery's `html()` method.

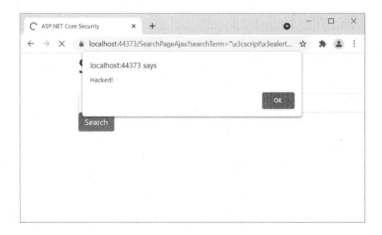

Figure 2.7 Cross-site scripting despite using the @ character

We once again have cross-site scripting. It's obvious that user-supplied data in a Java-Script context (or, to be more exact, within a JavaScript string) needs special handling. Luckily, ASP.NET Core has us covered. The `HttpUtility.JavaScript-StringEncode()` method properly escapes special characters for usage within a JavaScript string. Here is the amended code snippet:

```
let result = "@HttpUtility.JavaScriptStringEncode(Model.Result)";
```

When using the previously successful payload, the following output is generated:

```
let result = "\\x3cscript\\x3ealert(\\x27Hacked!\\x27)\\x3c/script\\x3e";
```

All the backslashes are now properly escaped, and the attack ceases to work.

> **TIP** Properly handling user data in JavaScript is especially crucial for single-page applications (SPAs), where the server routinely just handles API requests and JavaScript takes care of the rest. When the whole attack takes place on the client side (e.g., JavaScript reads data from the URL and then outputs it on the page), we talk about the third kind of cross-site scripting according to OWASP: DOM-based XSS (type 0).

More encodings

The `System.Text.Encodings.Web` namespace contains the `HtmlEncoder` and `JavaScriptEncoder` classes, which provide essentially the same functionality. This comes in handy when using Blazor because you usually do not use the `System.Web` namespace there. The following code would HTML-encode a string (JavaScript-encoding works in an analogous fashion):

```
var encoded = HtmlEncoder.Default.Encode(inputString);
```

There is no built-in functionality for CSS encoding, though. My best advice for using user-supplied data in dynamically generated CSS is simple: don't do it. And where you absolutely need this feature, validate the input as strictly as possible (e.g., use only lowercase letters from *a* to *z*, no special characters).

Our application is now, at least in theory, XSS-proof, but remember the defense-in-depth principle. There's always more that we can do, and in the case of XSS, there is an additional, and extremely effective, safeguard.

2.3   Content Security Policy

One of the most effective weapons against cross-site scripting is baked into all modern browsers (and some older ones). Content Security Policy (CSP) comes as an HTTP header that instructs browsers where to load (and, when we are talking about JavaScript, execute) content from. This may make it close to impossible to pull off an XSS attack.

> **WARNING** CSP is a defense-in-depth security mechanism, so it's not a replacement for the XSS countermeasures we have covered in this chapter so far. Instead, CSP will be your safety net in case you actually have cross-site scripting in your application.

At the time of this writing, Content Security Policy Level 2 is the latest version of the standard governed by the World Wide Web Consortium (W3C). There is also existing work on and early implementations of CSP 3 (https://www.w3.org/TR/CSP3/ has the latest version), but browser support is limited at best. Only Chrome is willing to add new features before the standard is finalized, probably fueled by the fact that the editor of CSP 3, Mike West, works for Google. That's why we stick with CSP 2 for now, but we'll also have a brief glimpse of version 3.

> **NOTE**   Read all about Content Security Policy Level 2 at https://www.w3.org/TR/CSP2/. The standard reached the "W3C Recommendation" state in December 2016.

Content Security Policy Level 2 is supported by all relatively recent versions of Chrome-based browsers (Chrome, Edge, Opera), Safari (since version 10), and Firefox. The preceding version, Content Security Policy 1, is also supported in old Microsoft Edge (the one based on Microsoft's own rendering engine), and Internet Explorer 10 and 11. Still, we skip CSP 1. The old Edge versions are no longer relevant in the market. Internet Explorer is also at the end of its life and, to make things worse, supports only one feature (I am not kidding) of CSP, and that's one that no one is actually using. Remember that CSP is a defense-in-depth mechanism: Internet Explorer will ignore CSP headers and miss the extra level of protection. The web application itself should be XSS-free anyway.

Before we can dive into Content Security Policy, we will first look at a trivial but typical web application to have something to apply CSP to.

2.3.1   Sample application

The sample application does not do much—it determines the current time and displays it. However, it is using several patterns that turn out to be a challenge once Content Security Policy comes into play. This time we use Razor Pages. Let's start with the page itself in the following listing.

> **Listing 2.7   Razor Page that will support Content Security Policy later**

```
@page
@model CSPModel

<div class="text-center">
    <h1 class="display-4">Content Security Policy</h1>
    <div class="mt-5 mb-5">
        <img src="https://www.manning.com/assets/manningLogoBlack-
            4ce2f7a38da67c986590975d7769f389.svg">
    </div>
    <div class="mb-3">
        <p id="timeSpan" style="font-size: xx-large">
            Current time:
        </p>
    </div>
</div>

@section Scripts {
<script src="https://cdn.jsdelivr.net/npm/underscore@1.13.1/
underscore-umd-min.js"></script>
```

Loads Manning logo from manning.com

Shows placeholder for time output

Loads the Underscore library from a CDN

```
<script src="~/js/csp.js"></script>          ◁─┐ Loads custom
<script>                                        │ JavaScript code
    window.setInterval(
        "updateTime(new Date().toLocaleTimeString())",
        1000);
</script>
}
```

Updates the current
time every second

The page basically contains an output placeholder that will later contain the current time. Custom JavaScript code will update the placeholder every 1,000 milliseconds, so once a second. The Underscore library will be used as the template engine. On top of it all, the Manning logo is displayed, but for budgetary reasons, it is directly linked from www.manning.com. The following listing shows the external JavaScript file we are using.

Listing 2.8   The JavaScript code for the Razor Page

```
var $timeSpan = document.getElementById("timeSpan");
var $tmpl = _.template("Current time: <%= time %>");

function updateTime(timeString) {
    $timeSpan.innerHTML = $tmpl({ time: timeString });
}
```

The code implements the `updateTime()` function called via `setInterval()` in listing 2.7. The Underscore library is used to display the current time in the HTML placeholder. For now, the application works as expected, as shown in figure 2.8.

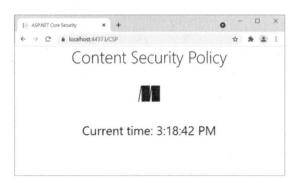

Figure 2.8   The current time is
shown and updated each second.

The Manning logo and the current time are shown. This will change, though, when we add Content Security Policy.

2.3.2   *How Content Security Policy works*

Content Security Policy comes in the form of an HTTP header called `Content-Security-Policy`. The header value consists of *directives* and associated values. A directive usually has a dash in its name.

NOTE   Previous versions of CSP used `X-Content-Security-Policy` or `X-Webkit-CSP`. If you find code with these header names, chances are that it and its description are severely outdated.

The "mother of all directives" is called `default-src` and provides the browser with a list of all valid origins or URIs for resources. As a value, Content Security Policy supports several constants, delimited by single quotes. One such constant is `'self'`, which stands for *current origin*—yes, the term origin as defined by the IETF is back. The following directive basically states, "Load everything from the current origin only":

```
default-src 'self'
```

Let's make sure that the sample application is using this Content Security Policy. The following listing shows the page model for the Razor Page.

Listing 2.9   Adding Content Security Policy to the page

```
using Microsoft.AspNetCore.Mvc.RazorPages;

namespace AspNetCoreSecurity.RazorSamples.Pages
{
    public class CSPModel : PageModel
    {
        public void OnGet()
        {
            var cspHeader = "default-src 'self'";       ⟵┐ Shows the variable
            HttpContext.Response.Headers.Add(             │ holding the CSP value
                "Content-Security-Policy",
                cspHeader);
        }
    }
}
```

The variable `cspHeader` contains the policy value for the `Content-Security-Policy` header.

Meta tag vs. HTTP header

We could also set the Content Security Policy on the client only, without any server interaction or HTTP headers. A `<meta>` tag serves as the alternative approach:

```
<meta http-equiv="Content-Security-Policy" content="default-src 'self'">
```

For a simple policy, this works equally well. However, there are some CSP features where the `<meta>` tag does not work, such as reporting (covered later in this chapter). Using the HTTP header is therefore recommended and is the approach used throughout this chapter.

When we reload the page with this new setting, the browser should display something similar to figure 2.9.

**Figure 2.9   This does
not look right.**

The current time is no longer displayed. Also, the Manning logo is missing, and the
font size of "Current time" is smaller than before. So, while Content Security Policy
may help protect us against cross-site scripting, it might also break our site. Let's gradually fix the code and the policy to make everything work again.

2.3.3   *Refactoring applications for Content Security Policy*

The first error on the page is probably the easiest one to fix. The Manning logo does
not show up, but this should not come as a surprise. We are lifting it from manning
.com, and since that's not the current origin, it does not satisfy the `default-src`
`'self'` policy.

One remediation would be to add the logo origin to the `default-src` directive,
but it's always better to be as specific as possible. Content Security Policy defines a
large variety of directives for different kinds of resources. Table 2.2 shows the most relevant ones (additional directives will be covered later in this chapter).

Table 2.2   Content Security Policy directives

Directive name	Type of content sources directive allows
`child-src`	iframes and web workers
`connect-src`	HTTP and WebSocket requests (`XMLHttpRequest`, `fetch()`)
`font-src`	Web fonts
`img-src`	Graphics and images
`media-src`	Audio and video files
`object-src`	Data executed by plugins (The `plugin-types` directive may contain a list of plugins that may be used on the current page.)
`script-src`	JavaScript code
`style-src`	CSS styles

Each directive in table 2.2 covers a specific type of content. If such a directive is set, it overrides any `default-src` directive for that type. On the other hand, if `default-src` is set and one of the directives in table 2.2 isn't, the former value applies for that type of content. To give a concrete example, `default-src 'self'` also applies to images, unless `img-src` is set to something else.

Back to the application. We need to allow the Manning logo to be loaded and displayed from manning.com, so we should consider using the `img-src` directive. The URL of the image is https://www.manning.com/assets/manningLogoBlack-4ce2f7a 38da67c986590975d7769f389.svg.

There are four options to choose from:

- *Use the protocol, host name, and possibly port (origin)*—https://manning.com.
- *Use a path*—https://www.manning.com/assets/. Note that you must not omit the trailing slash, because https://www.manning.com/assets would be treated as the file called assets on https://www.manning.com).
- *Use the full URI*—https://www.manning.com/assets/manningLogoBlack-4ce2f7 a38da67c986590975d7769f389.svg.
- *Use a wildcard (*)*—I recommend you don't do this, unless you really want to allow any images from anywhere (which usually is not the case).

WARNING Especially when working with CDNs, try to avoid greenlighting the whole CDN at once. It's very likely that the CDN also contains older versions of other libraries that either have security vulnerabilities in them or provide a JSONP (JSON with Padding—an endpoint that accepts user data and returns tailored JavaScript code) endpoint. You lose the cross-site scripting protection that Content Security Policy provides, since you trust all JavaScript code on that CDN. This is also called a *CSP bypass*. It's better to limit the policy to specific URLs or at least to specific libraries, if possible.

Adding `'self'` to the list of allowed sources is also a good idea—the website will probably use a favicon as well. This CSP looks like a reasonable approach (note that URIs do not need single quotes—they are for CSP constants like `'self'`):

```
default-src 'self'; img-src 'self' https://www.manning.com/assets/
```

Note that directives are separated by a semicolon, and there's a space character between directive values. When the `cspHeader` variable from listing 2.9 is set to this value, the Manning logo will reappear, which is a good first step. The other issues—no time being shown, font size too small—are still a problem, though.

Taking a closer look at the source code in the browser, we also notice that we are relying on other external resources:

- The CSS parts of the Bootstrap library are loaded from a CDN (the layout page has that by default when using the .NET project template).
- The Underscore JavaScript library is also loaded from a CDN.

Turns out that both libraries come from the same server: https://cdn.jsdelivr.net. But remember our rule: be as explicit as possible. Therefore, we do not add the site to the `default-src` directive, but to `style-src` and `script-src`. To facilitate updates to the libraries, we are not using the full URIs this time, but just the origin:

```
default-src 'self'; img-src 'self' https://www.manning.com/assets/
➥style-src 'self' https://cdn.jsdelivr.net
➥script-src 'self' https://cdn.jsdelivr.net
```

Still, that's not enough to fix the application; we have to take care of the JavaScript code next. One of the most important gotchas from using Content Security Policy, and the cause of most of the effort required when migrating a legacy app for it, can be summed up like this: *inline is dead.*

If there is a CSP directive that covers CSS styles (i.e., `default-src` is set and/or `style-src` is set), then inline styles cease to work. If there is a CSP directive that covers JavaScript code (`default-src` and/or `script-src` are set), then inline JavaScript code won't be executed any longer.

Before we talk about the implications and potential remedies, let's pause for a minute and focus on XSS. Assume that our web application has an XSS vulnerability. It can be exploited in one of three ways:

- By injecting `<script>/* malicious code */</script>`. This counts as inline code and is therefore prevented by CSP.
- By injecting `<script src="https://malicious.server/attack.js"></script>`. As long as https://malicious.server is not part of the allow list (and there is no reason to assume that it is), CSP prevents loading and executing this code. This also reinforces the recommendation to not put the complete CDN on the allow list.
- By injecting `<script src="attack.js"></script>`. This assumes that the malicious JavaScript code already exists on our server. In that case, cross-site scripting is the least of our problems.

If we manage to apply a CSP to a site, then cross-site scripting is essentially dead! With that in mind, let's see how inline code can be either refactored or allowed with CSP.

Usually, the best approach is to avoid inline code altogether. Externalize JavaScript and CSS and avoid inline styles (use appropriate selectors instead) and event handler attributes like `onclick` (use DOM event listeners instead). This sounds easy in theory and works really well when starting a website from scratch. Porting legacy applications can be much, much harder. Sometimes the code is riddled with inline styles, JavaScript event handlers, and `<script>` blocks with inline code. Even worse, sometimes the framework makes the endeavor close to impossible. If you have worked with ASP.NET Web Forms in a previous life, you know what I'm talking about—functionality totally relying on inline JavaScript code, without any options to change that behavior. I have managed to get even these kinds of applications ready for Content Security Policy, but it was a major undertaking. For new, greenfield applications, my advice is start "CSP first"—define a strict Content Security Policy, and then try to stick with it, or gradually add to the policy.

If migrating a legacy application to fit a CSP turns out to be too much of an effort, maybe fixing the policy is an option. In order to re-enable inline content, the standard offers a few options.

The first one is by using a *nonce* ("number used once") and describes a one-time token. The idea is as follows: the Content Security Policy is using a random, one-time token that is different each time so that an attacker cannot guess it. Then the value of that token is added to the <script> and <style> elements where inline JavaScript code and CSS styles are being used. The name of the associated attribute is nonce.

There is no strict rule how that token should be generated, as long as it's random and unpredictable. You could pick a GUID (globally unique identifier), or you could use the following approach:

```
var byteArray = new byte[32];
using (var random =
    System.Security.Cryptography.RandomNumberGenerator.Create())
{
    random.GetBytes(byteArray);
}
var token =  Convert.ToBase64String(byteArray);
```

The .NET random number generator yields 32 random bytes, which are then Base64-encoded. When I ran this on my machine, this is the token I got:

```
19UoXyUC5RHumWo7PyZ/8o9WmaquPDfD49Xx+EEekDI=
```

Using this token for Content Security Policy purposes is a two-step process. First, add an attribute with the token value to all inline <script> and <style> elements:

```
<style nonce="19UoXyUC5RHumWo7PyZ/8o9WmaquPDfD49Xx+EEekDI=">
...
</style>

<script nonce="19UoXyUC5RHumWo7PyZ/8o9WmaquPDfD49Xx+EEekDI=">
...
</script>
```

Then provide the token value in the appropriate CSP directives, using the following format (note the mandatory single quotes):

```
'nonce-<token value>'
```

Our policy could then look like this:

```
default-src 'self'; img-src 'self' https://www.manning.com/assets/;
➥style-src 'self' 'nonce-19UoXyUC5RHumWo7PyZ/8o9WmaquPDfD49Xx+EEekDI='
➥script-src 'self' 'nonce-19UoXyUC5RHumWo7PyZ/8o9WmaquPDfD49Xx+EEekDI='
```

This policy allows CSS and JavaScript from the current origin (excluding inline styles and inline code, of course) and from other sources if the correct one-time token is used.

Note that this approach allows any code (and styles, but we focus on JavaScript) to be run, as long as the `<script>` tag has the correct token value. An attacker should not be able to predict the token, so the application should be sufficiently protected. However, it is possible to tell the browser *which* code to run.

For this, we need to calculate the `SHA256`, `SHA384`, or `SHA512` hash of the content of the `<script>` or `<style>` element, including line breaks and other whitespace. One way to do this is to use the `SHA256`, `SHA384`, or `SHA512` class from the `System .Security.Cryptography` namespace. Then the hash value needs to be added to the appropriate CSP directive (`default-src`, `script-src`, `style-src`) in the following fashion:

```
'sha<algorithm name>-<hash>'
```

If we peek at the console as part of the browser developer tools, we even get pointed in the right direction when we take a closer look at the error message generated for the inline JavaScript code (figure 2.10).

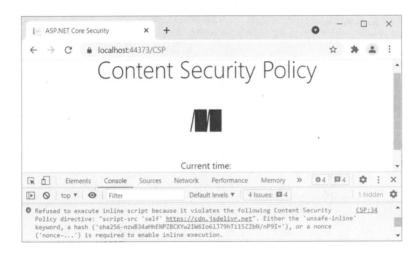

Figure 2.10   The Chrome error message even suggests a suitable hash.

The message even mentions a hash that would match our inline code! So here we are, with the next iteration of our Content Security Policy:

```
default-src 'self'; img-src 'self' https://www.manning.com/assets/;
style-src 'self' https://cdn.jsdelivr.net;
script-src 'self' https://cdn.jsdelivr.net
'sha256-nzwB34aHhENPZBCXYw2IW6Io61J79hTi15ZZbN/nP9I='
```

This policy now explicitly allows inline JavaScript code that matches the hash.

Verifying JavaScript code with Subresource Integrity (SRI)

When you are loading a JavaScript file via a `<script>` tag and want to make sure that it wasn't tampered with (especially if it's located on a third-party server you don't control), the SRI feature will come in handy. Just set the `integrity` attribute of the `<script>` tag to the hash value of the JavaScript file's content, like we did previously in this chapter when loading `jQuery`:

```
<script src="https://code.jquery.com/jquery-3.6.0.min.js"
        integrity="sha256-/xUj+3OJU5yExlq6GSYGSHk7tPXikynS7ogEvDej/m4="
        crossorigin="anonymous"></script>
```

If the content of the JavaScript file doesn't match the hash, then the browser refuses to execute. All modern browsers support SRI, except for Internet Explorer. As always, we can live with this limitation, since SRI is a defense-in-depth technique just like CSP.

The `crossorigin="anonymous"` attribute prevents credentials from being sent along with the request. It is not required for SRI to work.

Creating two different pieces of code that have the same hash is practically impossible, so an attacker cannot inject any code they choose. Problem solved!

Well, almost. What are *not* covered by using a hash are the following cases:

- Event handler attributes (e.g., `onclick`)
- `javascript:` links (`<a href="javascript:alert('Hacked!')">`)
- Style attributes (`style="font-size: xx-large"` in the sample application)

We can still calculate a hash for that—in case of `style="font-size: xx-large"`, one valid value is `'sha256-yckz1zrIL2HgQwm7x1ins99s5jndZE3XnmgOAk-JvDOg='`. However, we additionally need the `'unsafe-hashes'` constant to make the hash apply *only* to the style attribute:

```
default-src 'self'; img-src 'self' https://www.manning.com/assets/;
➥style-src 'self' https://cdn.jsdelivr.net;
➥'unsafe-hashes' 'sha256-yckz1zrIL2HgQwm7x1ins99s5jndZE3XnmgOAkJvDOg='
➥script-src 'self' https://cdn.jsdelivr.net
➥'sha256-nzwB34aHhENPZBCXYw2IW6Io61J79hTi15ZZbN/nP9I='
```

With these changes, we can see some progress (figure 2.11)—at least in Chrome-based browsers.

> **NOTE** Firefox does not support `'unsafe-hashes'` yet (track http://mng.bz/6XnD for progress on this matter), so you have to convert the inline style to external CSS and an appropriate selector.

Figure 2.11   The font size is back—still no time, though.

The large font makes a comeback, but we are still not seeing the current time. The browser console helps us solve the riddle: there is yet another side effect of having a Content Security Policy for JavaScript. Dynamic evaluation of code ceases to work, too. The following patterns are typical for this issue:

- Calling `eval()`
- Using `new Function()` with a string argument
- Calling `setInterval()`, `setTimeout()`, `sort()`, and other functions with a string argument instead of an anonymous function

The latter case applies to our sample application—the `setInterval()` code needs to be refactored (and should also be put in the external csp.js JavaScript file) like this:

```
window.setInterval(
    function() {
        updateTime(new Date().toLocaleTimeString());
    },
    1000);
```

Bad news: the application still does not run. There is one more catch. Remember the Underscore library we are using for templating? Turns out that it is relying on dynamic code evaluation—it is using `new Function()`, for instance. Obviously, we cannot fix the library itself, and we also cannot easily get rid of it (in the sample application we could, but in a more complex one it won't be so easy).

For this kind of situation, there is one last resort in CSP. The constant `'unsafe-eval'` allows the use of `eval()` and friends. Note that the value is not called `'enable-eval'` or something similar, but it is stressing that this might not be safe. You are supposed to feel the pain and some effects of a bad conscience while typing this.

> **NOTE**   If you can rule out that user-supplied data will be fed to `eval()` and similar calls, using `'unsafe-eval'` is an acceptable choice. There is another option called `'unsafe-inline'` that re-enables inline code. This might

make sense in a CSS context, when your existing app has lots of inline styles. When using `'unsafe-inline'` for `script-src`, though, you basically forfeit most of the XSS protection Content Security Policy is offering.

This leaves us with the following Content Security Policy:

```
default-src 'self'; img-src 'self' https://www.manning.com/assets/;
style-src 'self' https://cdn.jsdelivr.net;
'unsafe-hashes' 'sha256-yckz1zrIL2HgQwm7x1ins99s5jndZE3XnmgOAkJvDOg='
script-src 'self' https://cdn.jsdelivr.net
'sha256-nzwB34aHhENPZBCXYw2IW6Io61J79hTi15ZZbN/nP9I=' 'unsafe-eval'
```

Success—the application works again. Admittedly, the application was doctored a bit to cause us several issues when creating the CSP. On the other hand, you can see that applying CSP to an existing site does take some effort and depends a bit on whether you have previously followed best practices with regards to JavaScript and CSS, such as externalizing everything. Such advice will be covered in the next section.

NOTE If you look at the browser console while running the page, you may notice that one Content Security Policy remains. Visual Studio is injecting code that is opening a WebSocket connection to synchronize the browser with the IDE (e.g., to allow hot reload). You can use the `connect-src` directive and set it to the current origin plus the one Visual Studio is using. On my system, `connect-src 'self' ws://localhost:49326/` would work. A similar concern would apply for a Blazor Server application maintaining a WebSocket connection to the server, which would require `connect-src 'self'`.

More Content Security Policy directives

The Content Security Policy specification supports more directives. The following two do not limit content being loaded but instead impose restrictions on the page's behavior:

- `base-uri`—Which values or paths are allowed for `<base href="">`
- `form-action`—Which values are allowed for the `action` attribute of `<form>` elements on the page (target URL for form data submission)

Chapter 4 will also cover the `frame-ancestors` directive that limits which pages may load the current one in an iframe.

2.3.4 Content Security Policy best practices

Using Content Security Policy is a double-edged sword. You can effectively protect your application from cross-site scripting, but you can also break its functionality. During development, you need to ensure that everything works, but also in production, you are extremely interested in whenever the policy is violated. There can only be two reasons for this to happen: either you forgot to add some special case in your CSP, or you have a security vulnerability that is actively exploited.

The `report-uri` directive makes the browser send an HTTP POST request to an endpoint of our choosing whenever one policy is violated. The directive can then look similar to this:

```
default-src 'self'; img-src 'self' https://www.manning.com/assets/;
style-src 'self' https://cdn.jsdelivr.net;
'unsafe-hashes' 'sha256-yckz1zrIL2HgQwm7x1ins99s5jndZE3XnmgOAkJvDOg='
script-src 'self' https://cdn.jsdelivr.net
'sha256-nzwB34aHhENPZBCXYw2IW6Io61J79hTi15ZZbN/nP9I=' 'unsafe-eval'
report-uri /collect
```

This will send information about the policy violation in JSON format to the `/collect` endpoint on the server, using HTTP POST. The name of the endpoint, is of course, arbitrary, and it can also reside on a different server—you just have to implement it. (This is not covered in this book, but there are commercial options available; the most well-known one is probably https://report-uri.com. Of course, you have to decide first whether you want to send information about potential incidents to a third party.) Our application still has one remaining policy violation—the WebSocket connection for Visual Studio—and it generates the following JSON data (formatted for legibility) in Chrome:

```
{
    "csp-report": {
        "document-uri": "https://localhost:44373/CSP",
        "referrer": "https://localhost:44373/CSP",          ⟵─┐ Shows the violated
        "violated-directive": "connect-src",                  ◄──┘ directive
        "effective-directive": "connect-src",
        "original-policy": "default-src 'self'; img-src 'self'
        https://www.manning.com/assets/; style-src 'self'
        https://cdn.jsdelivr.net 'unsafe-hashes' 'sha256-yckz1zrIL2HgQwm7
        x1ins99s5jndZE3XnmgOAkJvDOg='; script-src 'self'
        https://cdn.jsdelivr.net 'sha256-nzwB34aHhENPZBCXYw2IW6Io61J79
        hTi15ZZbN/nP9I=' 'unsafe-eval'; report-uri /collect",
        "disposition": "enforce",
        "blocked-uri": "ws://localhost:49326",
        "line-number": 5,
        "column-number": 18,
        "source-file": "https://localhost:44373/_framework/aspnetcore-
    browser-refresh.js",
        "status-code": 0,
        "script-sample": ""        ⟵─┐ Shows a sample of the offending
    }                                 │ content (not filled here)
}
```

Firefox, on the other hand, reports this information to the server:

```
{
    "csp-report": {
        "blocked-uri":
        "ws://localhost:49326/AspNetCoreSecurity.RazorSamples/",
        "column-number": 17,
        "document-uri": "https://localhost:44373/CSP",
        "line-number": 5,
```

```
"original-policy": "default-src 'self'; img-src 'self'
➡https://www.manning.com/assets/; style-src 'self'
➡https://cdn.jsdelivr.net 'sha256-yckz1zrIL2HgQwm7x1ins99s5jndZE3
➡XnmgOAkJvDOg='; script-src 'self' https://cdn.jsdelivr.net
➡ 'sha256-nzwB34aAHhENPZBCXYw2IW6Io61J79hTi15ZZbN/nP9I='
➡'unsafe-eval'; report-uri https://localhost:44373/collect",
"referrer": "",
"source-file": "https://localhost:44373/_framework/aspnetcore-
➡browser-refresh.js",
"violated-directive": "default-src"
  }
}
```

Shows the violated directive

Shows the HTTP referrer of the current document (not filled here)

You can see subtle differences between the two browsers. Firefox reports that the `default-src` is violated. Chrome-based browsers correctly say that `connect-src` is the directive that is actually violated (`"violated-directive"`); since it is absent from the Content Security Policy, the value from `default-src` is used. The line number is a bit off, as well (`18` in Chrome, `17` in Firefox). Firefox is providing a field for the HTTP referrer (which is not set), whereas Chrome's JSON structure is ready for part of the violating script (`"script-sample"`), but this value is not filled yet—more on that later in this chapter.

So, the data coming from the browsers is not set in stone, but it is still valuable. And it's getting better. If you are replacing the `Content-Security-Policy` header with `Content-Security-Policy-Report-Only`, the browser does two things: (1) all policy violations are detected, and (2) they are sent to an endpoint if the `report-uri` directive is set. However, the Content Security Policy is not enforced, so your application behaves exactly as before CSP was added. When creating a new CSP for a site, start with the `Content-Security-Policy-Report-Only` header, and let it run for a week or two. Your users will unknowingly test the policy. You just have to monitor what your reporting endpoint receives. Once you are happy (i.e., no more reports are coming in), you are ready to arm the system and use the `Content-Security-Policy` header.

The end of the CSP-generation process is now clear, but the rest of the process is not, so how can we get there? As always, it depends on the circumstances and the actual project. However, here are two approaches that have often worked very well for me.

When you migrate a legacy site to cope with CSP, start with a policy that basically forbids everything. The `'none'` constant comes in handy here:

```
default-src 'none'; form-action 'none'; report-uri /collect
```

No resources may be loaded; no forms may be submitted. Then, while using the web application, monitor whatever is sent to the collection endpoint, and then either fix the site or expand the policy (preferably the former). To save some time, you might also just start with `default-src 'self' report-uri /collect` and see how far that gets you.

The end goal is a CSP that is as strict as possible, if that's feasible for the stack you are using. What you should definitely do is disable plugins and set the base URI:

```
object-src 'none'; base-uri 'none'
```

You may also want to consider restricting JavaScript content to those with a one-time token only:

```
script-src 'nonce-19UoXyUC5RHumWo7PyZ/8o9WmaquPDfD49Xx+EEekDI='
```

We intentionally omitted techniques to maintain backward compatibility with browsers that only understand Content Security Policy 1, since that is no longer relevant. We are not looking backward; in fact, we are looking forward, to Content Security Policy Level 3.

2.3.5   *Content Security Policy Level 3 features*

The upcoming CSP3 version is not yet a final standard, but work is ongoing, and Google Chrome and related browsers serve as early adopters. The current status of the CSP3 document is "working draft," so everything is subject to change. On the other hand, since Chrome started implementing some of those features already, the specification author (employed by Google) is probably not too inclined to introduce too many backward compatibility breaking changes.

> **TIP**   The best source for a browser compatibility list for CSP3 is this page at MDN Web Docs (formerly known as Mozilla Developer Network): http://mng.bz/o2rr.

We have already encountered one CSP3 feature, the `'unsafe-hashes'` constant, which makes CSP hashes also apply for event handler attributes. Another new constant is `'report-sample'`. This may be added to any directive and ensures that if a policy violation occurs, the report sent will also contain the culprit—the violating piece of code or markup. This is how the policy could look:

```
default-src 'self'; img-src 'self' https://www.manning.com/assets/;
➡style-src 'self' https://cdn.jsdelivr.net;
➡'report-sample' 'sha256-yckz1zrIL2HgQwm7x1ins99s5jndZE3XnmgOAkJvDOg='
➡script-src 'self' https://cdn.jsdelivr.net
➡'sha256-nzwB34aHhENPZBCXYw2IW6Io61J79hTi15ZZbN/nP9I=' 'unsafe-eval'
➡report-uri /collect
```

In this Content Security Policy, the `'unsafe-hashes'` constant was replaced with `'report-sample'`, so the inline CSS style (`style="font-size: xx-large"`) will cause a policy violation. The report sent to the collection endpoint will then look like this (edited for legibility):

```
{
    "csp-report": {
        "document-uri": "https://localhost:44373/CSP",
        "referrer": "https://localhost:44373/CSP",
        "violated-directive": "style-src-attr",
        "effective-directive": "style-src-attr",
        "original-policy": "default-src 'self'; img-src 'self'
        ➡https://www.manning.com/assets/; style-src 'self'
        ➡https://cdn.jsdelivr.net 'report-sample' 'sha256-yckz1zrIL2HgQwm7
        ➡x1ins99s5jndZE3XnmgOAkJvDOg='; script-src 'self'
```

```
➥https://cdn.jsdelivr.net 'sha256-nzwB34aHhENPZBCXYw2IW6Io61J79h
➥Ti15ZZbN/nP9I=' 'unsafe-eval'; report-uri /collect",
    "disposition": "enforce",
    "blocked-uri": "inline",
    "line-number": 20,
    "source-file": "https://localhost:44373/CSP",
    "status-code": 0,
    "script-sample": "font-size: xx-large"
  }
}
```

The `"script-sample"` entry in the JSON structure now contains the offender that caused the violation.

> **WARNING** The `'report-sample'` constant only works for inline styles and for JavaScript code—it won't have any effect on other violations, such as the WebSocket call to a third party, which our application still does.

Another useful addition in CSP3 is the `'strict-dynamic'` constant:

```
Content-Security-Policy: script-src 'self' 'strict-dynamic'
```

Once this is activated, JavaScript code is allowed to dynamically add more JavaScript to the page, usually with this pattern:

```
let js = document.getElementById("script");
js.src = "https://cdn.jsdelivr.net/npm/underscore@1.13.1/underscore-umd-min.js";
document.getElementsByTagName("body")[0].appendChild(js);
```

A new `<script>` element is created and then added to the DOM (the specification calls this *non-parser-inserted script*). The idea is compelling: if we trust a certain piece of JavaScript code—for instance, by using a hash to greenlight it—then we should also trust the code it dynamically loads. The `'strict-dynamic'` constant may be used in the `default-src` and `script-src` directives.

The remaining additions to CSP are also mostly useful but may be described in rather few words:

- The `navigate-to` directive restricts where the browser navigates to from the current page, no matter whether users click on a link, submit a form, or are redirected via JavaScript code.
- `script-src-attr` and `script-src-elem` work like `script-src`, but only for specific types of JavaScript: the former applies to event handler attributes, the latter to `<script>` elements. Similarly, `style-src-attr` and `style-src-elem` work for `style` attributes and for `<style>` elements only. Usually it is not necessary to make this distinction, so `script-src` and `style-src` are sufficient in most cases.
- `report-to` is the new name of the `report-uri` directive; for obvious compatibility reasons, the old name is still valid for the time being.

CSP3 adds useful new features without changing the general approach of the defense-in-depth mechanism. When we manage to apply a CSP to our web application, we have a very solid protection from cross-site scripting. But browsers place even more weapons at our disposal.

2.4   *More browser safeguards*

Adding security features into browsers is a trend that arguably started with Internet Explorer 8, which introduced some interesting ideas to provide more attack protection in web browsers. Some of these approaches turned out to be really useful (chapter 3 will describe one, the HttpOnly cookie flag), whereas others did not work so well in the long run.

Let's start with something deprecated and look at the X-XSS-Protection HTTP header. The prefix X- means that it's not an official, standardized header. The idea of the Internet Explorer 8 team was that browsers should be able to heuristically find out whether a cross-site scripting attack is currently taking place. One signal could be if there is something in the URL that also appears verbatim on the page and is executed as JavaScript code. When this feature was introduced, there were two design goals:

- *The XSS detection must be very fast.* Users don't accept slow browsers.
- *The XSS detection must not flag valid code as an attack.* No false positives!

Like Content Security Policy, the built-in XSS browser protection is a defense-in-depth mechanism. Its goal is not to be perfect, but just to add some extra security, without being detrimental to the performance and usability of the web browser.

By default, this protection is enabled, and you will not find any option in the browser settings to deactivate the XSS auditor. Remember that injected JavaScript code runs in the security context of the current page. If there is any person or entity that should be allowed to turn the protection off, it's the server. And this is where the X-XSS-Protection HTTP header comes in. To deactivate the protection, set it like the following:

```
X-XSS-Protection: 0
```

When the header was first introduced, some major sites like Google set it to 0 because they were afraid that the auditor might interfere with their applications. A few months later, however, they changed the header to this value:

```
X-XSS-Protection: 1; mode=block
```

This not only activates the protection feature (it's enabled by default anyway), but also prevents the browser from rendering the page if a potential XSS attack is determined. Without mode=block, an error banner like the one in figure 2.12 appears. Internet Explorer properly renders the page but does not execute the suspicious JavaScript code.

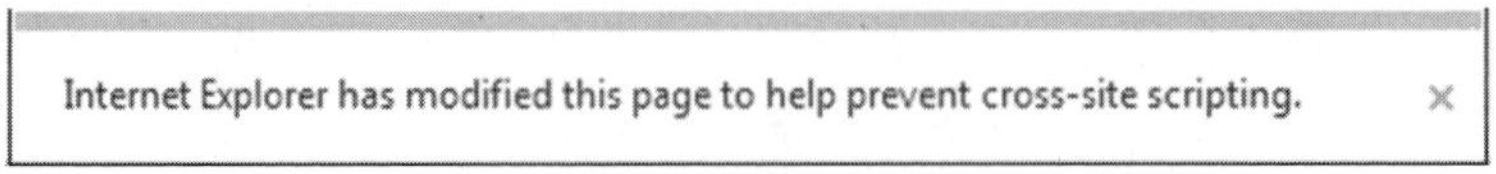

Internet Explorer has modified this page to help prevent cross-site scripting.   ✕

Figure 2.12   Internet Explorer thinks that cross-site scripting is taking place.

Safari, Google Chrome, and Microsoft Edge adapted this feature. Chrome-based browsers even provide reporting capabilities similar to Content Security Policy:

```
X-XSS-Protection: 1; report=/collect
```

Any detected XSS attacks will be sent to the collection endpoint (which has yet to be implemented).

With the rise of Content Security Policy, `X-XSS-Protection` became less popular. Eventually, the feature was deprecated and has been removed in recent versions of Chrome-based browsers. Firefox browsers never adapted the HTTP header. So long, `X-XSS-Protection`, and thanks for the fish—CSP has now taken your place in all modern browsers (and Internet Explorer users as least have some cross-site scripting protection).

The best XSS defense consists of properly escaping special characters. However, a frequent desire is to have the web application accept any input, including HTML, and "just strip out the JavaScript portion." This is much, much harder than it sounds. Here is a nice example from security researcher Gareth Heyes (http://mng.bz/nN1g):

```
<div='/x=&quot;&#39&gt;&lt;iframe/onload=alert(1)&gt;'>
```

This looks like a legitimate `<div>` element with a rather strange syntax. Internet Explorer, however, parses the entities within the x attribute so that the input mutates to the following elements in the DOM:

```
<div=' x="&quot;'"><iframe onload="alert(1)">'"&gt;</iframe></div='>
```

Note that there is now suddenly an iframe (which was previously "hidden" in the attribute) with an `onload` attribute set—typical cross-site scripting. This attack is commonly called *mutated XSS* because the input mutates into something dangerous.

If you want to sanitize user input so that it does not contain JavaScript code, my advice is don't do it. And if you do, don't roll your own implementation—use something preexisting:

- Internet Explorer introduced the `toStaticHTML()` helper function— `toStaticHTML(input)`—which, unfortunately, wasn't picked up by other browsers. This is an approach from the past.
- The W3C is currently working on the HTML Sanitizer API (http://mng.bz/ v6PJ), and Firefox can be configured to use the simple API—new `Sanitizer().sanitize(input)`. This API might be very relevant in the future once all recent browsers support it.
- The open source project DOMPurify provides a simple syntax to sanitize input—just call `DOMPurify.sanitize(input)`—with many configuration options. Read more at the project site on GitHub (https://github.com/cure53/ DOMPurify). This is, arguably, the best option currently.

Despite the best of intentions, all of those features have already been exploited (and, later, fixed—it's a game of cat and mouse). If you can afford it, be very strict in what input you accept, and do not open Pandora's box by trying to remove JavaScript components in HTML strings.

Summary

Let's review what we have learned so far:

- Cross-site scripting manifests in injecting JavaScript (and, sometimes, HTML) into the output of a page, running with the same privileges as the website's legitimate code, making the attack dangerous.
- Escaping five special HTML characters effectively secures the HTML portions of an application by making the browser render them as harmless text.
- When utilizing user-supplied data in JavaScript code, JavaScript special characters need to be escaped prior to output.
- Content Security Policy is a defense-in-depth mechanism that is extremely effective against XSS by restricting which code the browser executes and which resources it loads.
- Making legacy applications ready for CSP often requires major refactoring.
- Other browser approaches to prevent cross-site scripting, like built-in XSS detection, did not work well enough in practice.

One of the XSS consequences is that cookies may be stolen—especially session cookies. So next up, we will look at ASP.NET Core's session management, how it may be attacked, and what we can do to protect against that.

Attacking session management

In late 2010, software developer Eric Butler released a Firefox extension called *Firesheep*. It worked like this: you would connect to a public Wi-Fi network, like at a train station or a coffee shop. When installed and active, the extension would continuously analyze (unencrypted) data in the current wireless network. If someone else in the same network was logged into one of a select number of sites, a window popped up, prompting you to go to that site, as that other person. And indeed, one click later, you could access a third-party site as the person sitting close to you. Those sites included

- Amazon
- Facebook

51

- Google (including Google Mail)
- Hacker News
- LinkedIn
- Quora
- Reddit
- Stack Overflow
- Twitter
- Windows Live (including Windows Live Mail, previously known as Hotmail)
- Yahoo! (including Yahoo! Mail)
- And about 20 more

The extension was surprisingly simple: it scanned for certain cookies containing session identifiers. Once one was encountered, the extension could re-create this cookie in the user's Firefox instance. The attacker was then logged into their victim's account and could, for instance, read and write their emails, read and write tweets, or access their calendar. This attack is called *session hijacking*—the session is literally taken hostage—and exploits the session mechanism of many of today's web frameworks, including ASP.NET Core. In order to mitigate this risk, we need to analyze how sessions work and how we can make it harder for session cookies to be stolen. We will also need to discuss how we can detect an ongoing attack.

> **WARNING** If you are curious, Firesheep's source code is available at https://github.com/codebutler/firesheep. However, it has not been maintained for many years, only works with ancient Firefox versions (below 4), and very likely contains security vulnerabilities.

3.1 Anatomy of a session management attack

Session hijacking may be best explained by looking at a simple application that can be exploited. Let's start with the following listing, which is the page model for a Razor Page.

Listing 3.1   Persisting the browser identification string

```
using Microsoft.AspNetCore.Mvc.RazorPages;
using Microsoft.Net.Http.Headers;            Loads additional functionality for
                                             simplified HTTP header access
namespace AspNetCoreSecurity.RazorSamples.Pages
{
                                             Shows the page property for the
    public class SessionWriteModel : PageModel    browser identification string
    {
        public string UserAgent { get; set; } = string.Empty;

        public void OnGet()                  Reads out the user agent
        {                                    from the HTTP request
            this.UserAgent =
            ➥ HttpContext.Request.Headers[HeaderNames.UserAgent];
```

```
        HttpContext.Session.SetString(          Persists the user
            "browser",                          agent to the session
            this.UserAgent);
    }
  }
}
```

Upon page load, the browser identification string that clients routinely send as part of a request is read out. The code is checking the `User-Agent` HTTP header for that information. Next, this browser string is stored into the user's session, using the `Session.SetString()` method. The following listing shows the associated Razor Page.

Listing 3.2 The associated Razor Page

```
@page
@model AspNetCoreSecurity.RazorSamples.Pages.SessionWriteModel

<div class="text-center">
    <h1 class="display-4">Login</h1>
    <form method="post" action="">
        <div class="mt-5 mb-5">
            <p class="lead">Data written to session:
            ➥@Model.UserAgent</p>                     ◁──┐ Shows output data
        </div>                                             from session
        <div class="mb-3">
            <a asp-page="SessionRead">Read from session
            ➥</a>                             ◁──┐ Links to second page
        </div>                                     to read from the session
    </form>
</div>
```

Here, the browser identification string is shown, and there is also a link to a second page (*SessionRead.cshtml*), which you can see in full in the next listing.

Listing 3.3 The browser info from the session

```
@page
@using Microsoft.AspNetCore.Http

<div class="text-center">
    <h1 class="display-4">Login</h1>
    <form method="post" action="">
        <div class="mt-5 mb-5">
            <p class="lead">
                Data read from session:
                @(HttpContext.Session.GetString("browser")
                ➥?? string.Empty)                ◁──┐ Shows output browser identification
            </p>                                       string from the session, if any
        </div>
    </form>
</div>
```

Now it gets interesting: the page uses the `Session.GetString()` method to access the browser identification string that was just written to the session and outputs it. Bad news: if things go wrong, this application may be exploited.

3.1.1   Stealing session cookies

It's time for a quick experiment. Open an arbitrary browser, say Firefox, and load the *SessionRead.cshtml* page (figure 3.1). You will get a different browser information string.

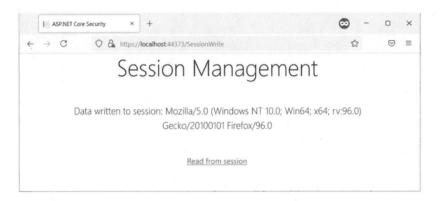

Figure 3.1   The Firefox user agent is written to the session.

You will see that the user agent for that browser is shown on the page, assuring you that the same information has been written to the session. Now open up the browser developer tools; in most browsers, you can access them by pressing F12 (figure 3.2).

Figure 3.2   The F12 tools display cookie information (among many other things).

There you can find all the cookies your browser has stored for the current site, usually in the Application or Storage tab. Note that there is one called `.AspNetCore.Session`, which we will need shortly.

Now open a different type of browser, say Google Chrome. Open the same page, and tend to the browser developer tools. Copy the name and the value of the ASP.NET session ID cookie from the first browser (Firefox) to the second one (Chrome). Then, in the second browser, click the link to get to the *SessionRead.cshtml* page. You should get a result similar to the one in figure 3.3.

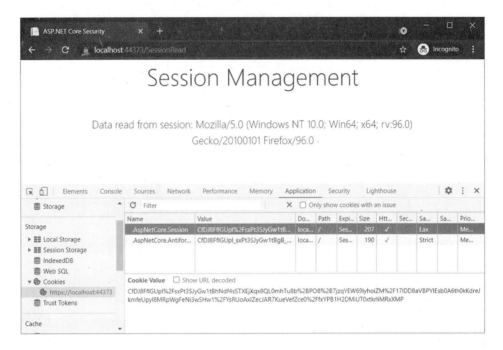

Figure 3.3 This Firefox looks suspiciously like Chrome (or the other way around?!).

In the exemplary setup for the screenshots, Google Chrome now claims that we are using Firefox, since the former browser is now using the session created in the latter one. The session was successfully hijacked.

In order to either prevent this kind of attack or to find out when it happened, we need to understand the underlying mechanism a bit better.

3.1.2 Cookies and session management

ASP.NET Core's session management relies on HTTP cookies, so let's look at them first. Cookies were initially conceived by the developers of the then-popular web browser Netscape Navigator in 1994. A preliminary specification was published, and Internet Explorer also implemented it later. There is also a proper standard, RFC 6265 (https://datatracker.ietf.org/doc/html/rfc6265), but the general process has not changed in the last 25-plus years.

NOTE The original Netscape website does not exist anymore, but there is an archived version of the cookie specification at https://curl.se/rfc/cookie_spec.html. As the page said back in 1994: "Use with caution."

Nowadays, cookies are an indispensable tool for creating web applications. This is because storing user-specific data was not a concern when the web and HTTP were created. Actually, the HTTP specification has stated since the beginning that the protocol is stateless. This means that it cannot store anything—there is no "state" that the client has when communicating with the server. Since almost all complex web applications need to store information, even if it's only regarding who is logged in, there is no viable alternative for cookies (we briefly discuss local storage and session storage later in this chapter). Figure 3.4 show how cookies work in general.

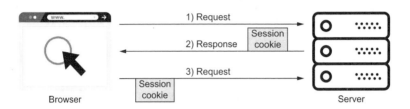

Figure 3.4   The process of sending and receiving cookies

The server is the entity that sends the cookies using the `Set-Cookie` HTTP header. It contains the cookie's name, its value, and optional attributes such as the expiration date (if there's none, the cookie expires when the browser is closed; otherwise, it expires no later than its expiration date).

```
Set-Cookie: PreferredLanguage=en-US; expires=Sat, 13 Jun 2026 12:34:56 GMT
```

The browser then has three options according to its configuration:

- Store ("accept") the cookie.
- Do not store ("deny") the cookie.
- Ask the user what to do.

To be honest, about 20 years ago, I opted for the third option, but nowadays, there are cookies everywhere, so browsers removed this option for good. The first option is almost always the one in effect. Disabling cookies in the web browser basically prevents you from using many web applications, so no one is doing that these days. Admittedly, most browsers offer specific settings for third-party cookies, which can be blocked, usually without affecting the core functionality of a site.

When the cookie is stored, it is sent back once the client sends the next HTTP request back to the server. This time, the `Cookie` header is used, and only the name and value of the cookie are sent:

```
Cookie: PreferredLanguage=en-US
```

NOTE   We are assuming that the cookie's domain flag is not set. Third-party cookies are out of scope for the discussion of this chapter. The way some clients implement their session restore feature might also give cookies without an expiration date a life past the closing of the browser.

Since cookies are stored in the browser, their values are easy to manipulate. It obviously does not make sense to store sensitive information in a cookie, such as the currently logged in username or user-specific privileges. But how can we persist vital information while a user is interacting with our application?

Enter session management. This mechanism piggybacks on cookies but mitigates the risks of data manipulation, at least to some degree. Figure 3.5 shows the process.

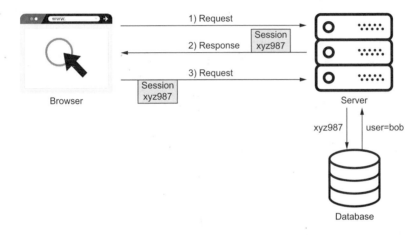

Figure 3.5   The process of session management with cookies

The server stores some information about the current user session. The figure visualizes a database, but this could very well be in-memory storage or other means of persisting data. Each dataset has a unique identifier, the *session ID*. This session ID is then sent to the client as a cookie. The session ID itself is generated on the server, is rather long, and is virtually impossible to guess. Therefore, data manipulation in the browser is less of a concern than when the cookie contained actual pieces of information.

The browser sends cookies back to the server with each subsequent request, so the server can always identify the session and access the correct session data. So as long as the session ID is not stolen, the process seems to be secure. On the other hand, once an attacker gets ahold of a session ID, they can impersonate the user when talking to the server. All the server needs and expects is the session ID. Luckily, ASP.NET Core supports some precautions to keep the session ID safe.

> **Session storage and local storage**
>
> There are two other technologies for storing data in the client: local storage and session storage. Data persisted here may only be read and written from JavaScript code, using the `localStorage` and `sessionStorage` objects. In this case, the server is out of the picture. That's why local storage and session storage are primarily used by single-page applications (SPAs). Session storage data is purged once the browser tab is closed, whereas local storage does not have an expiration date.
>
> If you are storing sensitive data in one of the two options, the main threat is XSS, since JavaScript code may access local storage and session storage data. Chapter 2 contains techniques and approaches to prevent XSS. Whereas you may protect cookies from JavaScript access with the `HttpOnly` flag, there is no such mechanism for local storage and session storage, as these are explicitly JavaScript APIs.

3.2 ASP.NET Core cookie and session settings

Earlier versions of ASP.NET came with session management support out of the box, without any additional mandatory configuration. This changed with ASP.NET Core, where all features have to be explicitly enabled. In the Program.cs file, we both need a call to `builder.Services.AddSession()` and `app.UseSession()`. If you have an existing project that started with a .NET version prior to 6 and middleware configuration resides in the Startup.cs file, add `services.AddSession()` to the `Configure-Services()` method, and `app.UseSession()` in the `Configure()` method (this is the first and last time we will mention this legacy approach). The pages or controllers, using session functionality such as `Session.SetString()` and `Session.Get-String()`, may need to import the `Microsoft.AspNetCore.Http` namespace to have access to those and related methods.

> **NOTE**   When using Blazor, you usually do not need session management; if you do, chances are that you are hosting the Blazor app within an ASP.NET Core app and therefore also have a Program.cs file.

There are three main approaches for an attacker to steal a session ID:

- On the client, usually with cross-site scripting. Chapter 2 provides a wealth of information about the attack, as well as about countermeasures.
- On the server, which is hard to pull off. SQL injection comes to mind, but only in case the session information is stored in a database. Chapter 6 will get you covered.
- During the transport between client and server, by sniffing traffic (usually only possible if HTTP is used instead of HTTPS). That's how the Firesheep extension worked.

The original author of the cookie specification foresaw the third attack vector and added a safeguard into his technical concept. A few years later, the team behind

Internet Explorer 6 added a protection for the first attack vector (and other browsers followed suit promptly). These two defenses come in the form of cookie flags:

- `HttpOnly`—This flag hides the cookie from direct JavaScript access, making XSS less useful for cookie theft (see callout).
- `secure`—This flag makes sure that this cookie is only sent from the client back to the server over a secured connection (HTTPS), preventing eavesdropping cookies.

> **NOTE** I say "less useful" because there is an attack vector that at least hypothetically works. If the HTTP `TRACE` method is activated on the web server (by default, it isn't, at least for the default configuration of modern web servers), then an XSS attack might inject JavaScript code that issues a `TRACE` request to the server. The browser automatically sends all cookies along this request. The server returns all HTTP headers, including those cookies—that's how `TRACE` works. In this specific scenario, the attacker can then access the session cookies.

Setting the session cookie flags can be done in Program.cs like this:

```
builder.Services.AddSession(options => {
    options.Cookie.HttpOnly = true;
    options.Cookie.SecurePolicy = CookieSecurePolicy.Always;
});
```

Note that you explicitly need to set both options if you elect to use these security features (and I recommend that you do!). By default, the `HttpOnly` flag is deactivated, and the `secure` flag is only being used if you access the application using HTTPS (the value for this default option is `CookieSecurePolicy.SameAsRequest`, and the enum is part of the `Microsoft.AspNetCore.Http` namespace).

> **WARNING** When enabling the `Secure` flag, make sure that you will always use the application via HTTPS, even during local development. Otherwise, you will not see the cookie when using plain HTTP.

Figure 3.6 shows the F12 developer tools once the application has the new cookie settings.

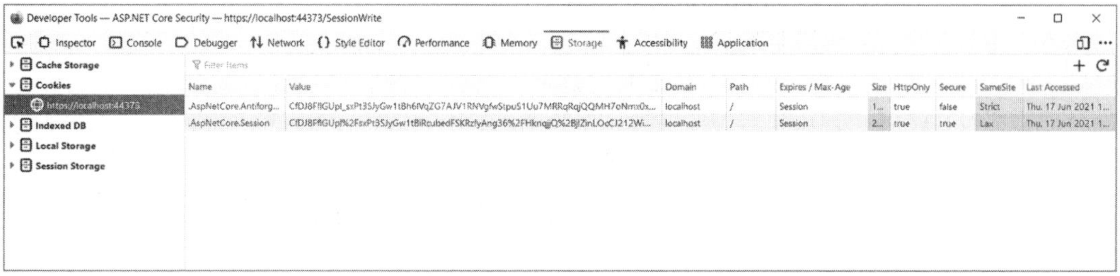

Figure 3.6 The session cookie now enjoys extra security.

Both the `secure` flag and the `HttpOnly` flag are now set for the `.AspNetCore.Session` cookie. Figure 3.7 proves that `HttpOnly` works as expected.

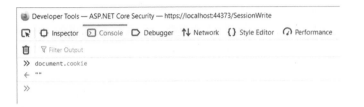

Figure 3.7
The session cookie is invisible to JavaScript.

The JavaScript variable `document.cookie` does not contain the session cookie, although it is there.

> **NOTE** There is another cookie flag called `SameSite`, which adds protection from another attack called *cross-site request forgery* (CSRF) and will be covered in detail in chapter 4.

Protecting cookies

Adding those settings in the `AddSession()` call in Program.cs applies them to all session cookies. If you want to have the same protection for the custom cookies you are setting, you can use a similar approach:

```
var cookieOptions = new CookieOptions()
{
    HttpOnly = true,
    Secure = true
};

Response.Cookies.Append("PreferredLanguage", "en-US", cookieOptions);
```

First create some cookie options (the Boolean `Secure` property is translated to the secure flag), and then apply them when adding a new cookie to the HTTP response.

In case a session is indeed stolen, it's helpful to limit the amount of time that a session can be exploited. By default, each session will be abandoned after 20 minutes of inactivity (meaning no HTTP requests with that session ID). This time span can be globally set in the `AddSession()` call in Program.cs as well:

```
builder.Services.AddSession(options => {
    options.IdleTimeout = TimeSpan.FromMinutes(5);
}
```

I often support companies in migrating their desktop applications to the web, and a common request is to set the session timeout to something in the ballpark of 8 hours (log in when the day starts, log out when the day ends). When I have my security hat on—and that is often the case—I have to decline. Especially for security-critical areas, a shorter timeout supports the security concept. On the other hand, users may need to log in more often, or might even lose unsaved work due to the session expiring, so try to find a compromise between security and usability.

Do you remember the three places where session IDs may be stolen—client, server, and in between? We will now make sure that the latter approach does not work by using HTTPS throughout.

3.3   *Enforcing HTTPS*

HTTPS is an end-to-end encryption, so in a nutshell, the client and the server negotiate the configuration of the encryption before they begin exchanging any data, including HTTP headers. Therefore, cookies are not sent in cleartext when HTTPS is being used.

> **NOTE**   Even the URL is protected when using HTTPS. The browser first uses the HTTP method `CONNECT` to negotiate encryption with the server; only then is the actual HTTP request, including the URL, sent.

With the `secure` flag being set, the cookie will not be transmitted when a regular HTTP request is sent. This is exactly what was missing when Firesheep had its 15 minutes of fame. Back then, only the login forms for the various services were using HTTPS, but afterward, the communication was done without encryption for "performance reasons." Turns out that security must trump performance, so these days, HTTPS is being used throughout, with browsers even warning users if a regular HTTP connection is being used, as you can see in figure 3.8.

Figure 3.8   Google Chrome makes it very obvious that HTTPS isn't being used.

After Firesheep was released, companies were essentially forced to speed up their efforts to move to "HTTPS only." It took some of them several months to do it, but in the end, the complete communication was encrypted, including the session IDs.

Securing cookies is an important step, but part of a complete security solution is to also prevent any HTTP requests. The ASP.NET Core templates provide a good starting point when you enable the Configure for HTTPS checkbox (figure 3.9).

Additional information

ASP.NET Core Web App   C#   Linux   macOS   Windows   Cloud   Service   Web

Framework ⓘ

.NET 6.0 (Long-term support)

Authentication type ⓘ

None

☑ Configure for HTTPS ⓘ
☐ Enable Docker ⓘ

Docker OS ⓘ

Linux

Back   Create

Figure 3.9   Visual Studio offers some HTTPS preparation when creating an ASP.NET Core project.

Apart from configuring the appsettings.json file to set up an HTTPS listener, two interesting pieces of code are added to Program.cs:

```
if (!app.Environment.IsDevelopment())
{
    app.UseExceptionHandler("/Error");
    app.UseHsts();                        Permanently
                                          uses HTTPS
}
                                   Redirects HTTP
                                   to HTTPS
app.UseHttpsRedirection();
```

Let's start with the app.UseHttpsRedirection() call. The name reveals what is happening—all incoming HTTP requests will be redirected to HTTPS. By default, this is done by sending the HTTP status code 307 Temporary Redirect. A more common HTTP status code for redirection is 302 Found, but this method does not maintain the HTTP method; a POST request would be redirected to GET, which should break many applications. HTTP 307 keeps the HTTP method, so a POST request to an HTTP resource will be redirected to a POST request to HTTPS. Technically, the server sends the HTTP 307 status code, and the browser then issues the new HTTP request. This initial HTTP request happens without encryption.

As usual, the behavior of this feature can be configured in Program.cs as well, in the AddHttpsRedirection() call (this call is not required if you are fine with the default values):

```
builder.Services.AddHttpsRedirection(options => {
    options.HttpsPort = 444; // default: 443
    options.RedirectStatusCode = 302; // default: 307
});
```

The values you can set are the port to be used for the HTTPS redirect and the HTTP status code.

> **TIP** When you have configured the HTTPS port in the appsettings.json file using "https_port" as the JSON key, ASP.NET Core automatically picks that value up for the redirection, but you can override it in the AddHttps-Redirection() call.

When using UseHttpsRedirection(), all requests to the server are encrypted, with one possible exception: the very first one, when the user enters the domain name into the browser. With some extra effort, even this request might use HTTPS, with the aid of one more HTTP header.

The secret ingredient is defined in IETF RFC 6797: HTTP Strict Transport Security (https://datatracker.ietf.org/doc/html/rfc6797), or HSTS. The central component is the Strict-Transport-Security HTTP header, which is supported in all recent browsers—even Internet Explorer 11 adheres to it. This HTTP header instructs the browser to exclusively use HTTPS to talk to a host, even if the user explicitly provides an http:// URL. Browsers remember this setting, so it's almost impossible to ever talk plain HTTP to that server again!

WARNING   This is a potential disadvantage of HSTS: if you are not absolutely sure that you will never send cleartext HTTP requests to your server in the future, think twice before activating this feature. HSTS requires HTTPS throughout and does not support a mix of both encrypted and unencrypted communication.

HSTS supports two major settings in the HTTP header:

- `max-age`—How long the browser shall cache these settings (in seconds)
- `includeSubdomains`—Whether subdomains should be included (e.g., api .example.com if the header is sent from example.com)

Here is a typical HSTS header:

```
Strict-Transport-Security: max-age=63072000; includeSubDomains;
```

The browser caches these settings for 730 days (roughly two years) and applies it to all subdomains.

You may have already guessed it—these settings can be applied directly in Program.cs by adding an (otherwise unnecessary) `AddHsts()` call to the `Program` class:

```
builder.Services.AddHsts(options =>
{                                             Enables HSTS for
    options.IncludeSubDomains = true;   ←──── subdomains too
    options.MaxAge = TimeSpan.FromYears(2);   ←── Caches this setting for
});                                               a maximum of 2 years
```

In addition to these two settings, ASP.NET Core allows us to exclude certain hosts from sending this header (which could facilitate testing in some cases):

```
options.ExcludedHosts.Add("insecure.example.com");
```

We have made some progress—now only the first request to a website can hypothetically be unencrypted; all future requests will use HTTPS. But there is one possible extra step. When you open Google Chrome and type http://www.google.com in the address bar (yes, with `http://` as a prefix), you should see something similar to figure 3.10 in the F12 browser developer tools' Network tab.

There is an HTTP 307 redirect, but this time, it's `307 Internal Redirect` (previously, we had `307 Temporary Redirect`). The `internal` refers to the browser—it's Google Chrome that's switching to HTTPS, without the server being involved! This could be HSTS at work, but even if you install a new machine and then add Chrome to it, you could witness this effect.

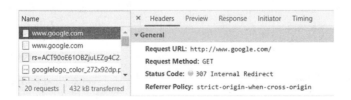

Figure 3.10 Where
is the HTTP request?

There is a simple, yet powerful reason: Google Chrome—and all other modern browsers—come with a preload list of domains where the browser should use HSTS (and, consequently, HTTPS) by default. It's not a big surprise that all Google domains are preloaded into Chrome that way, but there are thousands of others as well. Other browsers have their own lists and synchronize with the Chrome list from time to time.

> **NOTE** If you are curious, the Chromium project, the technological foundation of Google Chrome, provides the latest version of that list at http:// mng.bz/446a. At the time of writing, it was over 17 MB in size, so your browser might have a hard time rendering it.

But even better, you may become part of that list, too. The web application at https:// hstspreload.org/ allows you to add a domain to the Google Chrome list (which should later automatically put it in other browsers as well). You need to prepare your application first, though. Make sure that the `max-age` HSTS setting is greater than or equal to 31536000 seconds (one non–leap year), and then add the preload flag to the `Strict-Transport-Security` header like this:

```
builder.Services.AddHsts(options =>
{
    options.IncludeSubDomains = true;
    options.MaxAge = TimeSpan.FromYears(2);
    options.Preload = true;
});
```

The resulting HTTP header will then look similar to this one:

```
Strict-Transport-Security: max-age=63072000; includeSubDomains; preload
```

There is no functional difference compared to before; however, now the hstspreload.org application allows us to add this domain to the preload list. You have to explicitly greenlight this by adding the `preload` flag. Check out figure 3.11 to see the preload application when you check the status of facebook.com.

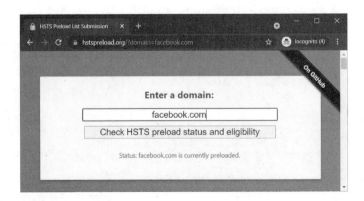

Figure 3.11 Facebook is among the preloaded sites in Google Chrome.

So Facebook is part of that list, and many, many others too. Last time I tried, a domain was added to the preload list in a few weeks. Removing a domain takes a bit longer and also requires all users to update their browser versions. For browsers other than Chrome, the delay will be even longer. I cannot stress this enough: only use HSTS, and especially the preload feature, when you are certain that you will never need plain HTTP ever again. Just in case, the removal form is at https://hstspreload.org/removal/.

> **TIP** When using Google Chrome, you can manually add domains to the HSTS list and later remove them (but not preloaded items). Just visit the internal URL chrome://net-internals/#hsts—if using another Chrome-based browser like Edge or Opera, adapt the protocol prefix appropriately (edge://net-internals/#hsts or opera://net-internals/#hsts). This may be useful for testing purposes and for some scenarios within a corporate setting (e.g., to preload URLs that should not be part of a publicly available list).

From a configuration standpoint, we have done everything we can to make session management attacks harder. Still, there is no 100% security, so depending on the sensitivity of the application, preparing for the worst might be required.

We've now seen how to protect against session management attacks, but how can we tell if a hijacking has already taken place?

3.4 *Detecting session hijacking*

Let's assume that somehow an attacker managed to actually hijack a session ID—for instance, by installing malware on the client. Could the application notice that? Or is the attacker indistinguishable from the legitimate user?

There is no bulletproof solution to this question, but there are a few criteria that could be an indication—but no proof!—of a successful attack:

- *Change of IP address*—This could be a suspicious sign, but there could be legitimate reasons for it, such as mobile devices switching from Wi-Fi to a data connection and back, internet load balancers within a company network, automated connection reset after 24 hours with some ISPs, or at random points in time after a reboot due to a power outage, and more. Even worse, in the scenario with Firesheep in a public network, both the attacker and the victim have the same external IP address. So, a different IP address might be an attack, but it is not guaranteed to be one. Perhaps flag an operation that a user is doing for manual review.
- *Change of other HTTP headers, such as the browser identification string (user agent)*— This is a stronger sign. Why would a user first use Firefox, and then, in the same browser session, use Chrome? This is almost certainly an attack (or, in rare cases, a side effect of testing or debugging). A common mistake is to just compare the user agents character by character. If a browser auto-updates and restores the session once the new version has been installed, the user agent string has changed, but the user is the same. Again, it's just an indication (albeit a strong one), not proof. The same thing is true for changed language settings.

Requiring login again before any extra-critical operations might be a good idea. Although session hijacking is unlikely if you implement the advice given in this chapter, the defense-in-depth principle should be motivation enough to add an extra layer of security where applicable.

Summary

Let's review what you have learned so far:

- Session management is based on HTTP cookies and involves using a unique identifier to recognize users between HTTP requests.
- A stolen session ID, called *session hijacking*, enables attackers to impersonate a current session of their victim.
- Using the `HttpOnly` cookie flag prevents cookie theft via cross-site scripting by hiding it from JavaScript access.
- Using the `secure` cookie flag prevents the cookie from being sent to the server via cleartext HTTP.
- Enforcing HTTPS prevents stealing session IDs when they are sent from the server to the client and back.
- HSTS instructs the browser to use HTTPS only when communicating with certain domains.
- Manually check for surprising changes in HTTP headers. This might be a strong indicator of a successful session-hijacking attack.

We have now protected ASP.NET Core's built-in session management, but we are not done with cookies yet. There are other attack vectors against them, requiring additional safeguards. Conveniently, both ASP.NET Core and modern web browsers can help us out again.

Cross-site request forgery 4

This chapter covers

- Learning how cross-site request forgery (CSRF) works
- Looking at consequences CSRF may bring
- Preventing CSRF
- Protecting cookies to prevent CSRF
- Clickjacking and how it's related to CSRF

In 2005, security researcher Samy Kamkar found a security vulnerability in the then-popular social network Myspace (if you've been around long enough, you might remember that service). He managed to inject JavaScript code into his profile page, a classical cross-site scripting (XSS) attack (explained in chapter 2). The JavaScript code, however, did something really interesting: when executed, it issued an HTTP request on the victim's behalf, adding them to Kamkar's friends list. This started a chain reaction, and less than 20 hours later, Kamkar had over one million friends on Myspace.

> **NOTE** Kamkar himself provided a detailed reconstruction of the events at https://samy.pl/myspace/, and a thorough technical description of the

attack at https://samy.pl/myspace/tech.html. However, I recommend that you read this chapter first so that you know all the required technical details about these kinds of attacks.

Completely unrelated, in 2018, a manufacturer of routers and other hardware issued a security advisory (http://mng.bz/XZV6) about "new attacks against web-enabled devices." It was possible to change DNS settings of routers, and the vulnerability had already been exploited. Turns out, this "new" attack was the same as in 2005 and is called cross-site request forgery (CSRF). Let's have a look.

NOTE   Sometimes CSRF is also dubbed XSRF—to go along nicely with XSS. This is less common, however. The pronunciation is usually "c-surf," or just the four letters.

4.1   *Anatomy of a cross-site request forgery attack*

The name of the attack pretty much describes its anatomy. Some other site (cross-site) prompts a client to send an involuntary, "forged" request. Figure 4.1 shows the process in a bit more detail.

Most commonly, CSRF looks like this: a user has previously visited a website (third-party site) and created a state with it—for instance, they logged in, or they added data to a shopping cart. This state is persisted, usually in the form of a cookie (say, a session cookie, and the session contains the login state or the contents of the shopping cart).

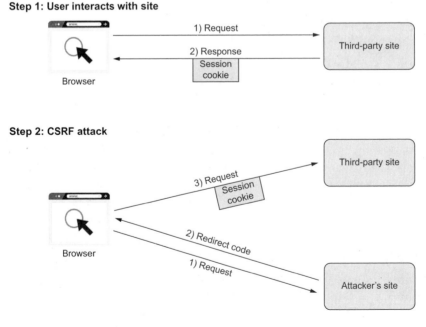

Figure 4.1   The most common form of cross-site request forgery

While the browser is still open and the session is still active, the user visits another website, controlled by the attacker. This site redirects the user to the site the user previously interacted with. This usually happens in one of two ways:

- For GET requests, the attacker's site contains JavaScript code that prompts the browser to issue the request. This is done by setting location.href, by adding an iframe with its href attribute set to the target URL, or by using an <img> tag with the href attribute set to the target URL.
- For POST requests, the attacker's site contains a <form> element with its method attribute set to "post" and its action attribute set to the target URL. Also, the page contains JavaScript code that submits the form.

Now put yourself in the (virtual) shoes of the target site (i.e., the third-party site). It receives an HTTP request issued by the user's browser. This request obviously contains the session cookie, so the target site can access the session information and will, for instance, identify the user. For GET requests, this is usually not much of an issue. According to REST (REpresentational State Transfer) principles, such a request must not change the state of an application. For POST (and all other "unsafe" HTTP methods except for GET, HEAD, OPTIONS, and TRACE), though, things look a bit different. These requests may indeed affect the application.

Let's look at a sample application that basically stores items in a shopping cart. This shopping cart is persisted in the user's session. We start with the model, shown in the following listing.

Listing 4.1 The model: A shopping cart item

```
namespace AspNetCoreSecurity.MvcSamples.Models
{
    public class ShoppingCartItem
    {
        public string Name { get; set; } = string.Empty;
        public int Quantity { get; set; }
        public double Price { get; set; }
    }
}
```

Our model is rather simple and is not backed by a database—a shopping cart item just consists of a name, a price, and a quantity. Next up, we create a static helper class to retrieve the shopping cart and add items to it, using ASP.NET Core's session management. The following listing contains the code.

Listing 4.2 The shopping cart helper class

```
using AspNetCoreSecurity.MvcSamples.Models;
using System.Text.Json;

namespace AspNetCoreSecurity.MvcSamples.Classes
{
```

```
public static class ShoppingCartHelper
{
    public static List<ShoppingCartItem> getCart()
    {
        var cartAsJson =
          ➡StaticHttpContext.Current?.Session.GetString("ShoppingCart");
        if (cartAsJson == null)
        {
            return new List<ShoppingCartItem>();
        } else
        {
            return JsonSerializer.Deserialize<List
              ➡<ShoppingCartItem>>(cartAsJson) ??
              ➡new List<ShoppingCartItem>();        ◁┐ Reads the shopping cart
        }                                              │ as JSON from the session
    }                                                  │ and deserializes it

    public static void addToCart(ShoppingCartItem item)
    {
        var cart = getCart();
        cart.Add(item);
        StaticHttpContext.Current?.Session.SetString(
            "ShoppingCart",
            JsonSerializer.Serialize
              ➡<List<ShoppingCartItem>>(cart));     ◁┐ Serializes the shopping
    }                                                  │ cart into JSON and writes
}                                                      │ it to the session
}
```

Note that the `StaticHttpContext` class that the preceding code is using is a little
helper class that allows session access in a static context.

With that out of the way, it is time to implement a user interface. First, the next listing shows the markup to add a new item to the shopping cart.

Listing 4.3   The HTML/Razor form to add an item to the shopping cart

```
@model AspNetCoreSecurity.MvcSamples.Models.ShoppingCartItem

<h1>Add to Cart</h1>

<div class="row">
    <div class="col-md-4">
        <form asp-action="AddToCart"          Makes sure that the form
          ➡asp-antiforgery="false">    ◁─── is posted to the AddToCart
            <div class="form-group">           action method
                <label asp-for="Name" class="control-label"></label>
                <input asp-for="Name"
                  ➡class="form-control" />    ◁┐ Shows the
            </div>                              │ item's name
            <div class="form-group">
                <label asp-for="Quantity" class="control-label"></label>
                <input asp-for="Quantity"
   Shows the       ➡class="form-control" />
item's quantity └▷ </div>
```

```
        <div class="form-group">
            <label asp-for="Price" class="control-label"></label>
            <input asp-for="Price"
            ➥class="form-control" />                      ⭠┐ Shows the
        </div>                                               │ item's price
        <div class="form-group">
            <input type="submit" value="Add to cart" class="btn btn-
    primary" />
        </div>
    </form>
</div>
</div>

<div>
    <a asp-action="ShowCart">Back to Cart</a>
</div>
```

The form was more or less generated by Visual Studio's scaffolding feature and was edited and shortened a bit for clarity. Users may enter the shopping cart item data. Upon form submission, the data is sent back to the server, where the shopping cart helper comes into play.

Let's look at the action methods for the view from listing 4.3. We have two of those methods—one for GET requests and one for POST requests. The following listing shows both of them.

Listing 4.4 The action methods for shopping cart views

```
using AspNetCoreSecurity.MvcSamples.Classes;
using AspNetCoreSecurity.MvcSamples.Models;
using Microsoft.AspNetCore.Mvc;
using System.Diagnostics;

namespace AspNetCoreSecurity.MvcSamples.Controllers
{
    public class HomeController : Controller
    {

...

        public IActionResult AddToCart()          ⭠┐ This is the Action method
        {                                           │ for the GET request.
            return View();
        }

        [HttpPost]
        public IActionResult AddToCart(           ┐ This is the Action method
        ➥ShoppingCartItem item)          ⭠┘ for the POST request.
        {
            ShoppingCartHelper.addToCart(item);
            return RedirectToAction("ShowCart");  ⭠┐ After adding the item
        }                                           │ to the cart, redirect to
                                                    │ the cart overview page.
        public IActionResult ShowCart()
        {
```

This is the Action method for the cart overview page. ⟶

```
                var cart = ShoppingCartHelper.getCart();
                return View(cart);
        }

}
```

The code also includes the ShowCart() action method, which will be used to show the shopping cart's contents. It retrieves the cart from the session using the ShoppingCartHelper class, and then submits it to the associated view, which can be seen in the next listing.

Listing 4.5   The HTML/Razor view for the shopping cart

```
@model IEnumerable<AspNetCoreSecurity.MvcSamples.Models.ShoppingCartItem>

<h1>Shopping Cart</h1>

<p>
    <a asp-action="AddToCart">Add new item</a>
</p>
<table class="table">
    <thead>
        <tr>
            <th>
                @Html.DisplayNameFor(model => model.Name)
            </th>
            <th>
                @Html.DisplayNameFor(model => model.Quantity)
            </th>
            <th>
                @Html.DisplayNameFor(model => model.Price)
            </th>
            <th>
                Total
            </th>
        </tr>
    </thead>
    <tbody>
@foreach (var item in Model ??              ⟵──┐ Iterates over all shopping
  new ShoppingCartItem[] { }) {                  │ cart items and outputs them
        <tr>
            <td>
                @Html.DisplayFor(modelItem => item.Name)
            </td>
            <td>
                @Html.DisplayFor(modelItem => item.Quantity)
            </td>
            <td>
                @Html.DisplayFor(modelItem => item.Price)
            </td>
            <td>
                @(item.Quantity * item.Price)
            </td>
```

```
        </tr>
}
    </tbody>
</table>
```

This view was also initially generated by Visual Studio and then adapted for our needs. As always with ASP.NET Core MVC applications, there are several files required for a working solution (and we didn't even look at the `StaticHttpContext` class and Program.cs!), but the way it works is straightforward.

Figure 4.2 shows the form to add an item to the cart, and figure 4.3 shows the now-filled cart.

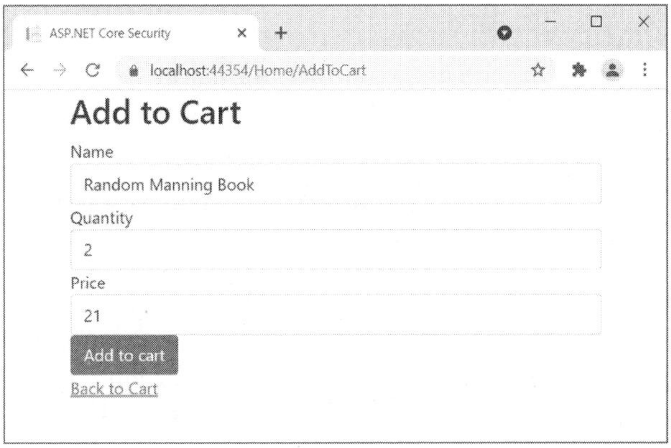

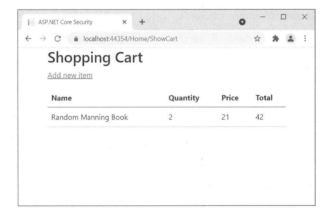

Figure 4.2 The user may add an item to the shopping cart . . .

Figure 4.3 . . . and it shows up on the overview page.

How can this process be exploited by an attacker? First, let's assume that putting an arbitrary item into someone else's shopping cart is undesired. If an attacker manages to pulls this off, we consider this a successful attack.

Let's analyze the HTTP request that is sent when we add an item to the shopping cart, using the HTML form provided in listing 4.3. You can use the F12 browser tools

to take a closer look, or a proxy on your local machine (Fiddler from https://www
.telerik.com/fiddler is a popular choice). Here is how it typically looks:

```
POST /Home/AddToCart HTTP/1.1
Host: localhost:44354
Content-Type: application/x-www-form-urlencoded
Content-Length: 44
Cookie: .AspNetCore.Session=CfDJ8FflGUpl%2FsxPt3SJyGwltBh83JWtqLoIGGCqd3lyMk1
JKOJVir4kPoFliKR5xV9fFe6U98ZlfmNE8lEyfmyzJ0nv8LTkvqMF11uXB6oxIDMVyQpbdfANqWm5
Eql6dnxATvtJMmdkU4iOnU1ZCzC2QQAWge8Ck4i55VOnyqI7OxdT

Name=Random+manning+book&Quantity=2&Price=21
```

I've removed additional headers that are not interesting at the moment and have left
only the relevant pieces of information intact:

- The HTTP method, endpoint, and HTTP protocol version
- The host (server)
- The content type that tells the server in which format the data is encoded
- The content length, which contains the length of the data being sent
- The session cookie
- The actual form data

It turns out that an attacker with access to the code of the application can fully predict
this HTTP request, with one sole exception: the session cookie, since it is unique to
each user session. Because of the way cookies work, this session cookie is sent to the
server automatically when the browser issues a request. The code in the next listing
exploits that by creating a form holding the same pieces of information.

Listing 4.6   The CSRF exploit

```html
<!DOCTYPE html>
<html>
    <head>
        <title>CSRF</title>
    </head>
    <body>
        <form method="post" action="https://localhost:44354/Home/AddToCart">
            <input type="hidden" name="Name"
            ➥value="Random Manning book">
            <input type="hidden" name="Quantity"
            ➥value="2">
            <input type="hidden" name="Price"
            ➥value="21">
        </form>
        <script>
            document.forms[0].submit();
        </script>
    </body>
</html>
```

**Shows the form fields
with the same names
as in the original form**

Note that there is a hidden form field for all three pieces of information for a shopping cart item (by convention, model binding puts individual input fields into a complex object). To the server, the resulting involuntary request looks more or less identical to a voluntary one. Therefore, the server is more than happy to oblige and to add a new item to the shopping cart.

> **NOTE** Of course, this attack has some prerequisites: the victim must have previously visited the target site, and the attacker has to have detailed knowledge of how that site works. As a principle, whatever can go wrong will eventually go wrong, so we can safely assume that *eventually* all these conditions will be met, and the attack will work.

And that is cross-site request forgery in a nutshell. The specific flavor of the attack presented is sometimes also called *session riding*—the attacker is riding piggyback on the victim's session. It took us about nine pages to thoroughly explain how this works, but now it should also be clear how Samy Kamkar got new friends on Myspace: he found a stored XSS vulnerability and injected JavaScript code that did a POST request to the "add user as a friend endpoint." For the example with the routers, all of them have a web-based administration interface, and the form to change the DNS settings was obviously not CSRF-protected, either.

Depending on which browser you are trying this in, the attack might work—or not. In a surprising twist of events, not only can (and should!) developers add CSRF protection to their apps, but web browsers can also lend a hand.

4.2 Cross-site request forgery countermeasures

When trying to defend a site against an attack, it is always wise to look at the prerequisites of the attack. If those cannot be met, the attack cannot be executed. In the case of CSRF, there are two aspects that make this attack possible.

The first one is that the attacker can precisely predict the HTTP request. In the preceding example, this was possible. If you ignore most of the other HTTP headers, the POST request basically contained the name, quantity, and price of the shopping cart item—all values that the attacker is able to provide. The HTTP method (POST) and the URL of the endpoint are also pieces of information available to the villain.

The only data that is not known to the attacker is the victim's session ID. This, in turn, is the second prerequisite for a successful CSRF attack: cookies are automatically sent to the server they belong to. There is no need for the attacker to steal the session ID; it comes for free.

> **NOTE** Of course, the user has to cooperate a bit as well. They usually need to be logged into the target site and must visit the attacker's site as well. We can safely assume that this can be achieved by social engineering or by spreading the malicious URL so much that it's likely there will be a matching victim.

4.2.1   *Making the HTTP request unpredictable*

Why can the attacker predict the HTTP request required to add an item to the shopping cart, add someone as a friend on a social network, or change the router's DNS settings? Because the server only expects the actual data—the shopping cart item, the friend ID, or the new DNS server info. If we instead add an additional, random token to the HTTP request, the whole attack collapses like a house of cards. The attacker cannot predict the token, so they cannot craft a proper request.

When it comes to implementing such a countermeasure, some aspects need to be taken into account. If the application uses one-time tokens, so each of those tokens is valid only once, simultaneously running the app in several browser tabs probably won't work reliably. Using the session ID as the token sounds like a good idea at first—the attacker does not know the session ID, and thus does not know the token. If, however, the session ID has been stolen before (because the developer of the site did not read chapter 3), CSRF might immediately work again (honestly, if the session ID is stolen, the attacker might already be able to talk to the website on the victim's behalf). A common approach consists of adding a random token, plus a matching cookie. The random token will be an explicit part of the HTML form, whereas the token in the cookie is sent automatically by the client anyway. On the server, both of these values are verified. If they are missing or incorrect, the application switches into an error state.

Conveniently, ASP.NET Core already comes with such a mechanism. Even better, it is enabled by default. If you look at listing 4.3, you may notice that it contained a special attribute within the <form> element:

```
asp-antiforgery="false"
```

This deactivates the anti-CSRF mechanism and was solely put in place to demonstrate the attack. Usually, you would not want to work without the built-in protection in place. If you remove this attribute or set it to `true`, you will notice that two things happen when loading the form in the browser:

- ASP.NET Core automatically adds an additional hidden field to the form (on your system, it will have the same name but a different value, of course):

  ```
  <input name="__RequestVerificationToken" type="hidden"
  value="CfDJ8FflGUpl_sxPt3SJyGw1tBgM8keVYHfkxE19T2rR10nRplOj4dAyr-
  yplT4caP6xPy807LVMrTzSRcOvRPOaUfJcqm6U8z4y3LePaCElCKCw0FVAz3z-
  3V694vTIYpGckc97w08oOQSCfxBrucwU90c" />
  ```

- At the same time, the server issues an HTTP cookie with the following name and value (both will be different on your system):

  ```
  .AspNetCore.Antiforgery.Za7zYHoQn5w=CfDJ8FflGUpl
  _sxPt3SJyGw1tBhPF5OXIg6aFVm0YmyUzF29aTY-OBqu9g9jGqOdsqSDWGCDrO1LadtSyRd
  BiKBZemMxW6znfiVY5IZ5F4JqGcBCwDl8UlQgB9iqQaoXz8HWbWsB8Ma7JFK3j8RRPVF0ueI
  ```

In this example, the first two dozen or so characters of the field value and the cookie value match, but the rest is different. When you reload the form a few times, the token will change, but the cookie will stay the same. This allows the application to run in several browser tabs with a shared cookie jar.

INFO Making sure that the client always receives a token that the server later can later verify (and reject the request if that fails) is also called *synchronizer token pattern* (STP).

This behavior works in ASP.NET Core out of the box for ASP.NET Core MVC, Razor Pages, and Blazor apps. No additional configuration is required as long as you are using a form in the following ways:

- `<form method="post">...</form>`
- `@Html.BeginForm(...)`

Technically, the anti-CSRF functionality comes as middleware that is automatically activated once you are using the responsible middleware for MVC (`AddMvc()`, `AddControllersWithViews()`, or `MapControllerRoute()`), Razor Pages (`AddRazorPages()` or `MapRazorPages()`), or Blazor (`MapBlazorHub()`) in the `Program` class.

The `FormTagHelper`, which serves as the class responsible for properly rendering the forms into HTML, has anti-CSRF features baked in. If you want to get rid of that feature (and you should really have a very good reason if you consider doing that—for instance, another application sending an HTTP request directly to your `POST` endpoint), make sure that you avoid the helper altogether by doing the following:

- Remove it from the page with `@removeTagHelper Microsoft.AspNetCore.Mvc.TagHelpers.FormTagHelper, Microsoft.AspNetCore.Mvc.TagHelpers`.
- Opt out of using the helper for your form with `<!form>...<!/form>`.
- Deactivate the CSRF token on a per-form basis by using `asp-antiforgery="false"` (as shown in listing 4.3).

The antiforgery mechanism can also be configured. The default name for the form field holding the token is `__RequestVerificationToken`, but this may be changed in the `Program` class like this:

```
builder.Services.AddAntiforgery(options => {
  options.FormFieldName = "__AntiXsrfToken";
});
```

If the token shall be transferred to the server in the form of an HTTP header, its name may also be configured individually:

```
builder.Services.AddAntiforgery(options => {
  options.HeaderName = "X-Anti-Xsrf-Token";
});
```

Note that by default, the token is generated and added to any form. That does *not* mean that the token is automatically validated—that's where the developers need to lend a hand. With filters, ASP.NET Core provides a mechanism to implement this. The following three options exist:

- `AutoValidateAntiForgeryToken`—Requires (and validates) antiforgery tokens for all HTTP requests that may change the state of the application (i.e., all except for `GET`, `HEAD`, `OPTIONS`, and `TRACE`)

- ValidateAntiForgeryToken—Ensures that a certain action or request needs a valid anti-CSRF token, independent of which HTTP method is being used
- IgnoreAntiForgeryToken—Disables the verification of antiforgery tokens (although the token and the cookie are still generated by default)

You can use all of these filters as attributes for action methods or controller classes like this:

```
[HttpPost]
[ValidateAntiForgeryToken]                        Requires a valid token when
public IActionResult AddToCart(ShoppingCartItem item)   this action method is called
{
    ShoppingCartHelper.addToCart(item);
    return RedirectToAction("ShowCart");
}
```

Alternatively, you define these filters globally like this in Program.cs:

```
builder.Services.AddControllersWithViews(options => {    Globally enables token
    options.Filters.Add(                                 validation for all requests
        new AutoValidateAntiForgeryTokenAttribute());    except for GET, HEAD,
});                                                       OPTIONS, and TRACE
```

The out-of-the-box support for CSRF protection should suffice in most scenarios. Once we enable it in the shopping cart application (e.g., by removing the asp-anti-forgery="false" attribute) and try running the exploit again, we get an error message, as figure 4.4 shows.

Instead of adding an item to the shopping cart, the server now returns an HTTP error 400—Bad Request. And indeed, the request had bad intentions, yet the application was prepared for it and refused it. It is safe to say that the website is now in good

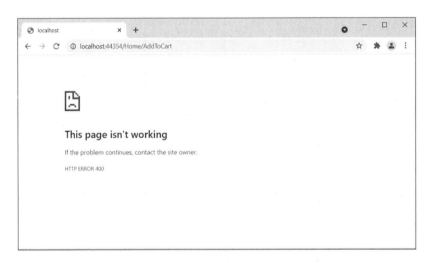

Figure 4.4   The CSRF attack does not work anymore.

shape with regard to cross-site request forgery. However, we can do even more with a little help from modern browsers.

4.2.2 Securing the session cookie

Let's go back a few steps to when we researched the prerequisites for a successful CSRF attack. Apart from the attacker accurately predicting the HTTP request, they also had to rely on the browser automatically sending the authentication cookie along with the request. This is exactly how cookies have worked since the mid-1990s—but this has recently changed.

The cookie specification resides in RFC 6265, as chapter 3 explained. Recent versions of that specification (e.g., http://mng.bz/yvoq) added a few new features, including something called *same-site cookies*. By adding the `SameSite` flag to a `Set-Cookie` header's value, you can instruct the browser whether or not to send that cookie once a cross-site request is executed. In other words, if the attacker's site is loaded into the browser and the client is then redirected to another site, then this very request will only send cookies with the appropriate same-site settings (subsequent, non-cross-site requests will behave as usual, without restrictions). The following three options exist:

- `Strict`—This kind of same-site cookie will never be sent with a cross-site request.
- `Lax`—This kind of same-site cookie will only be sent with cross-site requests if HTTP GET, HEAD, OPTIONS, or TRACE is used.
- `None`—This kind of same-site cookie will be sent with all cross-site requests, just like before there were same-site cookies.

This sounds extremely appealing, doesn't it? Most CSRF attacks rely on cookies being sent with the forged request. If, however, a cookie is marked as `Strict` or `Lax`, then it will not be part of the cross-site request. Another decisive blow against cross-site request forgery!

But it's getting even better—at least from a security perspective. The Google Chrome team planned to make all cookies default to `Lax` starting with Chrome 80. It actually took until version 85 of the browser to make it happen (they wanted to give developers a break during 2020, the first year of the pandemic), but from then on, you get CSRF protection for free in all recent Chrome-based browsers (including Opera and Edge). The Firefox team announced that they would also default to `Same-Site=Lax` in the future.

It makes sense to explicitly set this flag, at least for session cookies. This is easy to achieve in Program.cs. The call to `AddSession()`—which is required so that sessions are available at all—accepts cookie options. Apart from `SameSite`, we should also set the relevant cookie flags we already discussed in chapter 3, `secure` and `HttpOnly`:

```
builder.Services.AddSession(options =>
{
    options.Cookie.SameSite = SameSiteMode.Strict;
```

```
        options.Cookie.SecurePolicy = CookieSecurePolicy.Always;
        options.Cookie.HttpOnly = true;
});
```

Obviously, you can also secure other cookies that way, including those that you explicitly set, as well as the antiforgery cookie:

```
builder.Services.AddAntiforgery(options =>
{
    options.Cookie.SameSite = SameSiteMode.Strict;
    options.Cookie.SecurePolicy = CookieSecurePolicy.Always;
    options.Cookie.HttpOnly = true;
});
```

All modern browsers support same-site cookies, even legacy Internet Explorer 11 (on a recent enough version of Windows 10).

> **WARNING**   Make sure that you will never need any cookie information for cross-site requests. Some single sign-on mechanisms include a POST request from the sign-on server back to the application. If you need all the application's cookies on that request, you might consider SameSite=None, though. (There is a bug in older versions of Safari where SameSite=None was interpreted as SameSite=Strict! The associated bug ticket provides a good discussion of implications and workarounds: https://bugs.webkit.org/show_bug .cgi?id=198181.)

Same site vs. same origin

Same site does not mean "same origin." The latter term was discussed in chapter 2 and refers to identical scheme, domain name, and port. The former term is defined at https://html.spec.whatwg.org/#same-site, where you can see several examples of what is considered "same site" and what is not. Essentially, if two sites share the same scheme and the same registrable domain (e.g., manning.com and meap .manning.com), they have different origins but are still considered as the same site. Therefore, meap.manning.com redirecting to manning.com would prompt the browser to send all manning.com cookies along the request. In other words, if just one of your subdomains is taken over by an attacker, CSRF may be possible again. Therefore, same-site cookies are just a defense-in-depth mechanism and are not an excuse to waive other security measures like antiforgery tokens.

We can now successfully protect a web application from a forged request. But what happens if the request is actually (unknowingly) triggered by the user? Let's take a look at a related attack and how to fix the website.

4.3   *Clickjacking*

We have added a new feature to our application, allowing users to clear out their shopping cart with a simple click of a button. In order to achieve this, the helper class gets a new method:

```
public static void clearCart()
{
    StaticHttpContext.Current?.Session.SetString(
    ➥"ShoppingCart", "[]");
}
```

Sets the shopping cart to an empty list (in JSON format)

Next, the cart overview page receives a new button:

```
<form asp-action="ClearCart" asp-antiforgery="true">
    <input type="submit" class="btn btn-primary" value="Clear Cart">
</form>
```

The button is part of a form that is posting to the `ClearCart()` action method, which is implemented as follows:

```
[HttpPost]
public IActionResult ClearCart()
{
    ShoppingCartHelper.clearCart();
    return RedirectToAction("ShowCart");
}
```

The cart data in the session is cleared, and the client will be redirected back to the overview page. As you will certainly have noticed, we explicitly set `asp-antiforgery="true"` in the form to clear the cart, enabling the anti-CSRF token. The application also uses the `AutoValidateAntiforgeryTokenAttribute` filter, so we should be safe. But maybe we are not. The attacker has created the HTML page from the following listing and uploaded it to their server, as the next listing shows.

Listing 4.7 The clickjacking exploit

```
<!DOCTYPE html>
<html>
    <head>
        <title>CSRF</title>
        <link href="https://cdn.jsdelivr.net/npm/bootstrap@5.0.1/dist/css/
        bootstrap.min.css" rel="stylesheet" integrity="sha384-+0n0xVW2
        eSR5OomGNYDnhzAbDsOXxcvSN1TPprVMTNDbiYZCxYbOO17+AMvyTG2x"
        crossorigin="anonymous">
        <style>
            input[type=button] {
                position: absolute;
                left: 30px;
                top: 150px;
            }

            iframe {
                opacity: 0.15;
                height: 300px;
            }
        </style>
    </head>
    <body>
```

Position the button so that it matches the button in the iframe.

Make the iframe invisible (or, for demonstration purposes, almost invisible).

**This is the
button to
trick the user
to click on.**

```
            <input type="button" class="btn" value="Click here">
            <iframe src="https://localhost:44354/Home/ShowCart"></iframe>
        </body>
    </html>
```

**Shows iframe with the
cart overview page**

The idea is that the page with the Clear Cart button is loaded in an iframe, which is then made invisible by setting its opacity to 0% (or here, for demonstration purposes, to 15%). The iframe is still there and you can interact with it, but it cannot be seen. Also, the page contains a button that is placed exactly over the button in the iframe. As you can see in the markup, the button is loaded first, then the iframe—therefore, the iframe has a higher z-index and will be clicked on. The user, however, only sees the Click Here button and is unsuspicious.

Once the user intends to click the attacker's button, they click on the Clear Cart button instead. That's why this attack is commonly called *clickjacking*, a neologism merging *hijacking* and *click*. Figure 4.5 shows the result in the web browser.

Figure 4.5   The imperfect clickjacking attack (so that we can see what is happening)

Note that the new button is not exactly aligned, mainly so that you see what is going on (that's also the reason why the code uses an iframe opacity of 15%, instead of 0%). Also, the button is misplaced even more if there are actually items in the shopping cart. In other words, clickjacking is very hard to pull off for an attacker.

On the other hand, the attack is extremely effective. Our CSRF protection could be perfect and it still would not prevent clickjacking. The user is clicking the actual button on the actual web page, and the only oddity is that the site is loaded into an iframe on a third-party site. For the web server, the "clear cart" request cannot be distinguished from a regular, voluntary request (the referrer HTTP header could give an indication but is stripped in some recent browsers anyway, so the application cannot rely on it). All the attacker needs to do is set up the attacking page and then lure a user to it.

Once again, it's a good strategy to analyze the prerequisites of the attack. The attacked application is loaded in an iframe, and then the user is prompted to click the button. We cannot fix the human factor, but we can prevent the browser from loading the third-party page in an iframe. For this, the X-FRAME-OPTIONS HTTP header was introduced back in the day by Internet Explorer 8 (!) and later adapted by all other browsers. It supports two values:

- DENY—The page must not be loaded in an iframe at all.
- SAMEORIGIN—The page may be loaded in an iframe if the outer page (the one with the iframe) has the same origin as the inner page (the one loaded in the iframe).

There's good news: by default, ASP.NET Core emits X-FRAME-OPTIONS: SAMEORIGIN when the antiforgery middleware is activated. In order to demonstrate the security vulnerability, the demo application intentionally disabled the header by adding this code to Program.cs:

```
builder.Services.AddAntiforgery(options =>
{
    options.SuppressXFrameOptionsHeader = true;
});
```

If this option is set to `false` or not set at all, the X-FRAME-OPTIONS header will be added, so the exploit page will now look like figure 4.6.

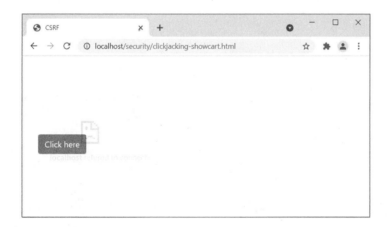

Figure 4.6   Thanks to the X-FRAME-OPTIONS header, the browser does not load the page in the iframe.

Depending on the web browser, the iframe either remains empty or shows an error message instead of the intended page. This one-line fix, which is enabled in the antiforgery middleware by default anyway, effectively prevents the attack.

TIP   When you are working with subdomains and would like to include your own content in iframes, there is not a good setting for the X-FRAME-OPTIONS header. DENY does not allow loading a page in an iframe at all, and SAMEOR-IGIN requires exactly the same scheme, domain, and port, so subdomains do not work. Content Security Policy (from chapter 2) supports the frame-ancestors directive, where you can explicitly allow certain hosts or pages to include your page in an iframe. On the other hand, this excludes Internet Explorer 11 and older browsers. As long as you still have to support them, there is no way to have both the iframe and sufficient clickjacking protection.

One more vector remains—hypothetically. Couldn't the attacker just issue HTTP calls with JavaScript to pull off the attack?

4.4   *Cross-origin resource sharing*

Luckily, it's not so easy. Remember the same-origin policy (SOP) from chapter 2? It limits JavaScript access to resources with the same origin. This also applies to HTTP requests—with some oddities. The following listing shows a simple Web API with a GET and a POST endpoint.

Listing 4.8   One API, two endpoints

```
using Microsoft.AspNetCore.Mvc;

namespace AspNetCoreSecurity.MvcSamples.Controllers
{
    [Route("api/[controller]")]
    [ApiController]
    public class CorsController : ControllerBase
    {
        // GET: api/Cors
        [HttpGet]                              GET
        public int Get()            ◁──┘      endpoint
        {
            return new Random().Next(10, 100);
        }

        // POST api/Cors
        [HttpPost]                             POST
        public void Post([FromBody] int value)  ◁──┘  endpoint
        {
        }
    }
}
```

Not much is happening in the API; the GET endpoint returns a random number between 10 and 99, whereas the POST endpoint does nothing.

In another project, in another origin, a Razor Page uses JavaScript to call that API. The following listing has all the details.

Listing 4.9   Cross-domain call to the API

```
@page

<div class="text-center">
    <h1 class="display-4">Cross-Origin Resource Sharing</h1>

    <div id="output"></div>
</div>

@section Scripts {
<script>
    fetch("https://localhost:44354/api/Cors")
        .then(response => response.json())
        .then(data => {
            document.getElementById("output").textContent = data;
        });
</script>
}
```

Use the URL of the
endpoint here.

The JavaScript code uses `fetch()` to call the API on the other server and then outputs the results. Running the code, however, leads to output like in figure 4.7.

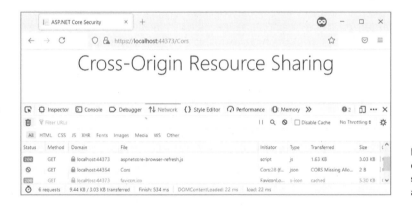

Figure 4.7   The cross-domain call succeeds and fails at the same time.

No random number appears, and the network tab shows the call to the API in red. However, curiously, the size of the data from the HTTP response is shown as 2 bytes (at least in Firefox—Chrome claims there were zero bytes transferred, but that's incorrect)—that would fit a response consisting of a double-digit number.

The request has been sent, but JavaScript did not receive any data. The reason: the same-origin policy. Let's just pretend for a minute that this request would work. In that case, an attacker could use JavaScript to send an HTTP request to the page to add an item to the shopping cart—automatically using the user's session ID cookie (we momentarily ignore `SameSite` cookies). As part of the HTTP response, the attacker could extract the token in the form and therefore would be able to circumvent the CSRF protection.

And even though cross-site request forgery was not even invented when the same-origin policy came about, since JavaScript cannot access the HTTP response (thanks to the SOP), the attack does not work.

But what if the JavaScript application has a legitimate interest in calling the API? The server is the one being attacked by CSRF, so the server needs to green-light this. When we look closely at the HTTP request that was generated when we tried to call the API with JavaScript, we will notice something curious. The `Origin` header is not something that is sent with each request—but the browser automatically adds it when there is a cross-domain request:

```
GET /api/Cors HTTP/2
Host: localhost:44354
User-Agent: Mozilla/5.0 (Windows NT 10.0; Win64; x64; rv:95.0) Gecko/20100101
    Firefox/95.0
Accept: */*
Accept-Language: en-US,en;q=0.5
Accept-Encoding: gzip, deflate, br
Origin: https://localhost:44373
Connection: keep-alive
Cache-Control: max-age=0
TE: Trailers
```

The header contains the origin—protocol, domain, port—of the calling page. The server can then take this information and decide whether the JavaScript code may have access to the data coming from the server. If so, the HTTP response needs to include the `Access-Control-Allow-Origin` header and set it to the origin that was sent (or to the placeholder *, but as always, better to be as explicit and restrictive as possible):

```
Access-Control-Allow-Origin: https://localhost:44373
```

This mechanism is called *cross-origin resource sharing* (CORS), and ASP.NET Core comes with great support for it—no need to manually implement this. If you search for "CORS" in the NuGet package manager, you will see a large selection like that shown in figure 4.8.

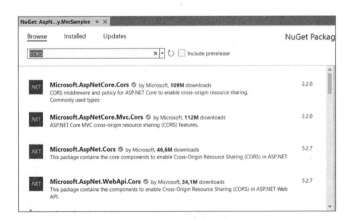

Figure 4.8 Many choices, but we need none of them.

However, you need to pick none of these options. The first two are for .NET Standard, and the next two are for the old .NET Framework. Instead, just go directly to Startup.cs, where CORS support may be activated. ASP.NET Core then automatically uses its own version of the `Microsoft.AspNetCore.Cors` package.

CORS comes as middleware in ASP.NET Core, so we have to both make it available and activate it. As usual, two steps in the `Program` class are required:

- We add CORS support (and will also configure it) by calling the `AddCors()` extension method.
- We activate CORS support by calling the `UseCors()` extension method.

Let's start with `AddCors()`. When calling the method, we can provide options. Usually, we want to configure at least one CORS policy (i.e., which origins are allowed). Here is how this can look:

```
builder.Services.AddCors(options =>
{
    options.AddPolicy(
        "CORS API Endpoint",        ⟵  Shows
        builder =>                      policy name
        {
            builder.WithOrigins("https://localhost:44373");   ⟵  Shows list
        });                                                       of origins
});
```

> **NOTE** Make sure that you are using the origin of the application calling the
> API, not the origin of the API itself! Also ensure that the origin consists only
> of protocol, domain, and port and does not have a trailing slash.

We can use an arbitrary number of policies, and each may have any number of origins. The `builder` variable (which is of type `CorsPolicyBuilder`) also provides methods to explicitly allow other pieces of information for a cross-domain JavaScript HTTP request:

- `WithExposedHeaders()`—List of HTTP response headers that are returned and thus made available ("exposed") to JavaScript
- `WithHeaders()`—List of allowed extra HTTP request headers that the server would like to get access to
- `WithMethods()`—List of allowed extra HTTP methods

If you want to blindly accept any request headers and HTTP methods, you may accept them all:

- `AllowAnyHeader()`
- `AllowAnyMethod()`

There is no such wildcard method for exposed headers, though. By default, no credentials like `Authorization` headers are sent along the cross-domain request—once again, CSRF protection is the cause. In scenarios where you do want to have this information available to the API, the `AllowCredentials()` method green-lights this to the browser (and `DisallowCredentials()` explicitly forbids it).

Finally, if you want one and only one CORS policy, you can avoid naming it and instead set a default one:

```
options.AddDefaultPolicy(
    builder =>
        {
            builder.WithOrigins("https://localhost:44373/");
        });
```

Now that the policy is set up, it's time to use it. Depending on your application, you may want the CORS policy to be globally applicable, or it should only be used for certain endpoints. Here are your options:

- CORS for all endpoints
- CORS for controllers or methods
- CORS for certain routes

To enable the CORS policy globally, we first need a default policy. Then the `Use-Cors()` call needs to be added to the code in Program.cs. However, as is often the case with ASP.NET Core middleware, the order of them is relevant. CORS needs to be activated after routing (`UseRouting()`) but before response caching, authentication, and authorization (`UseResponseCaching()`, `UseAuthentication()`, `Use-Authorization()`).

Since we have a default policy, just calling `UseCors()` is good enough:

```
app.UseCors();
```

Now all endpoints support the default CORS policy. For named policies, a different approach may be used to control when the policy applies. We still need a call to `Use-Cors()` in Program.cs, but we do not have a default policy this time.

Then the `[EnableCors]` attribute must be added to either the controller class (to make all action methods in them implement the CORS policy) or to individual methods only. As an argument, the policy name is used:

```
using Microsoft.AspNetCore.Cors;         ◁─┐ Loads the
using Microsoft.AspNetCore.Mvc;            │ namespace

namespace AspNetCoreSecurity.MvcSamples.Controllers
{
    [Route("api/[controller]")]
    [EnableCors("CORS API Endpoint")]      ◁─┐ Applies the policy to
    [ApiController]                          │ the whole controller
    public class CorsController : ControllerBase
    {
...
    }
}
```

Now all the methods in the API controller send the correct `Access-Control-Allow-Origin` header. When applying these changes to the API and running the page with the JavaScript `fetch()` call again, we get the desired result (figure 4.9).

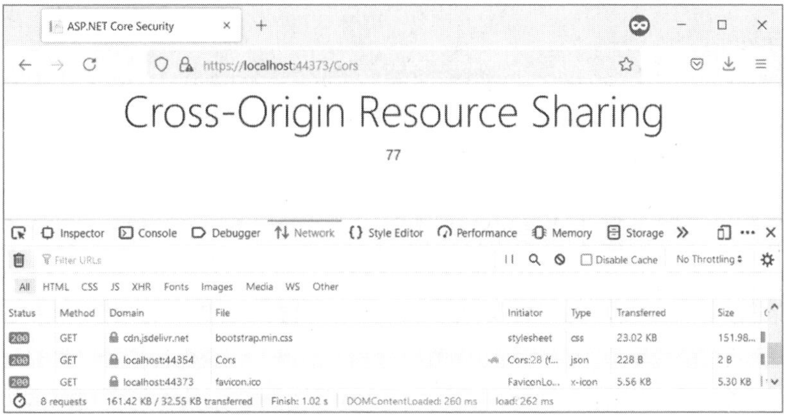

Figure 4.9 The lucky number (77) appears.

This time, not only does the HTTP request go through, but JavaScript can access the return value and display it.

TIP When enabling CORS for the whole controller, you may still use the [DisableCors] attribute to disable CORS for certain action methods.

The third CORS option is to use routing—we define named policies and apply them to the routes. In ASP.NET Core projects, the app.UseEndpoints() call is the right place to configure this. Just use the RequireCors() extension method after the appropriate call to MapControllers(), MapControllerRoute(), MapGet(), or similar methods:

```
app.UseEndpoints(endpoints =>
{
    endpoints.MapControllerRoute(
        name: "default",
        pattern: "{controller=Home}/{action=Index}/{id?}")
        .RequireCors("CORS API Endpoint");

});
```

CORS on steroids: Preflight requests

If you recall, even before adding the CORS support, the GET request was still issued—the 2 bytes return data seen in the developer tools prove it. But why did this work? According to the REST principle, a GET request does not change the state of the application. At least in theory, it's used for reading, not for writing. Therefore, browsers assume that a GET request does no harm, so it is issued—but JavaScript is not granted access to the data returned.

For POST requests (and other HTTP methods), things are a bit different. They may change the state of the application, so they can't just be sent. Often, the return data

(continued)

isn't even relevant. You can see that hinted at in the API, where the POST endpoint does not return anything.

In such cases, browsers send preflight requests that work as follows:

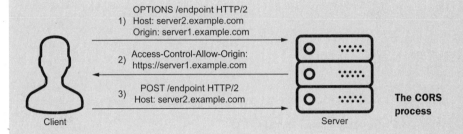

The browser first sends a request using the OPTIONS HTTP method. This should also not change anything on the server. If the HTTP response contains an Access-Control-Allow-Origin header with the appropriate value, the client then has the green light and sends the actual POST request. It's important to know that endpoint routing (using RequireCors() within UseEndpoints()) does not currently work with preflight requests. Using attribute routing or a default CORS policy is therefore recommended.

Summary

Let's review what we have learned so far:

- Cross-site request forgery is an attack that tricks a client browser into sending an HTTP request, which in turn causes the web application to change its state.
- By adding a unique piece of information, thus making it impossible for the attacker to predict the HTTP request, the threat is mitigated.
- Same-site cookies that are not sent when cross-site requests occur offer an additional layer of security.
- Clickjacking, as an attack related to CSRF, can be easily mitigated with a simple HTTP header.
- Cross-origin resource sharing protects web applications from some cross-site request forgery vectors by limiting what cross-domain JavaScript HTTP requests can do.
- For legitimate use cases, a server may re-enable cross-domain calls by configuring appropriate CORS settings.

All of the attacks in this book so far were exploiting the way web applications and browsers work. We will now switch over to more generic risks and how they relate to ASP.NET Core, starting with unvalidated data.

Unvalidated data

This chapter covers

- Understanding which parts of HTTP may be manipulated
- Using model validation in ASP.NET Core
- Preventing mass assignment

In 2012, Russian developer Egor Homakov started a discussion on the GitHub issue tracker for the Ruby on Rails framework (if you're interested, here is the whole thread: https://github.com/rails/rails/issues/5228). He was worried about a specific attack called *mass assignment,* and whether Ruby on Rails should change its default behavior to prevent developers from falling into this trap. Not happy with the arguably stern replies he got, he searched and found a mass assignment security issue in GitHub (which, in turn, has been developed in Ruby on Rails). As a result, he managed to grant himself full privileges for the Ruby on Rails project on GitHub. To make it obvious to others that he was indeed able to exploit such a vulnerability, he created a very interesting issue in the bug tracker. The issue has since been updated, but figure 5.1 shows an archived version (the URL of the issue is https://github.com/rails/rails/issues/5239, and the screenshot shows a version

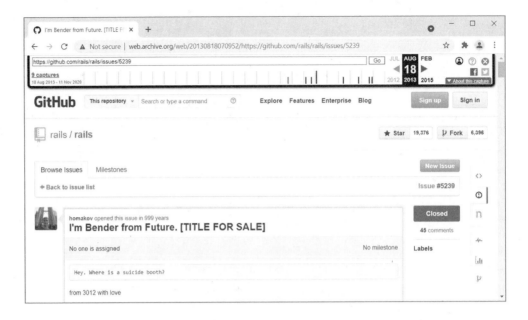

Figure 5.1   Bug reports from the future

from 2013, using Internet Archive's Wayback Machine: http://web.archive.org/web/20130818070952/https://github.com/rails/rails/issues/5239).

It looks like the issue was created in 3012, about 1,000 years in the future. The bug title and description refer to the *Futurama* TV series, which is set in the 31st century.

We will discuss the specific attack behind this later in the chapter, but let's look at the larger picture first. As with most attacks, the basic mistake was that input was not properly validated. Since HTTP is the dominant protocol used in web applications, we should look at it first.

5.1   *Looking at HTTP*

HTTP is the glue between web application frontends and backends, so that is where many attacks happen. Let's look what the browser is actually sending and whether this may be manipulated. Here is a typical HTTP GET request when loading manning.com into a browser:

```
GET / HTTP/1.1
Host: www.manning.com
Connection: keep-alive
Accept: text/html,application/xhtml+xml,application/xml;q=0.9,image/
    avif,image/webp,image/apng,*/*;q=0.8,application/signed-
    exchange;v=b3;q=0.9
Accept-Encoding: gzip, deflate, br
Accept-Language: en-US,en;q=0.9
Cache-Control: max-age=0
```

```
User-Agent: Mozilla/5.0 (Windows NT 10.0; Win64; x64) AppleWebKit/537.36
    (KHTML, like Gecko) Chrome/96.0.4664.110 Safari/537.36
```

And this is a typical HTTP POST request that the browser sends when trying to log into a Manning account:

```
POST /login HTTP/1.1
Host: login.manning.com
Connection: keep-alive
Accept: text/html,application/xhtml+xml,application/xml;q=0.9,image/
    avif,image/webp,image/apng,*/*;q=0.8,application/signed-
    exchange;v=b3;q=0.9
Accept-Encoding: gzip, deflate, br
Accept-Language: en-US,en;q=0.9
Cache-Control: max-age=0
Content-Length: 5650
Content-Type: application/x-www-form-urlencoded
Cookie: c_i=8b7d22e5-6297-4a72-a8c4-da4b349f7ea8;
    __cf_bm=796aaf6f8505ce143732cb0bf5fe5570704f9b70-1624959363-1800-
    AXD+HXmAXJF166DRun4wgMAN0pH32mzn/
    VVgFkyoNQNN3AlioVtMdTNbrx419oEGvHIGFH+TdpC1NW9Px6vtCqDsKKVl3zrISkXNEXKHp
    0ExULqnil0Y1ZfH+k7/G4KW4Gl1rxCcaksfxIVxA+cJ3KWTus8nZ/qxiKh1WK3P/
    iBNxb+IWbu7ggb03dWPj8tJPQ==
Origin: https://login.manning.com
Referer: https://login.manning.com/
    login?service=https%3A%2F%2Fwww.manning.com%2Flogin%2Fcas
User-Agent: Mozilla/5.0 (Windows NT 10.0; Win64; x64) AppleWebKit/537.36
    (KHTML, like Gecko) Chrome/96.0.4664.110 Safari/537.36
```

> **NOTE**   Both HTTP requests were edited for brevity; irrelevant HTTP headers were filtered out, some values were shortened, and the order of the HTTP headers was changed.

When a browser sends a request to https://example.com/page?param=value, the client and the server first negotiate encryption, if applicable (when using HTTPS, it is), and then the following headers are sent (assuming that GET is used; otherwise, the request starts with another method):

```
GET /page?param=value HTTP/1.1
Host: example.com
```

Even if other HTTP versions are used, for instance, HTTP 2.0, the basic approach remains the same. The Host header, required since HTTP 1.1, plus the actual URL of the page, are the bare minimum of information required for the server to handle the request. Most of the remaining HTTP headers provide metadata about the request, the client, or additional information.

Bad news: since all of these headers are sent by the client, any client, they all can be manipulated. An attacker does not need a browser to send such a request, but could even use telnet! (In practice, specialized tools with better usability are used.) Consequently, the application must never trust any data that comes as part of the request.

Let's look at some of the headers from the preceding requests and analyze when manipulation might take place and why.

- `Accept`—This header contains a list of MIME (Multipurpose Internet Mail Extensions) types that the browser accepts. In general, it contains HTML, some image formats, and (at the end of the list and less prioritized), "anything" (`*/*`). Some APIs use the value in this header to decide in which format to return the data. As you'll recall from chapter 2, an API might be prone to cross-site scripting if it is returning the `text/html` content type, so you'd better be explicit as to which formats you are returning.
- `Cookie`—As we discussed in chapter 3, cookies are stored on the client, are trivial to manipulate there, and will then be sent back in this HTTP header. The value in it is not trustworthy, so it either must be validated or changing it must make it invalid (e.g., session IDs).
- `Origin`—Especially when doing cross-domain requests, the browser automatically adds the `Origin` header. Chapter 4 covered CORS and how this header works. As we already stated there, this HTTP header is a security feature that is protecting the third-party domain. However, a malicious request can set this header to a different value. Do not trust the `Origin` header, and especially do not use it for authorization.
- `Referer`—This header contains the page the user is coming from (e.g., by clicking on a link or submitting a form). Also, when loading an image, the page referencing ("referring") the image is contained here. The application must not rely on this header since it can be manipulated, so don't use it for any kind of authorization. Also, modern browsers may shorten or skip this header (see chapter 9). (If you're wondering why this header is not spelled *Referrer*, there was a typo in the first HTTP specification, and for backward compatibility reasons, this was never changed.)
- `User-Agent`—The identification string of the client is put into this HTTP header. The format grew historically and is far from optimal. For instance, the user agents in the two example HTTP requests are from Chrome, but also contain "Mozilla" (the Netscape code name), "KHTML" (the rendering engine from the KDE project), "Gecko" (the Firefox rendering engine), "WebKit" (Apple's browser engine), and "Safari" (Apple's web browser). This was supposedly done to appease as many browser-detection scripts as possible. Do not expect anything from those user agent strings; they could be missing or contain random data or unexpected special characters (hint: XSS).

And while all of the preceding headers may (and will!) be manipulated, most of the attacks just tamper with the most obvious pieces of data: query string parameters and `POST` parameters.

No matter which HTTP method you are using, there might be parameters in the query string. Depending on which flavor of ASP.NET Core you are using, there are different approaches to access it:

- `HttpContext.Request.Query["name"]`
- `public IActionResult Get(string name) {}`
- `public IActionResult Get([FromQuery(Name = "name")] string nameFromURL) {}`
- Any other form of model binding (e.g., data from routes)

POST data does not show up in the URL but is sent after all HTTP headers, separated from them by a blank line. The formatting of the POST data depends on the `Content-Type` HTTP request header (not the response header of the same name!). The default value for POST requests is `application/x-www-form-urlencoded` and uses the same format as query string parameters (name-value pairs, separated by an ampersand). If file uploads are included, `multipart/form-data` is commonly used.

From an ASP.NET Core perspective, we do not care much, since the framework gives us access exactly as when using GET. The replacement for `HttpContext.Request.Query` is `HttpContext.Request.Form`, which is of type `FormCollection` and holds the name-value pairs. Other values in `HttpContext.Request` are also prone to manipulation, such as HTTP headers, including cookies.

> **NOTE** Session data cannot be as easily manipulated as data from the HTTP request. The only thing the client sends to the server that is related to sessions is the cookie with the session ID. That information may be manipulated, but it's virtually impossible to guess an existing session identifier unless it has been previously stolen (see chapter 3). If you are storing user-supplied data in a session, then yes, session data may also be manipulated and is not to be trusted.

Here's an easy rule of thumb: everything from `HttpContext.Request` is not trustworthy, and everything that is model-bound (action method parameters, page model parameters) is not trustworthy. Follow these two rules with all untrusted data:

- *Validate input*—If you can, check whether the input fits. You may check the data type, for instance.
- *Escape output*—When processing the data and stuffing it into an output format, escape special characters. Otherwise, you might fall victim to cross-site scripting when outputting HTML or JavaScript (see chapter 2), or to SQL injection (see chapter 6) or other attacks.

We will focus on input validation for now and look at what ASP.NET Core has in store for us.

5.2 ASP.NET Core validation

One of the central aspects of development with ASP.NET Core is model binding. Instead of manually plucking through GET and POST data, action methods may accept specific data types. The framework takes care of properly translating the request data into these types.

Once such a system is in place, validation may be declaratively added to the model. In other words, the model knows its validation rules; the application does not but is automatically using this information. Among other things, this decoupling facilitates reusing the model. The following listing shows a typical model class.

Listing 5.1   The issues model class

```
using System.ComponentModel.DataAnnotations;

namespace AspNetCoreSecurity.MvcSamples.Models
{
    public class Issue
    {
        public Issue()
        {
            this.CreationDate = DateTime.Now;          ◁── Sets creation date upon
        }                                                   class instantiation

        public int Id { get; set; }        ◁── The ID field is required for Entity
        public string Title { get; set; } = string.Empty;     Framework Core use later.
        public string Description { get; set; } = string.Empty;
        [Display(Name = "Creation Date")]
        public DateTime CreationDate { get; set; }
    }
}
```

The class already contains information about validation: the data types. The creation date must be `DateTime`, and the `ID`, if set, must be an integer. It is a common mistake to create action methods (or Razor handler methods) like this:

```
[HttpPost]
[ValidateAntiForgeryToken]
public async Task<IActionResult> Create(Issue issue)
{
    _context.Add(issue);
    await _context.SaveChangesAsync();
    return RedirectToAction(nameof(Index));
}
```

The model validation does take place, right after model binding and before the action method is called. However, our code is not handling the result of the model validation and will try to save the incorrect or incomplete data to the data context. The database will hopefully catch the error, but it is clearly preferable that we take care of the error handling. Here is a better approach:

```
[HttpPost]
[ValidateAntiForgeryToken]
public async Task<IActionResult> Create(Issue issue)
{
    if (ModelState.IsValid)
    {
        _context.Add(issue);
        await _context.SaveChangesAsync();
```

```
        return RedirectToAction(nameof(Index));
    }
    return View(issue);
}
```

The `ModelState.IsValid` property contains the Boolean result of the model validation and allows us to react properly. If validation failed, we can go back to the view and
show error messages there. (The `asp-validation-for` and `asp-validation-
summary` tag helpers come to mind, but that's beyond the scope of this chapter.)

Automated and manual validation

When using a Web API controller (`ApiController` class), the validation is enforced.
If it fails, an HTTP 400 error ("Bad Request") is returned without any extra code.

You may also run the validation manually; for instance, when changing the model
within your handler method:

```
ModelState.ClearValidationState(nameof(issue));
if (!TryValidateModel(issue, nameof(issue)) {
  return View(issue);
}
```

You can add additional validation rules to the model via attributes. They are defined
in the `System.ComponentModel.DataAnnotations` namespace—which is conveniently already present in the class, since we are already using the `[Display]` attribute that is defined in the same place—and can be associated with individual fields in
the model. Table 5.1 contains a list of the most relevant issues (more exotic features
such as credit card format validation or phone number formats that are not interna-
tionally recognized are omitted).

Table 5.1 ASP.NET Core validation attributes

Attribute example	Description
`[Required]`	Property must have a value.
`[StringLength(42)]`	Property must have a length of 42 characters max.
`[Range(10, 99)]`	Property must be a value between 10 and 99 (both inclusive).
`[Compare(nameof(RepeatValue))]`	Property must be identical to the one from the other field referenced in the attribute.
`[RegularExpression(@"^[a-zA-Z]{1,42}$")]`	Property must match the regular expression (between 1 and 42 uppercase or lowercase letters).
`[EmailAddress]`	Property value must be a valid email address.
`[Url]`	Property value must be a syntactically correct absolute URL.
`[Remote(action: "VerifyCustom", controller: "Validations")]`	Property will be validated with the `VerifyCustom()` method in the `ValidationsController` class.

All of these attributes (and all other missing validation attributes) support the `ErrorMessage` property where the error message may be defined and will then be picked up by the UI.

There are more advanced features available that we want to mention for the sake of completeness. From a security standpoint, it's more important that validation does takes place than how the implementation details look:

- *Custom validation with custom attributes*—A class that inherits from `Validation-Attribute` basically needs to override the `IsValid()` method and handle the validation there.
- *Custom validation with a custom method*—The model class needs to implement `IValidateObject` and then put the custom validation in the `Validate()` method.

Finally, if for some reason you do not want any validation at all for a property, the `[ValidateNever]` attribute has you covered.

Client-side validation

You may have noticed that we have discussed only server-side validation so far and have omitted the client side. Some Visual Studio templates even come with the jQuery validation libraries already set up. Microsoft has created the jQuery unobtrusive validation plugin, which is hosted on GitHub (http://mng.bz/aJVB). Don't be fooled by the generic name of this script—it's specifically tailored for ASP.NET Core MVC. With this plugin, the validation declared on the server also works on the client.

From a security standpoint, client validation is irrelevant. JavaScript may be deactivated, and HTTP requests with invalid data can easily be sent to the server. In-browser validation is just a usability feature. Even worse, since the code on the client may be analyzed, whereas the server code is usually a secret, any validation rules will be unveiled once the logic is made available to the browser. If no business secrets are involved, the usability benefits of having client validation in addition to server validations can be enormous, of course.

To reiterate the main point of this chapter: validate any user data the application receives. If you have a URL scheme like /Issues/42, where 42 is the ID of the issue to show, make sure that the current user has access to this ID (and did not guess it). If your UI has a selection list with three entries, verify that upon form submit, you do receive one of those three entries (or no entry at all), and not something the user made up. If you expect a certain input format, a data type, or a range, use the model validation features to have a simple yet effective validation mechanism in place.

TIP   The Fluent Validation library (https://fluentvalidation.net/) is a popular open source project that provides a nice, fluent API to implement custom validation in a .NET application.

Unfortunately, just validating the properties you are expecting is not always enough. One specific attack will send you more than you asked for.

5.3 *Mass assignment*

We will now reproduce the attack that this chapter started with, this time using our stack of choice. Remember the `Issue` class from listing 5.1? Once this was implemented in an ASP.NET Core MVC app, I ran the Visual Studio controller scaffolder (figure 5.2) to create controller actions and views using Entity Framework (for that to work, I had to install the `Microsoft.EntityFrameworkCore.SqlServer` NuGet package first—your mileage may vary).

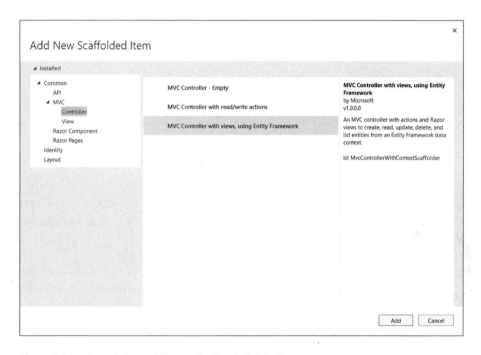

Figure 5.2   A few clicks, and the application is finished.

In the end, Visual Studio creates a controller with several action methods and associated views for CRUD (create, read, update, delete) operations based on the `Issue` model class. The following two commands, when run in Visual Studio's Package Manager Console, set up a matching database:

```
Add-Migration Initial
Update-Database
```

When the code is using the generated views to work with `Issue` values, the data is written to and read from a database.

Among the views generated, the Create.cshtml file provides a form to add a new issue to the system (see the following listing).

Listing 5.2   The view to add an issue to the database

```
@model AspNetCoreSecurity.MvcSamples.Models.Issue

@{
    ViewData["Title"] = "Create";
}

<h1>Create</h1>

<h4>Issue</h4>
<hr />
<div class="row">
    <div class="col-md-4">
        <form asp-action="Create">
            <div asp-validation-summary="ModelOnly" class="text-danger"></div>
            <div class="form-group">
                <label asp-for="Title" class="control-label"></label>
                <input asp-for="Title"
                    class="form-control" />
                <span asp-validation-for="Title" class="text-danger"></span>
            </div>
            <div class="form-group">
                <label asp-for="Description" class="control-label"></label>
                <input asp-for="Description"
                    class="form-control" />
                <span asp-validation-for="Description" class="text-danger">
                </span>
            </div>
            <!--
            <div class="form-group">
                <label asp-for="CreationDate" class="control-label"></label>
                <input asp-for="CreationDate" class="form-control" />
                <span asp-validation-for="CreationDate" class="text-danger">
                </span>
            </div>
            -->
            <div class="form-group">
                <input type="submit" value="Create" class="btn btn-primary" />
            </div>
        </form>
    </div>
</div>

<div>
    <a asp-action="Index">Back to List</a>
</div>

@section Scripts {
    @{await Html.RenderPartialAsync("_ValidationScriptsPartial");}
}
```

Annotations:
- **Shows the input field for the issue title** → `<input asp-for="Title" class="form-control" />`
- **Shows the input field for the issue description** → `<input asp-for="Description" class="form-control" />`
- **The input field for the creation date is commented out.** → `<!-- ... -->`

Note that I put the creation date field within an HTML comment, since this value is filled automatically in the model's constructor (see listing 5.1). Once the form is submitted, the `IssuesController` class kicks in, and the `Create()` action method handles the request. The next listing shows the relevant excerpt of that class.

Listing 5.3   The methods for the create issue view

```
#nullable disable
using AspNetCoreSecurity.MvcSamples.Data;
using AspNetCoreSecurity.MvcSamples.Models;
using Microsoft.AspNetCore.Mvc;
using Microsoft.EntityFrameworkCore;

namespace AspNetCoreSecurity.MvcSamples.Controllers
{
    public class IssuesController : Controller
    {
        private readonly AspNetCoreSecurityMvcSamplesContext _context;

        public IssuesController(AspNetCoreSecurityMvcSamplesContext context)
        {
            _context = context;
        }

...

        // GET: Issues/Create              Shows the action method
        public IActionResult Create()    ← for the GET request
        {
            return View();
        }

        // POST: Issues/Create                        Shows the action
        [HttpPost]                                  method for the
        [ValidateAntiForgeryToken]                    POST request
        public async Task<IActionResult> Create(Issue issue)  ←
        {
            if (ModelState.IsValid)
            {
                _context.Add(issue);
                await _context.SaveChangesAsync();
                return RedirectToAction(nameof(Index));
            }
            return View(issue);
        }

...

}
```

When the form is submitted to the server, the POST request is taken care of by the second `Create()` method. The data from the HTTP request is automatically converted into an instance of the `Issue` class (model binding, of course) and then added to the database. Figure 5.3 shows the input form in the browser.

Figure 5.3   The issue input form

As you can see, there is no field for the `CreationDate` property. This value is automatically set in the model, as figure 5.4 shows.

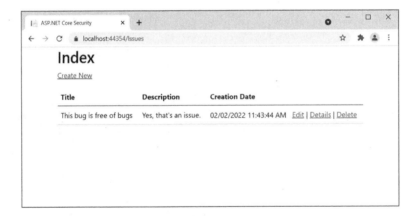

Figure 5.4   The page lists all issues in the database.

The overview page (Index.cshtml file and `Index()` action method) iterates over all issues in the database and displays them in a table-like format.

In theory, the application looks solid. Users cannot set the creation date themselves, since there is no UI for it. But aren't we using model binding? Let's look at the signature of the `Create()` POST method again:

```
public async Task<IActionResult> Create(Issue issue)
```

It expects something of type `Issue`. Everything coming in from the HTTP request—in this case, `POST` data—will be converted into an instance of `Issue` if possible. The form contains input fields with their name attributes set to `"Title"` and `"Description"`, respectively, so internally, the following code is executed (in reality it works in a more sophisticated fashion, so this is pseudocode for illustration purposes only):

```
var issue = new Issue();                                ◁──────┐  Constructor sets
issue.Title = HttpContext.Request.Form["Title"];               │  the creation date to
issue.Description = HttpContext.Request.Form["Description"];    │  the current date
```

But what if the HTTP request would additionally contain a field called `"Creation-Date"`? Then this pseudocode would run:

```
var issue = new Issue();
issue.Title = HttpContext.Request.Form["Title"];
issue.Description = HttpContext.Request.Form["Description"];
issue.CreationDate =
    Convert.ToDateTime(HttpContext.Request.Form["CreationDate"]);
```

The creation date is set, and that happens after the `Issue` constructor has run. Consequently, the user-supplied creation date is stored in the database. In order to replicate this, we could manually craft a suitable HTTP request. Since we did comment out the UI for the creation date, we can just comment it in, using the browser developer tools. Figure 5.5 shows how.

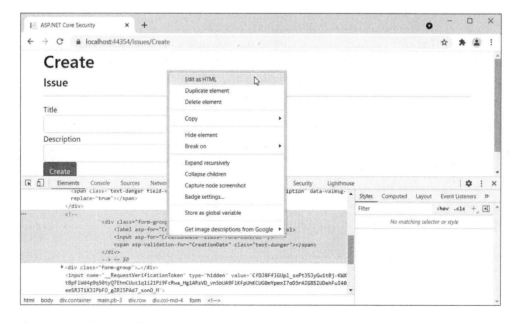

Figure 5.5 Reinstating the creation date input field

When editing the HTML within the browser, removing `<!--` and `-->` and adding `name="CreationDate"` to the input field does the trick. You may now enter a date and submit the form, and you will be presented with something like figure 5.6.

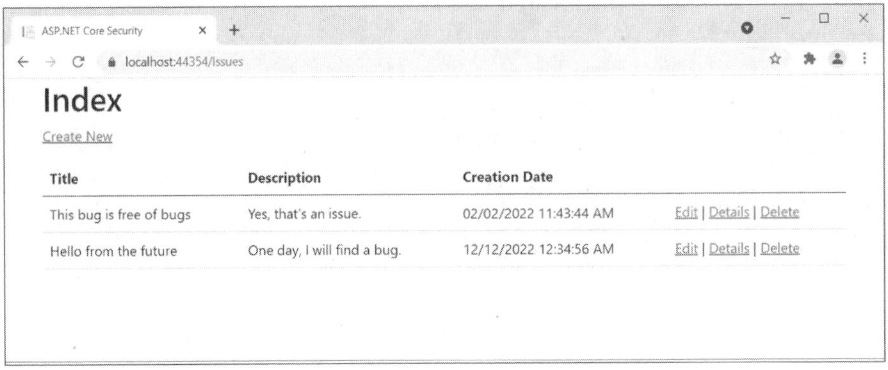

Figure 5.6   Hello from the future.

The issue was now created in the future (this screenshot was taken well before December 2022), quite similar to what happened on GitHub some years ago. The name of this attack is *mass assignment*—that explains pretty well what has happened. Thanks to model binding, all applicable data from the HTTP request was assigned to model properties. Essentially, we were able to set the creation date, which should not be available for users to write. Another term sometimes used for this attack is *overposting*—an attacker sends more POST data than expected.

In our example, finding this attack was rather trivial, since we knew the code and there was even commented-out markup showing us the name of the field. Yet the wording we used for the model property, `CreationDate`, is not very imaginative and could have been guessed rather easily by an attacker.

There are several ways to solve this. From an architectural point of view, a view model might come in handy. That's a model that's solely responsible for the view, and contains only properties for that view. For the *Create.cshtml* page, such a model class would require only a title and a description, but not a creation date. Here is how that could look:

```
public class CreateIssueViewModel
{
    public string Title { get; set; }
    public string Description { get; set; }
}
```

The class contains only the `Title` and `Description` properties. The action method then, in turn, expects this view model:

```
[HttpPost]
[ValidateAntiForgeryToken]
```

```
public async Task<IActionResult> Create(CreateIssueViewModel issueVm)
{
    if (ModelState.IsValid)
    {
        var issue = new Issue()
        {
            Title = issueVm.Title,
            Description = issueVm.Description,
        };
        _context.Add(issue);
        await _context.SaveChangesAsync();
        return RedirectToAction(nameof(Index));
    }
    return View(issue);
}
```

A new instance of the `Issue` class is generated and filled with the data from the view model—so title and description only! This effectively prevents mass assignment.

In fairness to the teams for ASP.NET Core and Visual Studio, I need to mention that recent versions add a comment to the template when views are scaffolded. Here is how the `Create` action method really looked before I tampered with it:

```
// POST: Issues/Create
// To protect from overposting attacks, enable the specific properties you
➥want to bind to.
// For more details, see http://go.microsoft.com/fwlink/?LinkId=317598.
[HttpPost]
[ValidateAntiForgeryToken]
public async Task<IActionResult>
➥Create([Bind("Id,Title,Description,CreationDate")] Issue issue)
{
...
}
```

The `[Bind]` attribute provides an explicit list of properties that may be bound, and a comment reiterates that you must select which of the model members you want to allow users to write. In our case, this may be limited to `Title` and `Description` (for the action method responsible for editing existing issues, you also need to allow the `Id` property).

This is basically an allow list—everything not on the list is not allowed. From a security perspective, that's the best approach, because if something is missing from that list, we may have a usability issue but not a security problem.

The `[Bind("Title,Description")]` syntax is actually a shorthand form for this more explicit option:

```
[Bind(Include="Title,Description")]
```

This makes it absolutely clear that the list contains properties that shall be included by the model binder. You can also use the opposite approach and disallow certain properties you do not want to be bound:

```
[Bind(Exclude="Id,CreationDate")]
```

This is a deny list. While it works here (and also on other very rare occasions, like the list of HTML special characters in chapter 2), we generally advise against going that route. If there is an element missing in the exclude list, we won't have a usability problem, but we will potentially have a security issue.

> **NOTE**   An attacker might also try to change the Id value in the request, trying to edit an item they do not have access to. You need to make sure that you authorize each request and validate that the current user does have access to the current item.

We cannot always easily parse formatted user input in our code, but defer that to .NET Core. When it comes to deserialization, this might become a problem.

5.4   *Secure deserialization*

Let's look at an attack that abuses deserialization. Many ASP.NET Core applications deserialize data all the time: HTTP POST data is transformed from the application/x-www-form-urlencoded MIME type into a list of values, and JSON data is accepted by API endpoints and is converted in the type provided. This mechanism is trusted and vetted and works well, and in a secure fashion.

When manually deserializing user-supplied data, though, there is a hypothetical chance that an attacker might find an opening in our defense. Due to the modular nature of the "new" .NET (previously called .NET Core) in comparison to the monolithic .NET Framework, these exploits are very rare. I would still like to demonstrate an attack and to deduce best practices from it.

The following Razor Page model is working with (predefined) JSON data and deserializing it, using the Newtonsoft.Json package.

Listing 5.4   Deserializing JSON data

```
using Microsoft.AspNetCore.Mvc.RazorPages;
using Newtonsoft.Json;

namespace AspNetCoreSecurity.RazorSamples.Pages
{
    public class DeserializationModel : PageModel
    {
        public void OnGet()
        {
            var payload = @"{
'$type':'System.Windows.Data.ObjectDataProvider, PresentationFramework,
Version=4.0.0.0, Culture=neutral, PublicKeyToken=31bf3856ad364e35',
'MethodName':'Start',
'MethodParameters':{
    '$type':'System.Collections.ArrayList, mscorlib, Version=4.0.0.0,
Culture=neutral, PublicKeyToken=b77a5c561934e089',
    '$values':['cmd', '/c notepad']
},
```

```
    'ObjectInstance':{'$type':'System.Diagnostics.Process, System,
    Version=4.0.0.0, Culture=neutral, PublicKeyToken=b77a5c561934e089'}
}";
        var data = JsonConvert.DeserializeObject(        ◁──── Deserializes the JSON
            payload,                                            string into an object
            new JsonSerializerSettings()
            {
                TypeNameHandling = TypeNameHandling.All   ◁──── Accepts
            });                                                  any type
    }
}
}
```

Figure 5.7 shows what happens when you run this code in the browser.

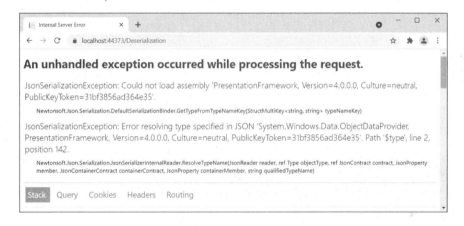

Figure 5.7   What is `PresentationFramework`?

The exception states that an assembly called `PresentationFramework` could not be loaded. That is part of Windows Presentation Foundation (WPF) and—of course—not part of a standard ASP.NET Core app. That's why the exception is triggered. But where does this `PresentationFramework` call come from? All we are doing is serializing data! Let's look at the payload string again:

```
{
    '$type':'System.Windows.Data.ObjectDataProvider, PresentationFramework,
    Version=4.0.0.0, Culture=neutral, PublicKeyToken=31bf3856ad364e35',
    'MethodName':'Start',
    'MethodParameters':{
        '$type':'System.Collections.ArrayList, mscorlib, Version=4.0.0.0,
    Culture=neutral, PublicKeyToken=b77a5c561934e089',
        '$values':['cmd', '/c notepad']
    },
    'ObjectInstance':{'$type':'System.Diagnostics.Process, System,
    Version=4.0.0.0, Culture=neutral, PublicKeyToken=b77a5c561934e089'}
}
```

The properties called '$type' provide the data type that is serialized. The `Object-DataProvider` class is responsible for creating the target object: `Presentation-Framework`. Unfortunately (for us), a WPF application may instantiate a class and call a method once it is initialized. The payload is using `System.Diagnostics.Process` for the class and `Start()` as its method. In the `MethodParameters` key, you can see which parameters are used in that call: `cmd` and `/c notepad`.

In a nutshell, once the data is serialized, Notepad is launched (if this is run under Windows—and you have a Windows version where this powerful IDE is still installed). In our specific scenario, that attack was futile, since `PresentationFramework` was not at our disposal. It would work, though, with a .NET Framework application on the command line. The previous payload was created using the YSoSerial.Net project from https://github.com/pwntester/ysoserial.net. The following command line call creates a `cmd /c notepad` payload for Json.NET and is deserializing it, causing the text editor to be launched (figure 5.8 shows the result):

```
ysoserial -f Json.Net -g ObjectDataProvider -o raw -c "notepad" -t
```

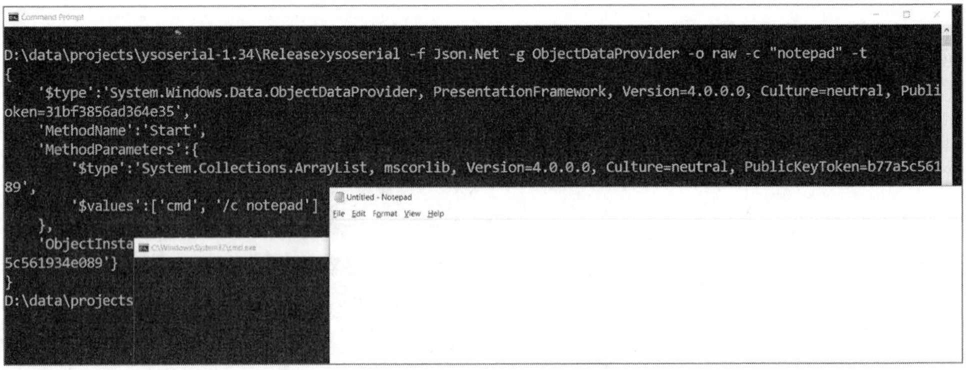

Figure 5.8   The text editor appears from out of nowhere.

Notepad pops up—the deserialization caused code injection. This is nice for demos, but in the real world, an attacker would call other commands, obviously, to create more harm.

When deserializing the string, we were allowing Json.NET to create any type that is contained in the JSON payload:

```
var data = JsonConvert.DeserializeObject(
    payload,
    new JsonSerializerSettings()
    {
        TypeNameHandling = TypeNameHandling.All
    });
```

A simple yet effective remedy is to disallow exactly that (and that's also the default value for that property):

```
var data = JsonConvert.DeserializeObject(
    payload,
    new JsonSerializerSettings()
    {
        TypeNameHandling = TypeNameHandling.None
    });
```

In that case, the '$type' values in the JSON string will not be used as the target type name, preventing the attack. .NET comes with its own JSON deserializer: the namespace System.Text.Json holds all functionality. The JsonSerializer .Deserialize() method takes care of deserialization. If you want to create a specific type, you can refer to the generic version of the method:

```
MyClass data = JsonSerializer.Deserialize<MyClass>(payload);
```

You have to explicitly provide the type. It is not inferred from the JSON string itself, rendering the attack toothless. As with many other aspects of .NET and ASP.NET Core, you are pretty secure by default. If you are doing any type of manual deserialization, always make sure that you define what kind of structure you are expecting, and verify that that's what you got.

Summary

Let's review what we have learned so far:

- Validate input and escape output to protect a web application against most attacks by being paranoid about any data that is sent to the application.
- ASP.NET Core comes with built-in data verification features, using model-based validation. Use data model attributes to put restrictions on the data, and don't forget verifying the Model.IsValid property.
- Model binding is an extremely convenient feature, but mass assignment attacks require that the list of properties that may be bound to must be at a minimum. Use [Bind(Include=...)] for an allow list, or [Bind(Exclude=...)] for a deny list.
- JSON deserialization may lead to code injection, but mainly in older versions of .NET. It is relatively trivial to defend against this attack by specifically setting the data type expected from deserialization.

The next attacks we will discuss are those against databases—effective countermeasures included, of course.

SQL injection
(and other injections)

This chapter covers

- Learning how string concatenations lead to SQL injection
- Understanding the consequences of SQL injection
- Avoiding SQL injection with prepared statements
- Using an OR (object-relational) mapper
- Other types of injection attacks

In early March 2021, Ars Technica reported (see the following callout) that 70 GB of data was supposedly stolen from the infamous social media platform Gab. This data included passwords and other user data, private messages, and more. The reason: the code was vulnerable to SQL injection. This allowed an anonymous attacker to access and download this vast amount of data and to make it available to selected researchers.

> **NOTE** See http://mng.bz/gwAE for the initial report, and http://mng.bz/5QOB for more details on the programming mistake.

6.1 Anatomy of an SQL injection attack

SQL stands for "Structured Query Language" and was invented in the 1970s to provide a language to communicate with a relational database to, among other things, read and write data to it. Even the creators (Donald D. Chamberlin and Raymond F. Boyce) probably could not imagine back then that their brainchild would still be in use almost 50 years later. That websites would send user input to a web server where it would be put in SQL queries that would then be executed against a database was certainly far from everyone's imagination back then.

However, SQL suffers from an architectural problem that many query languages have: data and commands are in the same string. If an SQL query is the result of a concatenation of strings, some of them contributed by the user, there might be a risk.

Let's look at a sample Razor Page where a simple login form is implemented. The following listing shows the login form.

Listing 6.1 The login form as part of a Razor Page

```
@page
@model LoginModel

<div class="text-center">
    <h1 class="display-4">Login</h1>
    <form method="post" action="">
        <div class="mt-5 mb-5">
            <p class="lead">@Model.SqlQuery</p>            ⟵┐ Later, the SQL query
        </div>                                                │ will be shown here.
        <div class="mb-3">
            <label for="inputEmail" class="form-label">User name</label>
            <input type="email" class="form-control" id="inputEmail"
            ➡name="email" placeholder="user@example.com">   ⟵┐ Shows the email
        </div>                                                │ address input field
        <div class="mb-3">
            <label for="inputPassword" class="form-label">Password</label>
            <input type="password" class="form-control" id="inputPassword"
            ➡name="password">                                ⟵┐ Shows the
        </div>                                                │ password field
        <div class="mb-3">
            <input type="submit" class="btn btn-primary mb-3" value="Login">
        </div>
    </form>
</div>
```

The associated page model class, shown in the next listing, includes the `OnPost()` method, which is executed once a `POST` request is sent—in our scenario, once a user submits the login form.

Listing 6.2 The page model with the (very limited) login logic

```
using Microsoft.AspNetCore.Mvc.RazorPages;

namespace AspNetCoreSecurity.RazorSamples.Pages
{
    public class LoginModel : PageModel
    {
        public string SqlQuery { get; set; } = string.Empty;

        public void OnPost(string email, string password)
        {
            this.SqlQuery = String.Format(
                "SELECT * FROM users WHERE email='{0}' AND password='{1}'",
                email, password);
        }
    }
}
```

The SQL query is assembled.

So far, there is no database involved, but we assume that there eventually will be one. In the first step, the user data is written in the SQL statement, and the statement is then shown.

The SQL string is concatenated. The base structure is a query against a (still hypothetical) user database, checking whether there is a user with the provided email address and password. Once a real database comes in, all matching records in it—ideally, zero or one—are returned, allowing the application to decide whether the user credentials are correct and whether to let the user in.

WARNING Of course, no application should store passwords in cleartext, as the code suggests here. The application should not store passwords at all. For the sake of demonstration, we still assume such an application architecture here. Chapter 8 will cover secure handling of passwords in greater detail.

Check out figure 6.1 to see what that page looks like in the browser.

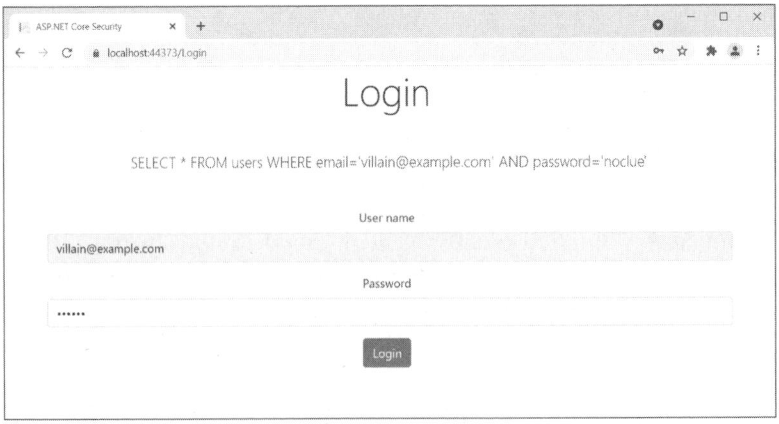

Figure 6.1 The login form in the browser

Let's say someone tries villain@example.com as the email address and `noclue` as the (highly improbable) password. This would result in the following SQL query:

```
SELECT * FROM users WHERE email='villain@example.com' AND password='noclue'
```

So far, so good. However, what would happen if the following password was used next (note that it includes four single quotes)?

```
noclue' OR ''='
```

Figure 6.2 shows the result and points out what was entered into the SQL query and how the database now interprets it.

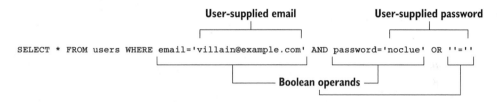

Figure 6.2   The malicious input alters the SQL logic.

The original SQL statement had only two Boolean operands—the check for the email address and the check for the password. But now there are three. The third operand is always `true` (empty string is always equal to empty string), so the `WHERE` statement does not restrict the result set. In the end, the SQL query is more or less equivalent to this one:

```
SELECT * FROM users
```

In other words, the attacker would now manage to log into the system without knowing a password or even a valid user email address! This attack is called *SQL injection*. In a nutshell, it may allow injecting any kind of SQL statement and run it against the database, with the privileges of the database user the web application uses. This makes SQL injection one of the most dangerous risks for websites. Now that we have seen the attack, it's time to protect the web application against it.

6.2   Prepared statements

SQL injection works because the attacker manages to switch the context within SQL—remember, an SQL statement is a string with commands and data. The preceding code assumed that the user would supply data and that it would be used in a data context (string within a `WHERE` clause, to be precise). However, by using a single quote and essentially ending the string, the attacker escaped the "string value" context and managed to add the third Boolean operand.

If you recall XSS from chapter 2, escaping output could be a promising strategy. Putting user data into an SQL query is also considered as output, so this rule may apply. However, it turns out that properly escaping special characters in SQL is tricky because there are so many options depending on the context. Within strings, single quotes come to mind (and replacing them with `\'` or `'`, depending on the database being used). The following query, when run against a MySQL database, would properly check for the `noclue' OR ''='` password:

```
SELECT * FROM users WHERE email='villain@example.com' AND
➥password='noclue\' OR \'\'=\''
```

But what about other special characters? Table 6.1 lists a few, and some of them depend on the specific database system.

Table 6.1   Some SQL special characters

Special character(s)	Function
( ) [ ]	Grouping
_ %	Wildcard characters
;	Ends a query
-- # /*	Starts a comment

There are several options, so it's easy to make a mistake. Why not let someone else do the heavy lifting? It turns out that all relevant database providers for .NET support prepared statements (also called *parameterized queries*). Here, the SQL is sent to the database in two steps. First, the statement is created and can contain placeholders. In the second step, values are assigned to those placeholders. Only then is the statement executed against the database.

This approach is simple yet effective, because it mitigates SQL's architectural issue: now it's clear what's a command and what's data. By assigning values to those placeholders, the database knows that the information submitted should only be considered as data. This essentially disabled the injection of unwanted SQL. A query with parameters can look like this:

```
SELECT * FROM users WHERE email=@email AND password=@password
```

Note that parameters are prefixed with the @ character and that there are no quotes around the parameters (otherwise, the parameter names would be used verbatim as strings).

Parameter syntax

There are different syntax options for prepared statements. The one we have been using so far (with the @ prefixes) is the most common and convenient one since every parameter can have a unique and memorable name. It's also possible to use the question mark (?) to denote parameters, and then assign values by position, not by name. This is obviously more error-prone, since the position of a parameter will change once another parameter is added somewhere before it.

Oracle is a well-known outlier since parameter names are prefixed with a colon. The SQL statement could then look like this:

```
SELECT * FROM users WHERE email=:email AND password=:password
```

For a long time, the most common way to send SQL statements to a database from within an ASP.NET application was to use ADO.NET (Advanced Data Objects for .NET). This approach also works with ASP.NET Core. For Microsoft SQL Server, the `Microsoft.Data.SqlClient` package from www.nuget.org/packages/Microsoft .Data.SqlClient contains the data provider. (There are similar packages for other major databases, but the way they implement prepared statements is so similar that we do not give them extra coverage.) The following listing shows how to use prepared statements with this package.

Listing 6.3 Using a prepared statement instead of concatenated SQL

```
using Microsoft.AspNetCore.Mvc.RazorPages;
using Microsoft.Data.SqlClient;
using System;

namespace AspNetCoreSecurity.RazorSamples.Pages
{
    public class IndexModel : PageModel
    {
        public void OnPost(string email, string password)
        {
            var connection = new SqlConnection(           Connects to
                "**connection string**");                 the database
            this.SqlQuery = "SELECT * FROM users WHERE email=@email AND
                password=@password";
                                                          Creates an SQL command
            var command = new SqlCommand(this.SqlQuery,   based on the SQL with the
                connection);                              placeholders/parameters

            command.Parameters.AddWithValue("@email",
                email);                                   Assigns values to
            command.Parameters.AddWithValue("@password",  the placeholders
                password);

            var reader = command.ExecuteReader();

            ...                        Login logic is
                                       omitted for brevity.
            reader.Close();
            connection.Close();
        }

        public string SqlQuery { get; set; }
    }
}
```

Essentially, you need to create a command object, feed the SQL to it, and then assign values to the placeholders in the query. Finally, the command must be executed to send the query to the database and optionally receive the requested records. We were using SQL Server here, but the command objects from other databases (e.g., `OracleCommand` from Oracle, `MySqlCommand` from MySQL, `SQLiteCommand` from SQLite, or `NpgsqlCommand` from PostgreSQL) use essentially the same syntax.

> **TIP** When going through existing code, look out for strings containing SQL queries, and analyze whether string concatenation takes place and whether some of those strings may be provided or manipulated by a user. Even better, make sure that whenever SQL is being used, prepared statements come into play, regardless of whether or not there is user data involved. That way, best practices are used throughout.

If you are indeed using SQL, prepared statements are likely your best bet against SQL injection. However, you might just skip SQL altogether.

6.3   *Entity Framework Core*

I routinely meet developers who haven't written one single SQL command in months, or even years. This is especially prevalent in the .NET space, where Microsoft seems to do almost everything to keep you away from SQL and instead lure you into the welcoming arms of Entity Framework Core. That's Microsoft's object-relational mapper (OR mapper or ORM). As the name suggests, this package lets you create objects and work with them. Entity Framework Core then maps those objects to a relational database. Here is some pseudocode that would query all users in a database for those with a specific email address/password combination:

```
db.Users.Where(user => user.email == email && user.password == password)
```

This does almost exactly the same thing as the SQL code from the previous section of this chapter (except for some special cases like case-sensitive databases); however, there is no string concatenation going on, and parameters are also absent. Instead, there is an object that represents all users in the data story (`db.Users`) and a LINQ syntax to select those users that fulfill certain criteria. There is no chance for an attacker to inject SQL that way since there is no SQL. Well, there is, but Entity Framework Core is automatically generating it. If you trust Entity Framework Core (and the OR mapper has a good security track record), you can feel sufficiently safe.

   I have not painted a complete picture, though. Entity Framework Core *does* allow sending verbatim SQL queries to a database. This would work similarly to the code snippet we just demonstrated:

```
var users = db.Users.FromSqlRaw("SELECT * FROM users WHERE
    email='villain@example.com' AND password='noclue'").ToList();
```

Entity Framework Core does not validate the SQL; it is just channeled through to the database. If you are using string concatenation and user data here, the application is suddenly prone to SQL injection again. Conveniently, there is support for parameterized queries. It uses a syntax similar to the one from .NET's `String.Format()`, but make sure that you are only using it directly in the `FromSqlRaw()` call:

```
var users = db.Users.FromSqlRaw(
  "SELECT * FROM users WHERE email={0} AND password={1}",
  email,
  password)
  .ToList();
```

Placeholders are numbered, starting with zero.

The preceding statement will have properly escaped the two values for the two placeholders. Alternatively, it is possible to use string interpolation like this:

This time, the FromSqlInterpolated() method needs to be used.

```
var users = db.Users.FromSqlInterpolated(
  $"SELECT * FROM users WHERE email={email} AND password={password}")
  .ToList();
```

Prefix with $ so that the variables within the curly braces are filled.

Again, the two placeholder values will be properly escaped.

> **NOTE** We are using Entity Framework Core in this chapter since it is the most commonly used OR mapper in the .NET space. If you are using another library, make sure you properly use parameters for any raw SQL you are sending, or just avoid creating SQL queries at all. In NHibernate, for instance, the `CreateSQLQuery()` method is the one to watch out for or skip completely.

Why use SQL at all?

Now that OR mappers like Entity Framework Core seem to solve the SQL injection problem for good, why is there any need to write SQL? It turns out that the convenience an OR mapper gives you does come at a cost. The SQL queries are generated based on the information you provide (e.g., the object and its relations). In some scenarios, the outcome is detrimental to performance. This can especially happen when several tables are joined as part of the query. When dealing with tables without a primary key, SQL might be a better approach as well.

Therefore, even the most die-hard fans of Entity Framework Core will always look for areas where verbatim queries are the way to go. In all of those cases, using static SQL without any user data in them, or parameters, or both is the way to go. Lightweight OR mappers like Dapper (https://dapperlib.github.io/Dapper/) can also be a good alternative.

So even though SQL injection is one of the most common web application security risks, we covered it last in this part of the book because the countermeasures are extremely easy to implement—if you know how.

This chapter would not be complete without at least mentioning a few of the other injections that may happen.

6.4   XML external entities

To be honest, XML parsing might not directly relate to injection, but it doesn't really fit into any other chapter. In the ASP.NET Core space, this attack is almost irrelevant, but since many consider the attack important (including OWASP; see chapter 16), we will touch the subject here.

The idea is as follows: let's assume we have a web application that expects XML and parses it. The XML is supplied by the user and is therefore not trusted. What could go wrong? First, let's look at the following listing, which shows an action method loading the XML content.

Listing 6.4   Processing XML

```
[HttpPost]
public ActionResult XmlEndpoint(string xml)
{
    var document = new System.Xml.XPath.XPathDocument(xml);
    var navigator = document.CreateNavigator();
    var output = navigator.InnerXml.ToString();

    return View(output);
}
```

The `XPathDocument` class is used to load the XML. Then the XML content is basically sent to the view (who might display it). Not much is going on there at a cursory glance, but unfortunately, some extra parsing might take place. The next listing shows an example of an XML payload that an attacker might send.

Listing 6.5   XML with a system entity

```
<?xml version="1.0" ?>
<!DOCTYPE attack [
  <!ELEMENT attack ANY >
  <!ENTITY xxe SYSTEM "file:///etc/passwd" >]          ⟵  Shows the definition
>                                                           of the &xxe; entity
<attack>&xxe;</attack>        ⟵  Shows the use of
                                 the &xxe; entity
```

Note that the XML uses the `&xxe;` entity—the name is completely arbitrary. Conveniently, the entity is defined in the same XML document as a system entity pointing to the local /etc/passwd file. When `XPathDocument` is loading the XML content, the system entity is found and resolved, so the contents of the local /etc/passwd file (on the server!) are put in place of `&xxe;`. If the view does output the XML, the attacker can access the contents of the file on the server. (This is a contrived example, of course, since on all relatively recent Linux systems, that specific file does not contain any password information anymore but might still be interesting for an attacker.)

This attack is called XML External Entities (XXE) because the XML payload contains entities that can be used to access local content (which is "external" for the attacker).

Server-side request forgery

Depending on the XML parsing component used and on the configuration of the system, it's also hypothetically possible for the attacker to let the entity point to a URL:

```
<!ENTITY xxe SYSTEM "https://mainserver/actions/shutdown">
```

In that case, the server would send the HTTP request to a system that might not be available to the outside but that is within the same secure network zone as the web server. In that case, we are talking about server-side request forgery (SSRF). It's related to cross-site request forgery but is a bit different.

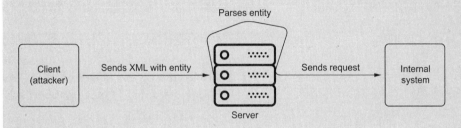

Server-side request forgery in action

The XML payload with the system entity in it prompts the server to send an HTTP request when that entity is resolved.

XXE is a somewhat surprising and theoretically dangerous attack. Yet, the stars have to be aligned properly for it to happen. First of all, the web application has to parse XML (which seems to become more and more rare these days). Then the attacker needs to have intimate knowledge about either the web application or the internal network. When trying to access a local file via XXE, the full URI to that file has to be known. When attempting to forge an HTTP request, the URL for that request must be known. It will be a GET request, so the endpoint needs to either return sensitive data or take an action like deleting an item (which should never be done via GET anyway). If the data in that file or from that internal service are of interest, the endpoint handling the XML must return the XML so that the attacker can actually see that information.

Only if all of these prerequisites are met does the attack make sense for the villain. There are some interesting proofs of concept that work in practice (here is one that I find pretty interesting: http://mng.bz/6XYo), but from what I am personally seeing in audits, XXE is rather exotic (at least for now).

But there is even better news. There are many ways to parse XML in .NET—XmlDocument, XmlNodeReader, XmlReader, XmlTextReader, XPathNavigator, and a few more. All of them are secure by default, since they do not resolve system entities. Although most attacks against web applications are technology-agnostic, choosing ASP.NET Core provides sufficient protection out of the box.

XXE is a special, and (luckily) rare, kind of attack. There are also other types of injections, which occur much more rarely.

6.5   Other injections

All query languages or formats might be prone to injection if user data is not properly filtered or escaped. However, rest assured that when talking about injections in web application security, SQL injection is the actual topic in almost all cases. Here are a few more exotic options:

- *XPath injection*—This can happen when an XPath query is generated with user input. The language looks similar to SQL. Escaping special characters depending on the context will help (usually, single quotes within a string also delimited with single quotes).
- *LDAP injection*—This takes place if LDAP (Lightweight Directory Access Protocol) queries (typically, the Distinguished Name entry) are using user input. The best approach is to use very strict filtering or an allow list with a limited set of valid input values. There is no built-in escaping helper method in .NET Core, unfortunately.
- *Regular Expression injection*—This is an "invention" of yours truly. It turns out that some technologies support the e modifier in regular expressions. This modifier runs code when replacing a match. If the replacement string (i.e., the code that is run during replacement) can be manipulated by an attacker, code injection is possible. Luckily, .NET refused to implement this modifier, and no one is missing it.

There are other kinds of injections as well, all of them equally rare, at least in the .NET space. However, by applying defensive programming, you should be well prepared for any of those attacks. Always remember to properly escape output—to be precise, escape input values when you output them in a query format. Creating a specific query format *is* outputting data. Identify the current context (e.g., within a string delimited with single quotes), and then consider which special characters exist in that very context (e.g., single quotes and backslashes) and how to properly escape them (possibly prefixing them with a backslash). Whenever you are processing user-supplied data and feeding it into any kind of query language, be extremely paranoid and validate the data as well as you can.

Summary

Let's review what we have learned so far:

- SQL injection is an attack that may lead to the execution of malicious SQL code.
- Concatenating strings with user data into an SQL query is the most common pattern for SQL injection.
- Prepared statements or parameterized queries help distinguish commands from data and can prevent SQL injection.

- An OR mapper like Entity Framework Core makes custom SQL queries unnecessary, effectively eliminating the risk of SQL injection. If you do use custom SQL queries there, ensure that you use parameters.
- Using entities in a carefully crafted XML payload could lead to data leakage or server-side request forgery, but requires an ancient version of .NET and is very hard to pull off.
- Other types of injections exist, but they are very rare.

Now that we have looked at the most common attacks, it is time to explore other security-related topics. The next part of the book will look at secure data storage and will also solve one of the issues from this chapter: secure password handling.

Part 3

Secure data storage

Most web applications need to store secret data in one way or another—database credentials, tokens, or other types of keys. This data should never fall into the hands of invaders in the event of an attack.

In order to mitigate this risk, chapter 7 discusses several approaches to storing secrets in an ASP.NET Core application. Chapter 8 takes a specific look at passwords and how to store (or rather, not to store) them.

7

Storing secrets

This chapter covers

- Exploring different kinds of encryption
- Securely storing configuration settings
- Using the Secret Manager to store data
- Using secure cloud storage options
- Protecting data stored locally by a Blazor app

In 2020, it was discovered that a piece of software by IT company SolarWinds contained a back door that was abused by attackers. Part of the attack involved downloading a malicious software update. The password for the FTP server containing those updates was "solarwinds123" (at least, at some point in 2019). Famously, the CEO blamed it on "an intern."

A security researcher found this password within a public GitHub repository of the company (see http://mng.bz/1oBj for background information on the attack and its aftermath). We will discuss secure passwords in the next chapter, but this chapter will focus on better ways to store secrets, such as passwords, within an application. There does not seem to be an obvious, simple solution for this task, as numerous examples prove:

- In 2014, AWS warned its customers that they must not store application keys publicly on GitHub; a trivial search found thousands of results (http://mng.bz/Pn5n).
- In 2018, security researcher Giovanni Collazo found many open etcd servers (a distributed key-value database) on the internet where he could extract about 750 MB worth of data, including passwords and other sensitive information (https://gcollazo.com/the-security-footgun-in-etcd/).
- A 2019 study found that over 100,000 repositories contained API tokens and cryptographic keys (see http://mng.bz/J2GV).
- An experiment undertaken in 2020 discovered that once there are AWS credentials stored in a GitHub repository, it only takes 1 minute until someone starts an attack, and 4 minutes until they are done (http://mng.bz/woDP).

Nowadays, there are several tools and services that try to mitigate the risk, offering scanning services for repositories (GitHub now does this automatically; see http://mng.bz/qYPr, but there are independent options such as https://github.com/trufflesecurity/truffleHog) and Git hooks (e.g., https://github.com/awslabs/git-secrets or https://github.com/auth0/repo-supervisor). The general guidance is not to store secrets in a public place, but that's an overly simple answer to a complex problem. Depending on the application, there are several options available, and we will discuss the most relevant ones for ASP.NET Core applications. How about encryption, for instance? But before we can use that, we need to discuss which kinds of encryption are available. Most of the time, the services and frameworks will transparently use encryption without bothering us with too many details, but it is valuable to understand the basics.

7.1 *On encryption*

Encryption is a process that transforms original information, plaintext, into ciphertext, the encrypted representation of that information. The basic idea is that if the ciphertext is somehow leaked, it is not valuable to the attacker since the plaintext cannot be retrieved easily (or at all). Encryption algorithms often use mathematical operations that are relatively easy to do but very hard to reverse. Without knowing the decryption key, retrieving the data is extremely time-consuming, or virtually impossible.

The two most common types of encryption are public-key encryption and symmetric-key encryption. Let's start with the latter, which is shown in figure 7.1. Here, one key is responsible for both encrypting data and decrypting it.

A symmetric-key approach requires that both the sender and the recipient use the same key, so it needs to be exchanged earlier. This is a potential disadvantage of that concept—for instance, when that exchange happens insecurely; say, via email. Examples of common symmetric-key encryption algorithms are as follows:

- *AES (Advanced Encryption Standard, formerly known as Rijndael)*—A NIST (National Institute of Standards and Technology; a US government agency) standard.

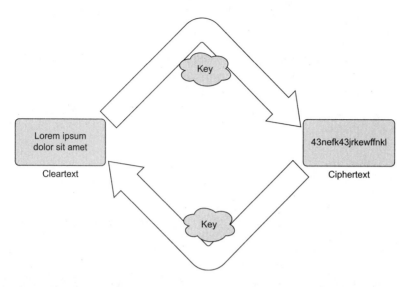

Figure 7.1 Symmetric-key encryption

- *Blowfish and Twofish*—Not patented, and in the public domain.
- *DES (Data Encryption Standard) and its more secure successor, 3DES (Triple DES)*—Its use is declining.

In contrast, public-key encryption uses two keys (figure 7.2).

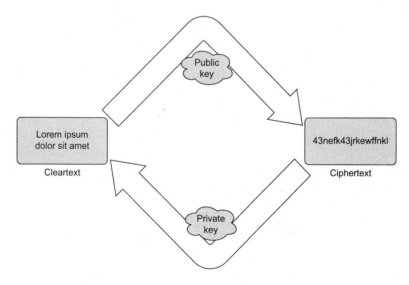

Figure 7.2 Public-key encryption

The encryption key is generally known (thus, *public-key*). The decryption key, however, is known only to the receiver (and is called a *private key*). In contrast to symmetric-key encryption, there is no secret key that needs to be exchanged; instead, the one key that needs to be known to the sender is public.

This approach is used by a variety of protocols—for instance, when accessing a resource via HTTPS (and thus using TLS, and formerly SSL) or when encrypting data via PGP or using SSH.

Hashing vs. encryption

Depending on the type of information to be encrypted, two different approaches come into play. When using symmetric-key or (asymmetric) public-key encryption, the encryption can be reversed, which means that the ciphertext can be decrypted. This is the essence of public-key encryption and symmetric-key encryption. For information such as database connection strings and API tokens, this approach should be used.

For passwords, things are a little bit different, which leads to the second approach. If users may authenticate against an application using a password, the application does not need to know that password—it only needs to know whether it is the correct one. This distinction is crucial. Instead of storing the password, the application can store a hash value (imagine a fingerprint) of that password. The hash value is easy to compute but virtually impossible to reverse. This mitigates the consequences of a data leak. A stolen password is known to the attacker, while a stolen hash—if done right—is more or less useless. Chapter 8 will discuss password hashing in great detail.

There are other means besides encryption to make sure that the secrets used by an application are not accessible to an attacker. A built-in .NET tool that comes in handy is Secret Manager. As we will see, there is no encryption involved, but it is a good start to handle secrets in an application, at least during development.

7.2   Secret Manager

Secret Manager provides an easy mechanism to store application secrets outside the directory structure of the project (and, hopefully, also outside of any public repositories). There are two ways to initiate that feature, either within Visual Studio or from the console. When using Visual Studio, look for Manage User Secrets hidden in the context menu when right-clicking on a project in Project Explorer (figure 7.3).

This option does two things. First, it adds an extra line to the project's .csproj file (assuming you are using C#—for other languages, use the appropriate file extension), which looks like the highlighted one here:

```
<Project Sdk="Microsoft.NET.Sdk.Web">

  <PropertyGroup>
...
    <UserSecretsId>18b55eaa-cb11-4793-bd55-e0cdd4e86063</UserSecretsId>
...
```

The GUID will be different in your case, of course. At the same time, a folder named exactly like the GUID will be created. On Windows, it will be in the roaming AppData folder (%AppData%, which usually resolves to C:\Users\<user-name>\AppData\Roaming), in the Microsoft\UserSecrets subfolder. The GUID folder will contain a file called secrets.json that will later hold the application secrets (but is not encrypted). Make sure to save the project to persist the .csproj changes.

Alternatively, you can use the console and issue the following command in the project folder:

```
dotnet user-secrets init
```

This adds the `<UserSecretsId>` element to the .csproj file but does not create the GUID folder or the secrets.json file. This approach also works on macOS and Linux, of course; there, the path will be ~/.microsoft/usersecrets/<GUID> (the tilde character points to the user's home folder).

> **NOTE** Using `dotnet user-secrets set` creates the secrets.json file if it doesn't exist.

When using Visual Studio, you can just add secrets to the JSON file by providing name-value pairs:

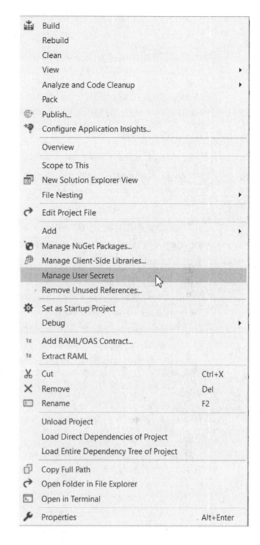

Figure 7.3 Initializing Secret Manager in Visual Studio

```json
{
  "ConnectionString": "Server=(localdb)\\Shop;Integrated Security=true;"
}
```

It is also possible to group entries:

```json
{
  "Shop": {
    "ApiToken": "abc123def456ghi789",
    "ConnectionString": "Server=(localdb)\\Shop;Integrated Security=true;"
  }
}
```

You can also add such entries to the file via the command line and the dotnet tool:

```
dotnet user-secrets set "ConnectionString":
➡"Server=(localdb)\\Shop;Integrated Security=true;"
dotnet user-secrets set "Shop:ApiToken": "abc123def456ghi789"
dotnet user-secrets set "Shop:ConnectionString"
➡"Server=(localdb)\\Shop;Integrated Security=true;"
```

Adds the ConnectionString key and associated value

Adds the ApiToken and ConnectionString keys within the Shop element

Accordingly, dotnet user-secrets remove deletes entries from the secrets.json file. Once everything we need is stored in the JSON file, the application is ready to retrieve this information. When in development mode, the call to CreateDefault-Builder() automatically sets up everything. Otherwise, a call to the AddUser-Secrets() of the IHostBuilder interface is required. However, we advise against using that feature in production—the data is not encrypted and will not automatically be deployed as part of the project (refer to the techniques in the following sections for alternatives).

The IConfiguration interface, as part of the .NET Configuration API, then provides easy access to values from the configuration. When using a Razor Page, use dependency injection to access the interface and, thus, the stored secrets. The following listing shows the minimal approach, using inline code.

Listing 7.1   Reading out user secrets in a Razor Page

```
@page
@using Microsoft.Extensions.Configuration;     Injects the
@inject IConfiguration Configuration           configuration object

<div class="text-center">
    <h1 class="display-4">Secret Manager</h1>
    <form method="post" action="">
        <div class="mt-5 mb-5">
            <p class="lead">API Token:
            ➡@Configuration["Shop:ApiToken"]</p>     Outputs data from
        </div>                                        the configuration
    </form>
</div>
```

When using the code-behind approach, or ASP.NET Core MVC, use dependency injection, or constructor injection, to be more precise, to access the configuration data as shown in the next listing.

Listing 7.2   Reading out user secrets in a Razor Page with a separate page model class file

```
using Microsoft.AspNetCore.Mvc.RazorPages;

namespace AspNetCoreSecurity.RazorSamples.Pages
{
    public class SecretManagerCodeBehindModel : PageModel
    {
        private readonly IConfiguration Configuration;
```

```
    public SecretManagerCodeBehindModel(
    ➥IConfiguration configuration)           ◁──┐  Shows constructor
    {                                            │  injection
        Configuration = configuration;
    }

    public string ApiToken = string.Empty;

    public void OnGet()
    {
        ApiToken = Configuration["Shop:ApiToken"];
    }
  }
}
```

The class constructor receives the configuration data when you provide a parameter as shown in the listing. When using ASP.NET Core MVC, use the constructor of the controller class to achieve the same result.

By the way, prior to .NET 6, the `Startup` class constructor from the default project templates used that approach as well:

```
public Startup(IConfiguration configuration)
{
    Configuration = configuration;      ◁──┐  Store the configuration in a
}                                          │  class member for easy access.

public IConfiguration Configuration { get; }
```

You could therefore also access configuration information within the `Startup` class. In .NET 6 and up, `builder.Configuration` in Program.cs grants access to the configuration data.

So far, we have created a file with secret information; that file resides outside the project folder, which hopefully prevents someone from carelessly checking it into the repository. But let's take a more general look at application setting files in ASP.NET Core applications.

7.3   The appsettings.json file

The main configuration file of ASP.NET Core applications is appsettings.json. By default (i.e., when using the standard templates), it contains settings on logging (see chapter 11) and a list of valid hostnames:

```
{
  "Logging": {
    "LogLevel": {
      "Default": "Information",
      "Microsoft": "Warning",
      "Microsoft.Hosting.Lifetime": "Information"
    }
  },
  "AllowedHosts": "*"
}
```

There is also a file called appsettings.Development.json, which contains the same information, except for the AllowedHosts entry. As the name already suggests, this version of the app settings file comes into play when the application is run in development mode.

ASP.NET Core automatically picks the suitable appsettings.json file when the Host.CreateDefaultBuilder() method is used (this usually happens in Program.cs). It first loads all configuration settings from appsettings.json and then from appsettings.<Environment>.json. Settings of the same name in the latter file overwrite those from the former file. The current environment is pulled from IHost-Environment.EnvironmentName and can be set in a variety of ways.

First, the launchSettings.json file in the project's Properties folder will define the Development environment. Here's a sample file; the port numbers may be different on your system:

```
{
  "iisSettings": {
    "windowsAuthentication": false,
    "anonymousAuthentication": true,
    "iisExpress": {
      "applicationUrl": "http://localhost:40000",
      "sslPort": 40001
    }
  },
  "profiles": {                              Shows the IIS
    "IIS Express": {                    ◁──┘ Express settings
      "commandName": "IISExpress",
      "launchBrowser": true,
      "environmentVariables": {                Defines the Development
        "ASPNETCORE_ENVIRONMENT": "Development",  ◁──┘ environment for IIS Express
        "ASPNETCORE_HOSTINGSTARTUPASSEMBLIES":
     "Microsoft.AspNetCore.Mvc.Razor.RuntimeCompilation"
      }
    },
    "AspNetCoreSecurity.RazorSamples": {    ◁──┐ Shows the Kestrel (built-in
      "commandName": "Project",                │ .NET web server) settings
      "dotnetRunMessages": "true",
      "launchBrowser": true,
      "applicationUrl": "https://localhost:5001;http://localhost:5000",
      "environmentVariables": {
        "ASPNETCORE_ENVIRONMENT": "Development",  ◁──┐ Defines the Development
        "ASPNETCORE_HOSTINGSTARTUPASSEMBLIES":        │ environment for Kestrel
     "Microsoft.AspNetCore.Mvc.Razor.RuntimeCompilation"
      }
    }
  }
}
```

No matter how you launch the ASP.NET Core application locally from Visual Studio—using IIS Express or the .NET web server Kestrel—the environment will be set to

Development, and the contents of the appsettings.Development.json file will be picked up.

As the launchSettings.json file already suggests, all Visual Studio does is set the `ASPNETCORE_ENVIRONMENT` environment variable. This will properly fill the `IHost-Environment.EnvironmentName` value. You can also configure this behavior on the project's property page in the Debug section. Since Visual Studio 2022, there is a dedicated UI for the launch profiles where these settings may be changed (figure 7.4).

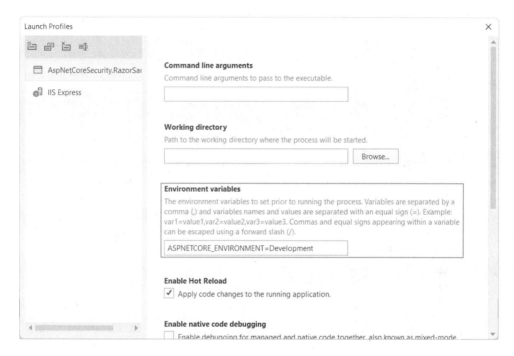

Figure 7.4   Configuring the environment variables that set the ASP.NET Core environment

Obviously, you can add more build configurations and set individual environment variables there. A typical approach is to use, for example, `Staging` and `Production` (and appsettings.Staging.json and appsettings.Production.json). Each of these environments might have specific settings—database connection strings tied to the environment or staging/production versions of APIs to use. By providing application settings for each environment, the application uses the correct settings wherever it runs. As long as the environment variable is correctly set, `CreateDefaultBuilder()` will load appsettings.json first, and then will automatically load the environment-specific file.

Programmatically loading the correct settings files

When you are not using `CreateDefaultBuilder()`, you need to instruct .NET to correctly retrieve and process them. Here is some sample code to achieve this:

```
var env = Environment.GetEnvironmentVariable(
    "ASPNETCORE_ENVIRONMENT");
var builder = new ConfigurationBuilder()
    .SetBasePath(Directory.GetCurrentDirectory())
    .AddJsonFile("appsettings.json", optional: false,
        reloadOnChange: true)
    .AddJsonFile($"appsettings.{env}.json", optional: true);
```

Determines the current environment

Uses the current directory as the location for settings files (change as needed)

Loads appsettings.json first and makes it mandatory

Loads the environment-specific settings file, if available

The code loads the main settings file first and then the specific ones. You can also use this approach if you are using additional settings files with different names.

Accessing those values then works exactly like accessing Secret Manager's settings: inject `IConfiguration`, and then access the values by their names. Still, the data in those files is not encrypted, which might not be feasible for some scenarios. Using environment variables might be an alternative (at least then there's nothing in the filesystem that could leak), but the information is not protected in memory. So how about storing the data securely somewhere else?

7.4 *Storing secrets in the cloud*

All major cloud providers offer APIs for storing secrets. They basically allow you to set up a storage for key-value pairs. There is an API to write secrets to that store and to retrieve them. How the data is stored is up to the cloud provider, but usually, asymmetric encryption will be used.

Using the cloud for storing secrets is a good option if the application is stored in the cloud as well. If yours isn't, then you might as well just glance at this section to get an overview (or, hopefully, get interested in learning more), or even skip it. Many ASP.NET Core applications work really well on your own servers. If, however, you are using one of the major clouds, feel free to dive into the section that covers your choice. Each of those sections assumes that you have at least some basic working knowledge of the cloud of choice.

Let's look at what Azure, AWS, and Google Cloud have to offer, starting with Microsoft's cloud (since they are also the driving force behind .NET, so API and tooling support is very good).

WARNING   Cloud providers are innovating (or breaking things) all the time, so there is a chance that some of the details we are about to describe will change in the future. The UI might look different, the path through the cloud administration could change, or there might even be new APIs, deprecating the existing ones. We will attempt to keep the book's code repository up to date. Pricing might change as well, so please verify the costs before attempting to use secret cloud storage options. For this reason, we will describe the most common use case but will not cover more specifics.

7.4.1   Storing secrets in Azure

The place to store secrets within Microsoft Azure is called Key Vault. It provides secure storage of key-value pairs and a web-based UI, a command-line tool, and a .NET API to write and read the data. In the Azure portal, create a new resource and choose the key vault type (figure 7.5).

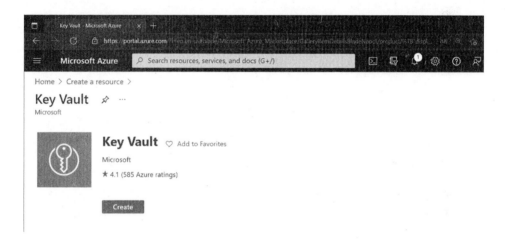

Figure 7.5   The Key Vault resource template

After clicking Create, the key vault will be configured. The following settings are required (figure 7.6):

- An Azure subscription
- A resource group where the key vault will reside
- A name for the key vault
- The region in which the key vault will be hosted
- The pricing tier to use (the premium tier offers additional features not covered here)

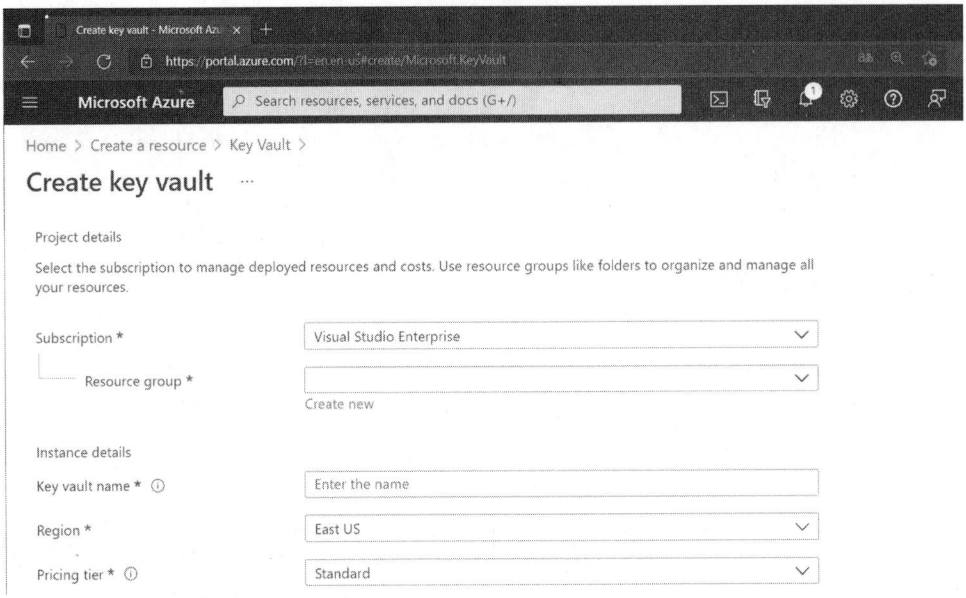

Figure 7.6   Creating the Azure Key Vault

Filling out the form will start a process that creates the key vault (and might take a few seconds). You may also use the Azure CLI to create a key vault; the command will look like this, depending on your desired settings:

```
az keyvault create --name "aspnetcoresecurity-vault" --resource-group
    "AspNetCoreSecurityRG" --location "eastus2"
```

Finally, you can add data to the key vault. Pick the Secrets option in the left column, which will get you to the UI shown in figure 7.7.

You may also use the Azure command-line interface again: `az keyvault set` will do the trick. Next up, create a key vault reference that will then be used from within the application to get access to the value in the vault. For this, a new resource needs to be created: an App Configuration store. There, in the Configuration explorer, you can set up a new key vault reference (figure 7.8).

The newly created key vault reference points to the secret that you have previously added to the vault. You provide a unique key and can then use this key in the application. Go to the App Configuration's *Settings/Access keys* page and retrieve the connection string to that configuration. For the ASP.NET Core application, we need two NuGet packages first:

- `Azure.Identity`—Part of the Azure SDK client library
- `Microsoft.Azure.AppConfiguration.AspNetCore`—A package that facilitates using Azure as a configuration source

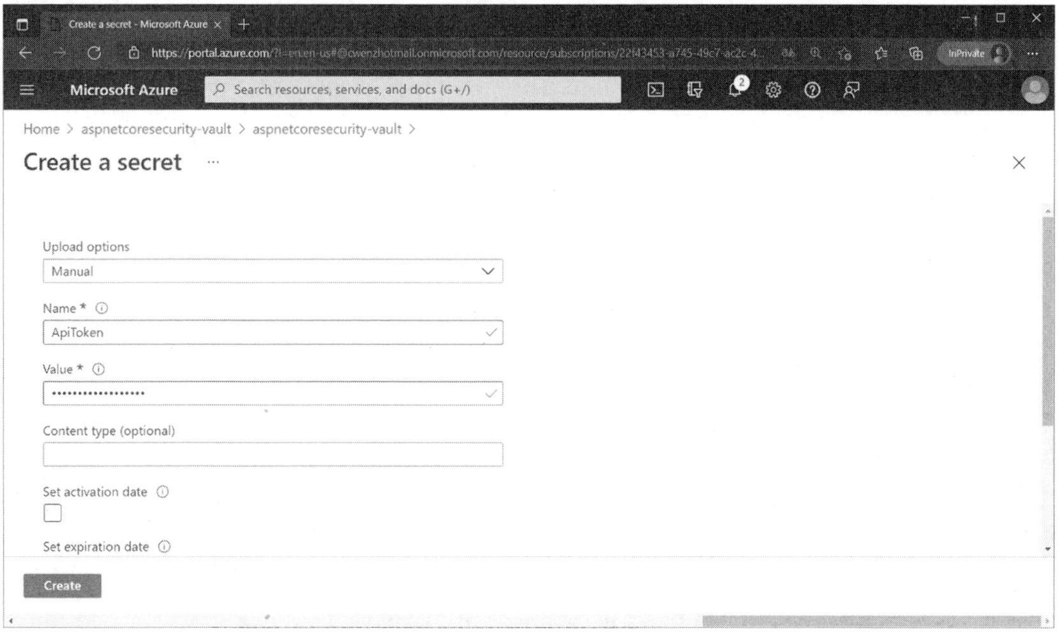

Figure 7.7 Adding a secret to the vault

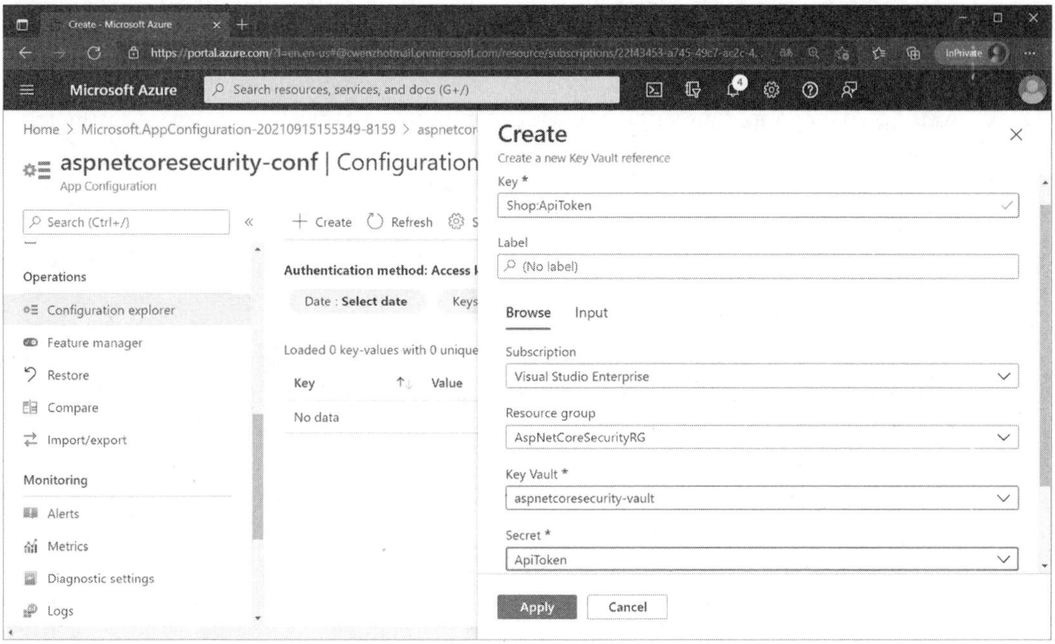

Figure 7.8 Creating the key vault reference

Then, in Program.cs, retrieve the configuration settings from Azure. Remember: the sole setting we have right now points to the key vault. Therefore, we can access the key vault data as a configuration option. Here is how that will look in code:

```
using Azure.Identity;

var builder = WebApplication.CreateBuilder(args);

builder.Configuration.AddAzureAppConfiguration(options =>
{
    options.Connect("...")
        .ConfigureKeyVault(vault =>
        {
            vault.SetCredential(
                new DefaultAzureCredential());
        });
});
```

Uses Azure App Configuration ← (pointing to `AddAzureAppConfiguration`)

Shows connection string from the "Access keys" ← (pointing to `options.Connect("...")`)

Uses the default Azure credentials (assuming the application is hosted there, too) ← (pointing to `vault.SetCredential`)

The application connects to the App Configuration resource using the connection string we previously noted (you may actually want to store that connection string in the appsettings.json file). Then it accesses the key vault, using the default Azure credentials. And that's it—whenever you are injecting `IConfiguration`, you may access the key vault value using the key chosen in the Azure App Configuration (in our example, `Shop:ApiToken`; see figure 7.8), as if it was a value from appsettings.json.

> **NOTE** We are assuming here that the application is running in Azure as well. Otherwise, you need to set up new credentials and then configure the key vault so that it may be accessed that way.

As you have seen, once everything is set up and configured, using it from within an ASP.NET Core app is a seamless process. When using other cloud providers, the experience is similar; for instance, when using AWS.

7.4.2   Storing secrets in AWS

In Amazon's cloud, AWS, the Azure Key Vault pendant is the AWS Secrets Manager. You can use both the AWS console and the CLI to add secrets to it. We will later use an API to retrieve the values from the store.

Go to https://console.aws.amazon.com/secretsmanager/home to access the Secrets Manager within the AWS Console (which is actually their web interface, but I digress). Your browser will then redirect you to the region of choice (e.g., to https://us-east-2 .console.aws.amazon.com/secretsmanager/home; it doesn't matter functionality-wise, of course). Then you can add a new secret, at least if you have `secretsmanager :CreateSecret` privileges. A wizard guides you through the process (figure 7.9).

When you are using a database within AWS, there are templates for several of them (including RDS and DocumentDB). For other secrets such as API keys, the "Other type of secrets" option is a good choice. You can then add secret key-value pairs (or plaintext) and provide the encryption key that will be used. The standard option, `DefaultEncryptionKey`, will suffice in most cases (and incur no extra costs).

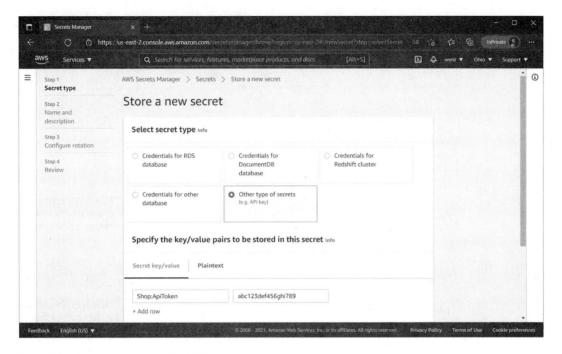

Figure 7.9 Storing a new secret in AWS

In the next step, you will need to provide a name for the secret(s) you want to store. You will use that name to later access the AWS Secrets Manager data. You can also enable the rotation of secrets, which means that the data is re-encrypted after a period of time, increasing the security even more.

After successfully completing the wizard, you will get code samples to retrieve the secrets in several languages. C# is one of them, but we will guide you through the implementation process anyway.

> **NOTE** When you prefer using the AWS CLI, the command to create a secret will look like this: `aws secretsmanager create-secret --name "Name-OfSecret" --secret-string "SecretData"`.

Amazon publishes an AWS SDK for .NET (https://aws.amazon.com/sdk-for-net/), which is the go-to solution for almost anything AWS. Since we "only" want to work with the Secrets Manager, the individual NuGet package `AWSSDK.SecretsManager` (www.nuget.org/packages/AWSSDK.SecretsManager/) will be used—which, in turn, depends on the Core package of the AWS SDK. Install it into the project, using either Visual Studio's NuGet package manager or the `Install-Package` PowerShell command. The code from the following listing shows how the secret value(s) may be retrieved.

Listing 7.3   Reading out AWS Secrets Manager data in a Razor Page

```
using Amazon;
using Amazon.SecretsManager;
using Amazon.SecretsManager.Model;
using Microsoft.AspNetCore.Mvc.RazorPages;

namespace AspNetCoreSecurity.RazorSamples.Pages
{
    public class AWSSecretsManagerModel : PageModel
    {
        public string ApiToken = string.Empty;

        public void OnGet()
        {
            string secretName = "AspNetCoreSecurityAWS";
            string region = "us-east-2";

            var client = new
        AmazonSecretsManagerClient(RegionEndpoint.GetBySystemName(region));

            var request = new GetSecretValueRequest()
            {
                SecretId = secretName
            };

            var response = client.GetSecretValueAsync(request).Result;
            ApiToken = response?.SecretString ??
                string.Empty;
        }
    }
}
```

> This is the configuration of the stored secret—change accordingly.

> Configures the request for the secret value

> Reads out the result from the request

We first need to instantiate the `AmazonSecretsManagerClient` class, using the region where the secrets are stored. When the application is running on AWS, the associated credentials are used to access the secrets, so make sure that these privileges have been assigned. Then the `GetSecretValueRequest` class will actually request the data, using the name of the secret(s).

The AWS documentation contains exhaustive information on the Secrets Manager, at https://docs.aws.amazon.com/secretsmanager/. Not surprisingly, Google's cloud offerings also include a store for secret information.

> **TIP**   If you would like to integrate the data from the AWS Secrets Manager in the IConfiguration data in your ASP.NET Core application, a third-party NuGet package may come in handy. Renato Golia is the author of `Kralize.Extensions.Configuration.AWSSecretsManager`, which implements a configuration provider. Refer to http://mng.bz/mOda on GitHub for more information about the package, usage information, and source code.

7.4.3 Storing secrets in Google Cloud

In Google Cloud, the Secret Manager is responsible for managing secrets (note the similar, but different name in comparison to AWS' Secre*t*s Manager). You obviously need a Google Cloud account and must fulfill a few prerequisites:

- Create a project with billing enabled.
- Enable the Secret Manager API for that project (https://console.cloud.google .com/marketplace/product/google/secretmanager.googleapis.com; figure 7.10).
- Make sure that your user has at least the Secret Manager Secret Accessor role to read data from the Secret Manager. You can configure that in IAM (identity and access management; https://console.cloud.google.com/iam-admin/iam).

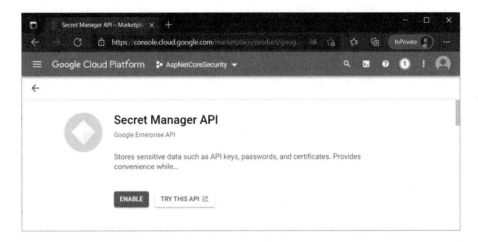

Figure 7.10   Enabling the Secret Manager API

If you try to enable the Secret Manager API for a project without billing, you will be prompted to add your billing information. That's obviously a good opportunity to verify the costs associated with that feature.

Then, go to the Google Cloud Secret Manager at https://console.cloud.google .com/security/secret-manager to add a secret. Figure 7.11 shows the first step of the associated wizard.

You have to provide the name and the value of that secret and can then configure additional settings, such as an optional expiration date of the secret or whether it will be rotated (similar to the approach the AWS Secrets Manager provides). In the end, the Secret Manager creates a secret version. That's not a version that is secret, but a version of a secret. Eventually, the value of secrets will change. In that case, the name

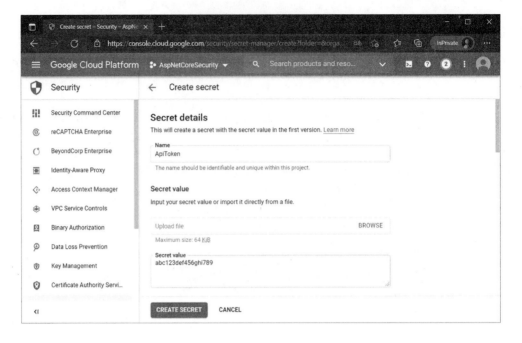

Figure 7.11   Storing a new secret in Google Cloud

of the secret can stay the same, but a new version of it will be generated. When accessing that secret, you need to know three things:

- The project ID (numeric)
- The ID of the secret (which is the name we have chosen in the wizard)
- The ID of the version (starting with 1, counting upward)

The Google Cloud console also provides the option to generate a resource ID of a secret version, but it basically looks like this:

```
projects/<project ID>/secrets/<secret ID>/versions/<version ID>
```

The .NET SDK for Google Cloud requires these three values to get access to the stored data. In the ASP.NET Core project, add the `Google.Cloud.Secret-Manager.V1` package, which is part of the aforementioned SDK. Once it is installed, reading out a secret is just a few lines of code, as shown in the next listing.

> **Listing 7.4   Reading out Google Cloud Secret Manager data in a Razor Page**

```
using Google.Cloud.SecretManager.V1;
using Microsoft.AspNetCore.Mvc.RazorPages;

namespace AspNetCoreSecurity.RazorSamples.Pages
{
```

```
public class GoogleSecretManagerModel : PageModel
{
    public string ApiToken = string.Empty;

    public void OnGet()
    {
        var smsClient = SecretManagerServiceClient.Create();

        var secretVersionName = new SecretVersionName(
            "projectId",
            "secretId",
            "secretVersionId");

        var result = smsClient.AccessSecretVersion(secretVersionName);

        ApiToken = result.Payload.Data.ToStringUtf8();
    }
}
}
```

Configures the secret version using the project ID, secret ID, and version ID

Converts the binary data to a string

Basically, all it takes is four steps:

1 Create a `SecretManagerServiceClient`.
2 Configure a `SecretVersionName` object.
3 Access the secret version using the service client.
4 Decode the (binary) data so that you get the string data stored in the secret.

The application itself must run within the Google Cloud as well since we did not provide any credentials. There is much more documentation on the Google Cloud website at https://cloud.google.com/secret-manager/docs.

But what if we do not want to use a cloud (as cynics say, someone else's computer)? Encryption may also take place directly in our ASP.NET Core application.

7.5   Using the data protection API

It is, of course, possible to use custom encryption and decryption for data within our application. However, when storing secrets within that web app, it needs to know how to decrypt the data. The decryption key, whether it's symmetric-key or public-key encryption, needs to be available to the application. When checking the source code into GitHub or any other version-control system, you need to mitigate the risk of a data leak. You should refrain from checking those credentials in, but then needing to store them somewhere else—or let .NET do the work.

Back in the Windows 2000 days, Microsoft introduced the data protection API (DPAPI). This interface could encrypt and decrypt data, so a symmetric cryptographic approach was chosen. In the .NET Framework days, when ASP.NET applications were tied to the Windows platform, this was a feasible solution. A machine key was used to encrypt and decrypt data, using Windows' DPAPI functionality. It was even possible to protect parts of the main configuration file (then called web.config) with a simple command-line tool.

Given today's cross-platform nature of .NET, this is not feasible any longer. So, Microsoft got to work and implemented a new data protection system, including a set of new data protection APIs. With them, encrypting and decrypting data is a simple method call. The encryption itself uses AES, certainly a solid choice. We will use MVC this time and start with the input form from the following listing.

Listing 7.5   Input form for the data to be encrypted

```
@model AspNetCoreSecurity.MvcSamples.Controllers.DataProtectionModel

<h1>Data Protection API</h1>

<div class="row">
    <div class="col-md-4">
        <form asp-action="Index">
            <div asp-validation-summary="ModelOnly" class="text-danger"></div>
            <div class="form-group">
                <label asp-for="Data" class="control-label"></label>
                <input asp-for="Data" class="form-control" />
                <span asp-validation-for="Data" class="text-danger"></span>
            </div>
            <div class="form-group mt-3">
                <input type="submit" value="Encrypt" class="btn btn-primary" />
            </div>
        </form>
    </div>
</div>
```

Shows the input field → (points to the `<label asp-for="Data"...>` and `<input asp-for="Data"...>` lines)

The form basically consists of an input field for data. Upon form submission, the data will be sent to the server to be encrypted. But first we need to define the model for that page:

```
using System.ComponentModel.DataAnnotations;
...
public class DataProtectionModel
{
    [Required]
    public string Data { get; set; } = string.Empty;
}
```

The class contains only one property, called `Data`, which will then hold the data. The `Microsoft.AspNetCore.DataProtection` namespace then contains everything we need. The `IDataProtector` interface contains methods for data encryption and decryption, whereas .NET does the heavy lifting and handles all of the details, including the cryptographic algorithms. In the controller's constructor, the data protector is created by using the `IDataProtectionProvider` interface; the latter is automatically injected via constructor injection:

```
public class DataProtectionController : Controller
{
    private readonly IDataProtector _protector;

    public DataProtectionController(IDataProtectionProvider provider)
```

```
    {
        _protector = provider.CreateProtector(
        ➥"DataProtectionController");          ◁─┐  Creates the
    }                                              protector
...
}
```

The argument for the CreateProtector() method is a unique string that identifies
the consumer of the protected data. That identifier is also called the *purpose string*
because it defines a purpose. Code for different purposes cannot see each other's
encrypted data. We are using the name of the controller class here, but that's just a
personal convention, not a mandatory requirement.

Once the form is submitted, the data from the input field will be encrypted with
the protector's Protect() method. The application then redirects the client to
another action method. The URL will have the format . . ./Decrypt/abc123, where
abc123 is the encrypted string. This facilitates accessing that information later:

```
[HttpPost]
public IActionResult Index(DataProtectionModel model)
{                                                           │  Encrypts
    var encryptedData = _protector.Protect(model.Data);  ◁─┘  the string
    return RedirectToAction("Decrypt",
    ➥new { id = encryptedData });          ◁─┐  Redirects to another action, with
}                                              the encrypted data in the URL
```

In the action method of the decryption page, the Unprotect() method reverses the
encryption, allowing the application to access the plaintext data. The following listing
contains the full code of the controller, with the decryption action method in bold.

Listing 7.6   Encrypting and decrypting data

```
using Microsoft.AspNetCore.DataProtection;
using Microsoft.AspNetCore.Mvc;
using System.ComponentModel.DataAnnotations;

namespace AspNetCoreSecurity.MvcSamples.Controllers
{
    public class DataProtectionController : Controller
    {
        private readonly IDataProtector _protector;

        public DataProtectionController(IDataProtectionProvider provider)
        {
            _protector = provider.CreateProtector("DataProtectionController");
        }

        public IActionResult Index()
        {
            return View();
        }

        [HttpPost]
```

```
        public IActionResult Index(DataProtectionModel model)
        {
            var encryptedData = _protector.Protect(model.Data);
            return RedirectToAction("Decrypt", new { id = encryptedData });
        }

        public IActionResult Decrypt(string id)
        {
            var decryptedData = _protector.Unprotect(id);
            var model = new DataProtectionModel() { Data = decryptedData };
            return View(model);
        }
    }

    public class DataProtectionModel
    {
        [Required]
        public string Data { get; set; }
    }
}
```

Decrypts the data from the URL ⟶ (points to `public IActionResult Decrypt(string id)` / `var decryptedData = _protector.Unprotect(id);`)

Finally, the next listing shows the associated view for displaying the decrypted information.

Listing 7.7   Displaying the decrypted data

```
@model AspNetCoreSecurity.MvcSamples.Controllers.DataProtectionModel

<h1>Data Protection</h1>

<div>
    Decrypted data: @Model?.Data
</div>
<div>
    <a asp-action="Index">Back to encryption</a>
</div>
```

Shows the data output ⟵ (points to `Decrypted data: @Model?.Data`)

Since the `Decrypt()` action method writes the retrieved, unencrypted data into the model, the view only needs to output the model's `Data` property. When trying out the code in the browser, the result after the form submission will look like figure 7.12.

Figure 7.12   The data from the URL has been successfully decrypted.

Notice the encrypted data in the URL and the plaintext information shown on the page. The default behavior of the data protection APIs works very well for most cases; however, additional configuration may be required in some scenarios. This is especially important if an app is spread across multiple servers. In that case, the encryption keys need to be made available to all instances of the application—for example, by putting them on a network share or by storing them in Azure or similar services.

When relying on the filesystem, .NET comes with suitable extension methods. In Program.cs, we add and configure the middleware as follows; this provides a local target file on the server:

```
builder.Services.AddDataProtection()
    .PersistKeysToFileSystem(new DirectoryInfo("..."));
```

When you want Azure to take care of your secrets, there is an extension method for both storing the keys in Azure Blob Storage and protecting them using Azure Key Vault, instead of storing them in cleartext (there is also an extension method for DPAPI protection, `ProtectKeysWithDpapi()`, but that only works on Windows):

```
builder.Services.AddDataProtection()
    .PersistKeysToAzureBlobStorage("Connection string", "Container", "Blob")
    .ProtectKeysWithAzureKeyVault("Key URI", new DefaultAzureCredential());
```

NOTE   Since `IDataProtectionProvider` and `IDataProtector` are interfaces, it is also possible to plug in your own custom implementations. For instance, there is a data protection provider for AWS, the `Amazon.AspNet-Core.DataProtection.SSM` NuGet package (http://mng.bz/6Xre).

This data protection mechanism can, somewhat surprisingly, also be used within a Blazor application.

7.6   *Storing secrets locally with Blazor*

For secrets stored on the server, Blazor applications behave comparably to regular ASP.NET Core applications. Things are a bit different for client-side storage options, though. When using Blazor WebAssembly, access to storage mechanisms like cookies, local storage, and session storage is possible. However, since the WebAssembly-powered app completely runs on the client, an attacker who successfully exploits a cross-site scripting vulnerability (see chapter 2), will also get access to this data if the application has it. Using encryption does not help much: the application will need to decrypt the data, and injected JavaScript code may be able to interfere.

When using Blazor Server, though, things are different. Secret data will be stored on the client in encrypted form, but the decryption will take place on the server, using the SignalR connection maintained by Blazor. There are two options (and objects):

- `ProtectedLocalStorage`, which uses JavaScript's `localStorage` API
- `ProtectedSessionStorage`, which relies on JavaScript's `sessionStorage` API

Both classes are defined within the `Microsoft.AspNetCore.Components.Server` `.ProtectedBrowserStorage` namespace.

A sample application will store the timestamp of the time when the Razor component was last accessed. When navigating back and forth from the page, the value will be maintained. The actual UI is trivial:

```
<p>Last access: @LastAccess.ToLongTimeString()</p>

@code {
    public DateTime LastAccess = DateTime.Now;
...
}
```

The `LastAccess` variable is initialized with the current time, but then the protected storage comes into play. The example uses session storage, but it would work exactly the same when using local storage (with the difference being that data in session storage is available only in the current tab and will be purged once it is closed). First of all, the namespace will be loaded, and the associated class (`ProtectedSessionStorage` in our case) will be injected:

```
@using Microsoft.AspNetCore.Components.Server.ProtectedBrowserStorage
@inject ProtectedSessionStorage ProtectedSessionStorage
```

Then it is possible to both read and write from and to the session storage, and ASP.NET Core data protection will take care of encryption and decryption (remember, when using Blazor Server, the C# code runs on the server). The helper methods `GetAsync()` and `SetAsync()` can be used for reading and writing. The following listing shows the complete code.

Listing 7.8   Reading and writing to protected session storage

```
@page "/protectedstorage"

@using Microsoft.AspNetCore.Components.Server.ProtectedBrowserStorage
@inject ProtectedSessionStorage ProtectedSessionStorage

<h1>Protected Storage</h1>

<p>Last access: @LastAccess.ToLongTimeString()</p>

@code {
    public DateTime LastAccess = DateTime.Now;

    protected override async Task OnInitializedAsync()
    {
        var lastAccess = await ProtectedSessionStorage        ⟵ Reads the current value
          ➡.GetAsync<DateTime>("lastAccess");                      from session storage
        LastAccess = lastAccess.Success ? lastAccess.Value : DateTime.Now;  and decrypts it
        await ProtectedSessionStorage
          ➡.SetAsync("lastAccess", DateTime.Now);            ⟵ Encrypts the new
    }                                                              value and stores it
}                                                                  in session storage
```

First, the `GetAsync()` call retrieves the time of the last access from session storage (if available) and decrypts it. Later, the `SetAsync()` call updates this value in session storage—the data protection feature automatically applies the encryption.

This feature requires that the component is not prerendered on the server. Look at the Pages/_Host.cshtml file and verify whether it contains markup like this:

```
<component type="typeof(App)" render-mode="ServerPrerendered" />
```

If that is the case, change the render mode as follows:

```
<component type="typeof(App)" render-mode="Server" />
```

Figure 7.13 shows the result in the browser after navigating from the page to another one and back.

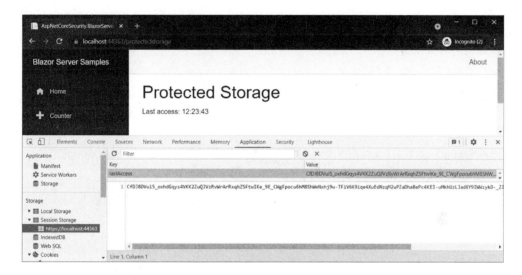

Figure 7.13   The decrypted value in the browser and the encrypted value in the developer tools

Upon the first load of the component, the current time is written to session storage. After navigating back and forth, that value is retrieved again and displayed. You will notice that it shows the time of the last access, not the current system time.

Summary

Let's review what we have learned so far:

- The ASP.NET Core Secret Manager is less secret than its name suggests and is just a convenient feature for storing secrets during development.
- Data stored in the appsettings.json and related files is not directly exposed via HTTP.

- Different versions of appsettings.json can be applied to different deployed versions of the application (e.g., staging and production systems).
- Every major cloud provider offers a mechanism to securely store secrets—we've looked at Microsoft Azure, AWS, and Google Cloud.
- ASP.NET Core data protection offers an infrastructure and several specific implementations for easily encrypting and later decrypting secrets to be used in the application.
- These data protection features may also be used within a Blazor Server app.

After we have seen all these different methods of handling secrets, using various kinds of encryption (or no encryption), there is still an elephant in the room: What about passwords? It turns out that we do not need to use encryption to securely manage them, as we will see in the next chapter.

Handling passwords

This chapter covers

- Learning how passwords may be stolen
- Learning how attackers retrieve encrypted or hashed passwords
- Exploring why hashing is best for password handling
- Implementing password hashing with ASP.NET Core
- Changing default password hashing behavior of ASP.NET Core

In early October 2013, Adobe reported a security incident on their servers. The original blog posts are no longer available (only using a web archive), but independent news sources paint a very clear picture. According to security journalist Brian Krebs (http://mng.bz/o2DZ), attackers were able to access the source code of a few Adobe products. Also, personal customer information was stolen. As the Verge reported (http://mng.bz/nND5), the number of affected accounts was initially estimated at around 3 million, but the actual number turned out to probably be over 150 million. To be fair, it is unclear how many of those accounts were inactive or test accounts. The numbers are still staggering, though.

Among the data extracted were, among other things, passwords. Luckily, they were not stored in plaintext. However, it was still possible to access many of them due to the way the application worked. Let's look at this case study to learn what went wrong (and to make it better).

8.1   *From data leak to password theft*

The passwords were encrypted with a symmetric-key block cypher (3DES), using the same key for encrypting and decrypting data (see chapter 7). The encryption was also deterministic: if two users had the same password, the same value was stored in Adobe's database.

This turned out to be a real problem given the sheer amount of data stolen. If someone has access to the data dump, one way to decipher passwords is to group the encrypted values by the count of their occurrence. The more often an encrypted password occurs, the more popular the password is—not only in the hacked application, but in many other websites, too.

There are several lists of the most commonly used passwords available. The best-known list is probably by NordPass, the developers of the password manager of the same name. Here are the top ten entries from 2020 (https://nordpass.com/most -common-passwords-list/ will contain the most up-to-date list at the time of checking the URL):

1   `123456`
2   `123456789`
3   `picture1`
4   `password`
5   `12345678`
6   `111111`
7   `123123`
8   `12345`
9   `1234567890`
10   `senha` (In case you are wondering, that's Portuguese for *password*.)

Very creative, isn't it? Note that the NordPass page also estimates the time required to crack such a password. Whereas the most commonly used one, `123456`, may be cracked in less than a second, the number 62 entry, `ohmnamah23`, takes 12 days. That password still isn't very good, but you see the difference.

Choosing a secure password

Obviously, `123456` is not a secure password for a variety of reasons. It's rather short, only uses digits, and is predictable (and holds the top spot on both the Nord-Pass and the Adobe list). For many years, a common suggestion was to use letters, digits, and special characters to avoid passwords that were easy to guess or part of a dictionary. The downside of this approach is that such passwords were hard to remember, so users routinely wrote them down and were also reusing them (so if a password was stolen once, the attacker might try it at many different services).

The most important aspect of a password is the entropy, a value that depends on the number of guesses a brute-force attack would require to find out the password. The password `123456` has an entropy of almost 20 bits, so it would take at most 2^{20} attempts (a bit more than 1 million) to guess it. Obviously, that number is not very high—for a computer, at least. A password consisting of six lowercase characters, six uppercase characters, and six digits would have an entropy of over 100 bits, requiring a number of guesses that is 33 digits long. So, the longer the password, the better.

NIST issues requirements for "digital identities," which also include passwords. For a while, the use of special characters was recommended, but that was eventually dropped. The current version, at the time of this writing (http://mng.bz/v6Dp—look for section 5.1.1.2, "Memorized Secret Verifiers"), recommends a minimum password length of 8 characters but also prompts developers to expect up to 64 characters. I'd aim at the latter.

Since password safes—software that stores a number of passwords and uses one passphrase to get access to them—are a commodity nowadays, there is no excuse not to use long, secure passwords. All these password safes offer to autogenerate such passwords. Even web browsers play their part, as the figure here shows (apologies for ruining the party, but that's not the password I'm actually using).

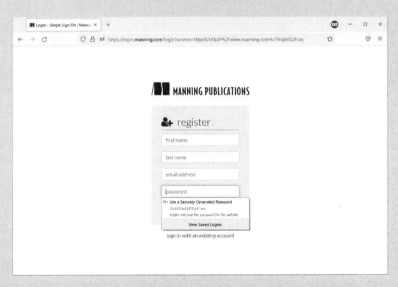

Firefox suggests a secure password.

If you are not using a password manager, you may use the advice of Randall Munroe's popular webcomic, XKCD. Just take a few unrelated words and use them as a password: His example is `correct horse battery staple`; this gives about 44 bits of entropy (see https://xkcd.com/936/ for the details).

Back to the list of Adobe encrypted passwords. Chances are that the most commonly used passwords at the Adobe site are also high up on the NordPass list (or any other comparable list). This facilitates guessing those passwords, even though the encryption itself has not been broken yet (see the following note). But in reality, things were even worse. Adobe also stored a security question that allowed users to remember their passwords. Note that I wrote "remember," not "retrieve." Instead of "What was the color of your first car?" users were prompted to provide a passphrase that would remind them of their passwords! These passphrases were stored in plaintext and were also part of the data dump.

> **NOTE** A group of researchers successfully recovered many of the Adobe passwords. The original page is no longer available, but the Internet Archive's Wayback Machine still has a copy: http://mng.bz/44ER. As you can see, there are many overlaps with the NordPass list.

Here's a little quiz. The following passphrases were used by various people who all had the same password:

- `let me in`
- `knock`
- `lmi`
- `open sesame`
- `let who in?`
- `the usual`
- `standard`

Would you take an educated guess what the associated password is? Spoiler: it's `letmein`.

Developer Ben Falconer took this one step further and created a crossword puzzle (https://zed0.co.uk/crossword/) containing some of the top 1,000 passwords from the Adobe leak. Figure 8.1 shows one based on the top 100 passwords.

The Adobe password leak is certainly not the only high-profile incident where user data has been stolen en masse. The "Have I Been Pwned?" service (https://haveibeen pwned.com/) contains the data from countless leaks, large and small, and tells you which data may have been stolen. I checked one throwaway email address I was using for nonessential services. It was part of 30 breaches (so far)—figure 8.2 shows the first three, including details about the data stolen.

Retrieving passwords from dumps is the effect of the actual problem: data being leaked. Often, this occurs using SQL injection, which we can properly defend our applications against (see chapter 6). There are other attack vectors, too, such as malware, accessing a back door in an application, or an internal attacker. Remember that we are always aiming at defense in depth! If data is being stolen, we need to make sure that the attackers can do as little as possible with it. When talking about passwords specifically, we must never store them, and we need to make it virtually impossible to retrieve those passwords from the stolen pieces of information. This is where hashing comes in.

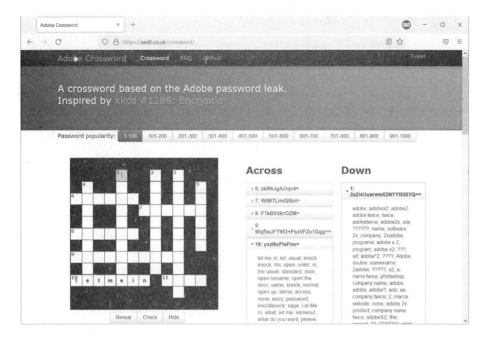

Figure 8.1   1 down: What could `adobex2`, `adobe twice`, and `2xadobe` hint at?

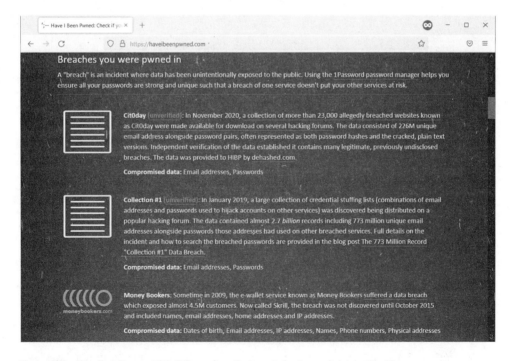

Figure 8.2   The first three of 30 (!) breaches that contained a certain email address

8.2   *Implementing password hashing*

Not storing passwords in cleartext goes without saying—if there is a data leak, the password is gone. Symmetric encryption does not really work, either. If the decryption key is stolen along with the encrypted passwords, the latter are gone, too. There is no real good solution if a website needs to access the passwords of the users. If the application can somehow get ahold of the password, an attacker may, too. That's why you should run if a website asks you to email a "forgotten" password (instead of providing you with a means to reset it).

But how can an application implement a login form if there is no way to retrieve a stored password? A common best practice is to not store the password itself but to store a hash of it. Imagine the hash as being like a fingerprint. If police find a fingerprint at a crime scene, they usually do not know the person it belongs to. However, if they have a list of suspects, they can take their fingerprints and then compare them with the one found. Someone's fingerprint is unique and does not change significantly. Hashing passwords works in a similar fashion, as figure 8.3 shows.

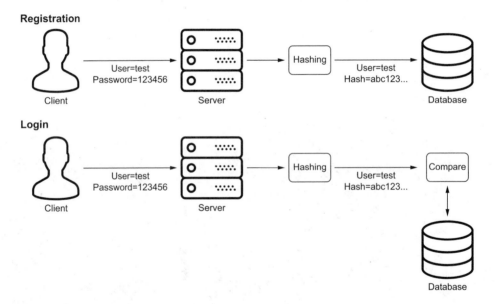

Figure 8.3   Password hashing in action

When a user registers with a site, their password is not stored. Instead, its fingerprint is generated (as a kind of one-way encryption) and then put into the database. Whenever that user tries to log in using their password, the application calculates the hash of the provided password and compares it with the one from the database. If they match, the application assumes that the password was correct and grants access.

There are many options for hashing algorithms. However, not all of them are suited for usage with passwords. First of all, the hash should have a certain length; otherwise, an attacker might manage to find a hash collision—two passwords having the same hashed value. Imagine that an attacker manages to get ahold of a password hash—for instance, via a leak. They now know the hash they need and just have to find a password that has exactly this hash. With a very insecure hashing algorithm, that password might not even be the one chosen by the user! Let's start with a hashing algorithm that has been used for a very long time, MD5.

8.2.1   MD5 (and why not to use it)

Spoiler alert: MD5 should be avoided these days. It creates a hash that is 128 bits, or 16 bytes, long. Back in the mid-1990s (!), it became obvious that MD5 might be broken beyond repair, since some research could prove that finding a collision might be feasible. In 2012, a research paper by Marc Stevens demonstrated an approach to construct such a collision using one single block (64 bytes) of input data (http://mng.bz/Qv66). Since then, relying on MD5 hashes to verify the validity of critical data such as passwords is futile.

Before we look at how to better hash algorithms, let's talk about some other reasons why MD5 should be avoided. We'll use the password from the aforementioned XKCD comic:

```
correct horse battery staple
```

The following simple console program calculates the hash of that password:

```
using System;
using System.Security.Cryptography;
using System.Text;

public class Program
{
    public static void Main()
    {
        using (var md5 = new MD5Cng()) {        ⟵  Uses the MD5 functionality
            var enc = new ASCIIEncoding();          built into .NET
            var hash = md5.ComputeHash(
                enc.GetBytes(
                    "correct horse battery staple"));
            var sb = new StringBuilder();
            foreach (var b in hash) {
                sb.Append(b.ToString("x2").ToLower());   ⟵
            }
            Console.WriteLine(sb.ToString());       ⟵
        }
    }
}
```

Computes the MD5 hash of a byte array

Creates the byte array from the input string

Converts the calculated hash into a hex string

Outputs the result

The desired password is converted into a byte array, which is the required input data type for .NET's MD5 calculation. The result is then converted into a hexadecimal string and looks like this:

```
9cc2ae8a1ba7a93da39b46fc1019c481
```

So how do we find a password that has the same MD5 hash? Using brute force, we would not live long enough to await the end result (unless, of course, there are revolutionary advances when it comes to calculation speed). However, there are databases of precalculated hashes available. For everything on the NordPass list or other lists, there is already an available hash. Depending on the hashing algorithm used, a technique called *rainbow tables* can speed up the password guessing significantly. The technical details are beyond the scope of this book, but here's a simplified explanation: rainbow tables cache intermediate results when generating hashes to save potentially many CPU cycles.

There are password/hash lists and rainbow tables consisting of many, many gigabytes of data, and there are also websites that look up hashes in their database. I tried a few better-known ones, and surprisingly, they did not find the previous MD5 hash. However, entering the hash into Google yielded the result shown in figure 8.4.

Over two dozen websites already know that hash—this is a sign that you should avoid the password. Some web applications tried to mitigate this kind of attack by using a technique called *salting*. The application added a piece of information to the password, a

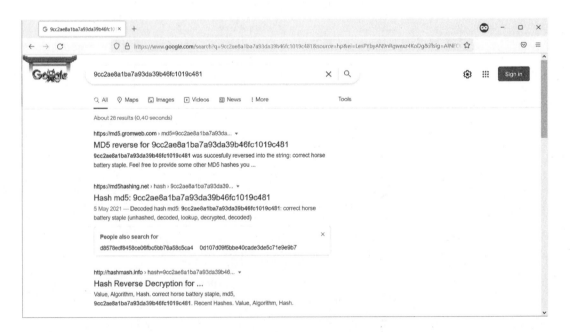

Figure 8.4   The "correct horse battery staple" password hash is common knowledge.

"salt," and then calculated the hash. This salt was known only to the application. Let's try a salt of `Manning`, which could lead to the following data prior to hashing:

```
correct horse battery stapleManning
```

That leads to the following MD5 hash:

```
06c8cc9cb28ea9e1224efcb2cc96b8d5
```

Google now reports zero matches (this will, of course, change once the e-book is indexed).

Salting provides protection to some degree from the aforementioned attacks. However, in our example, we made a few mistakes that torpedo our security efforts:

- The salt is rather short.
- The salt is predictable.
- The salt is constant.

A better approach would be to generate a long, random salt for each password and store the salt along with the hash. There is no direct way to retrieve the password from those two pieces of information. Also, if two users pick the same password, their hashes will be very different.

You might add some extra precautions by also adding pepper to the salt. Yes, that's really the terms that are being used. "Peppering" adds another security layer in case the database has been leaked (which means that the hashes and the salts are now known to the attacker). The hashes could be signed or encrypted. The application needs to know the appropriate data to validate the signature or to decrypt the hash. So if the application itself is not stolen, the extra defense layer might protect the hashes.

Now that we have established that MD5 is not secure any longer, let's look at alternatives. Another popular algorithm, SHA1, is also considered unsuitable. Other SHA-based algorithms, such as SHA256, SHA384, or SHA512, are better, but basically, the following four options are viable:

- Argon2—The winner of a password competition running from 2013 to 2015 (see www.password-hashing.net/ for details).
- PBKDF2 *(Password-Based Key Derivation Function 2)*—The recommendation by NIST; also fulfills the FIPS-140 standard (NIST's Federal Information Processing Standard for cryptography).
- scrypt—A hashing algorithm that uses more resources than many of the alternatives to make it more costly for attackers to brute-force a hash.
- bcrypt—An older password hashing algorithm dating back to 1999, but considered secure. There are some limitations, though, including a maximum length of 72 bytes for the data to be hashed.

.NET comes with support for PBKDF2; there are third-party implementations for the other algorithms, which we will talk about in a bit. But first, on to PBKDF2.

8.2.2   *PBKDF2*

The IETF republished PBKDF2 as RFC 2898 (see www.ietf.org/rfc/rfc2898.txt), so that's why the .NET class responsible for that algorithm is aptly, but probably surprisingly, called Rfc2898DeriveBytes and resides in the System.Security .Cryptography namespace. The class constructor expects three parameters:

- The password (or value) to hash.
- The size (in bytes) of the salt (it's also possible to provide a custom salt).
- The number of iterations the algorithm should use. The more iterations, the more secure the hash, but the longer hashing takes. This value is optional, but we will set it, and you will see why in a bit.

The following listing shows a username/password form that mimics the two essential aspects of using a password hash: generating the hash upon registration and validating the hash upon login.

> **Listing 8.1   The combined registration/login form as a Razor Page**

```
@page
@model HashingModel

<div class="text-center">
    <h1 class="display-4">Password Hashing</h1>
    <div class="mt-5 mb-5">
        <form method="post" action="">
            <div class="form-group">
                <label class="control-label" for="UserName">User name</label>
                <input type="text" id="UserName" name="UserName"
                  ⮑class="form-control" value="@Model.UserName" />
            </div>
            <div class="form-group">
                <label class="control-label" for="Password">Password</label>
                <input type="password" id="Password" name="Password"
                  ⮑class="form-control" value="@Model.Password" />
            </div>
            <div class="form-group">
                <label class="control-label" for="HashToVerify">Hash to
                  ⮑verify</label>
                <input type="text" id="HashToVerify" name="HashToVerify"
                  ⮑class="form-control" value="@Model.HashToVerify" />
            </div>
            <div class="form-group">
                <label class="control-label" for="SaltToVerify">Salt to
                  ⮑verify</label>
                <input type="text" id="SaltToVerify" name="SaltToVerify"
                  ⮑class="form-control" value="@Model.SaltToVerify" />
            </div>
            <div class="form-group">
                <input type="submit" asp-page-handler="Register"
                  ⮑value="Register" class="btn btn-primary" />
                <input type="submit" asp-page-handler="Login" value="Login"
                  ⮑class="btn btn-primary" />
            </div>
```

Annotations (left margin):
- Shows the username field → `<input type="text" id="UserName" name="UserName" class="form-control" value="@Model.UserName" />`
- Shows the password field → `<input type="password" id="Password" name="Password" class="form-control" value="@Model.Password" />`
- Shows the hash field (for mimicking the login) → `<input type="text" id="HashToVerify" name="HashToVerify" class="form-control" value="@Model.HashToVerify" />`
- Shows the salt field (for mimicking the login) → `<input type="text" id="SaltToVerify" name="SaltToVerify" class="form-control" value="@Model.SaltToVerify" />`
- Shows the Registration button → `<input type="submit" asp-page-handler="Register" value="Register" class="btn btn-primary" />`
- Shows the Login button → `<input type="submit" asp-page-handler="Login" value="Login" class="btn btn-primary" />`

```
            </form>
        </div>
        <div class="mb-3">
            @Model?.Message
        </div>
</div>
```

The form fields are filled with the values from the model, including the password field. That's not best practice, of course, but it helps us test the hash creation and verification without any extra copy-and-paste efforts. The associated page model class is shown in the next listing.

Listing 8.2 The page model class for the combined registration/login form

```
using System;
using System.Security.Cryptography;
using Microsoft.AspNetCore.Mvc;
using Microsoft.AspNetCore.Mvc.RazorPages;

namespace AspNetCoreSecurity.RazorSamples.Pages
{
    public class HashingModel : PageModel
    {
        public string Message { get; set; } = string.Empty;

        [BindProperty]
        public string UserName { get; set; } = string.Empty;
        [BindProperty]
        public string Password { get; set; } = string.Empty;
        [BindProperty]
        public string HashToVerify { get; set; } = string.Empty;
        [BindProperty]
        public string SaltToVerify { get; set; } = string.Empty;

        public void OnPostRegister()          ⟵──┐ The Handler method
        {                                          │ for the Register button
            // TODO
        }

        public void OnPostLogin()             ⟵──┐ The Handler method
        {                                          │ for the Login button
            // TODO
        }
    }
}
```

We will fill in the blanks—the code that runs after clicking the Register or Login buttons—individually for all the algorithms we will cover. First, the PBKDF2 hash creation:

```
public void OnPostRegister()
{
    var rfc2898 = new Rfc2898DeriveBytes(
        this.Password,              Instantiates the
        32,                         Rfc2898DeriveBytes class
        310_000);
```

```
    var hash = Convert.ToBase64String(rfc2898.GetBytes(20));    ◄──────   Pulls out the
    var salt = Convert.ToBase64String(rfc2898.Salt);    ◄──────            hash (and
                                                                           Base64-encodes it)
    this.HashToVerify = hash;                      Pulls out the salt (and
    this.SaltToVerify = salt;                      Base64-encodes it)
    this.Message = "Hash created";
}
```

The `Rfc2898DeriveBytes` class creates the hash that is available by calling `Get-Bytes(20)`, 20 being the default length in bytes of the hash. The automatically generated salt is more conveniently available by accessing the `Salt` property. Both values are then Base64-encoded and written in the page model properties so that they show up in the form fields.

Figure 8.5 shows one possible outcome of this code. Yours will most certainly look different since the hash is so random that a collision is highly unlikely.

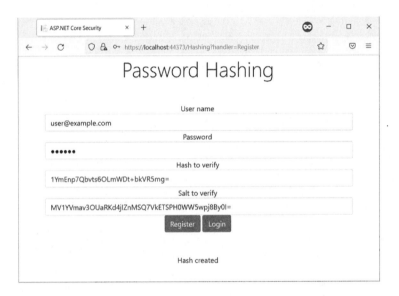

Figure 8.5   One possible set of salt/hash pairs for the most popular password, 123456

> **NOTE**   If you feel so inclined, you may also generate your own secure salt by calling `new RNGCryptoServiceProvider().GetBytes()`.

Since the hash and salt input fields are now conveniently prepopulated, we can implement the password verification method:

```
public void OnPostLogin()
{
    var salt = Convert.FromBase64String(             Converts the salt from
    ➡this.SaltToVerify);                    ◄──────  the form to a string
```

```
var rfc2898 = new Rfc2898DeriveBytes(
    this.Password,
    salt,
    310000);
var hash = Convert.ToBase64String(
    rfc2898.GetBytes(20));
var isValid = hash == this.HashToVerify;

if (isValid)
{
    Message = "Login successful";
} else
{
    Message = "Login failed";
}
}
```

Calculates the hash using the same salt as before

Converts the generated hash to a Base64-encodded string

Compares the stored hash with the generated one

Using the same password with the same salt and the same number of iterations will generate the same hash. So, if both the old and the new hash match, the password must be the same and the login was successful. In a real-world application, both the hash and the salt (and, if you intend to change that eventually, the number of iterations) will be stored in the database and then used later to verify the password. At no point did the application persist the password itself.

The OWASP maintains a password storage cheat sheet at http://mng.bz/XZy9, which they continuously update according to advances in password-cracking techniques. Among other things, they recommend the number of iterations to use for PBKDF2. That's precisely where the value of 310,000 came from. Make sure that you revisit that page and possibly update the number of iterations accordingly. The OWASP cheat sheet also covers other relevant algorithms, so let's look at their .NET implementations.

8.2.3 Argon2

Argon2 is—at least for now—the best option for password hashing. The algorithm is modern and efficient, but there is no built-in support in .NET (yet). The most common library implementing Argon2 is libsodium (see https://doc.libsodium.org/ for more details). There are a few .NET ports and wrappers for that library, with *libsodium-core* from https://github.com/tabrath/libsodium-core being the best maintained version at the moment. (This is not to be confused with the original from https://github.com/adamcaudill/libsodium-net. This version does not seem to be maintained any longer and is not compliant to .NET Standard, so we are using a fork.)

In order to use the library, the Sodium.Core package needs to be added to the project, either by using the command line

```
dotnet add package Sodium.Core
```

or by using the NuGet Package Manager console:

```
Install-Package Sodium.Core
```

Or, even easier, by referring to the NuGet package manager GUI in Visual Studio (figure 8.6).

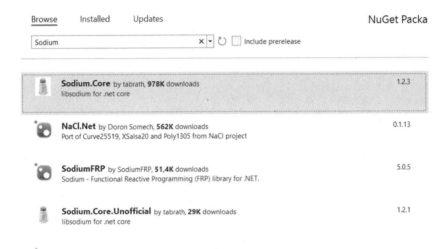

Figure 8.6   Adding `Sodium.Core` in Visual Studio's NuGet package manager

Here, you can easily install the package in the Visual Studio solution. Then a simple call to the `ArgonHashString()` method creates the hash:

```
using Sodium;

...

public void OnPostRegister()
{
    var hash = PasswordHash.ArgonHashString(       ◁─┐ Hash the string
        this.Password,                                 using Argon2.
        PasswordHash.StrengthArgon.Interactive)
        .TrimEnd('\0');                            ◁─┐ Removes excessive
    var salt = string.Empty;                           null bytes

    this.HashToVerify = hash;
    this.SaltToVerify = salt;
    this.Message = "Hash created";
}
```

Note that the code removes null bytes at the end of the hash. Otherwise, the validation may fail later. There are four predefined strength levels for `Argon2`; we use the default. Figure 8.7 shows the possible output for a call to this code.

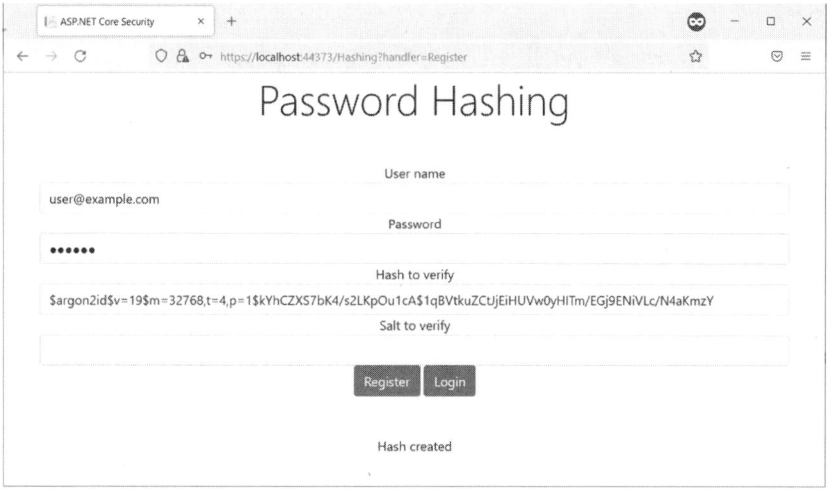

Figure 8.7 **Hashing using `Argon2`**

The hash contains all the information about the algorithm—which one was used (`Argon2`, or `Argon2id`, to be exact), the parameters being used (e.g., `t` is the minimum number of iterations, and `m` is the minimum memory size), and the salt. In this case, there is no need to store any extra values since the hash is basically self-descriptive. Verifying a hash is also not much more than a simple method call:

```
public void OnPostLogin()
{
    var isValid = PasswordHash.ArgonHashStringVerify(          Verifies the hash
        this.HashToVerify, this.Password);

    if (isValid)
    {
        Message = "Login successful";
    } else
    {
        Message = "Login failed";
    }
}
```

The `ArgonHashStringVerify()` method is "smart" enough to accept the complete hash and the password to verify against it; all the metadata about the algorithm, settings, and salt is extracted from the former.

8.2.4 scrypt

The best bet for `scrypt` support under .NET is the `Scrypt.NET` package from https://github.com/viniciuschiele/Scrypt, which can be installed similarly to `Sodium.Core`: command line, NuGet package manager console, or NuGet package manager UI. Afterward, hashing a password requires just minimal coding (shown in bold):

```
using Scrypt;

public void OnPostRegister()
{
    var scryptEncoder = new ScryptEncoder();
    var hash = scryptEncoder.Encode(this.Password);
    var salt = string.Empty;

    this.HashToVerify = hash;
    this.SaltToVerify = salt;
    this.Message = "Hash created";
}
```

Here is a typical resulting hash, once again using the password 123456 as an input:

```
$s2$16384$8$1$gduLm6gW+tVEC3V68FVNFSqprYi+rylX6tgJ2FqoE+E=$RhN0FWmgf5vXqgfQCo
    eIiG6nZyXXQp8CkZsBuIb1VfM=
```

Once again, all the relevant information about the hashing is part of the hash:

- s2 stands for the scrypt algorithm.
- 16384 is the number of iterations.
- 8 is the block size.
- 1 is the number of threads.

The OWASP password storage cheat sheet recommends higher values, so we should increase the default values. There are a few different suggestions in the document, but one is to increase the number of threads to 4, and another one is to increase the iterations to 65536. This may be achieved in the class constructor:

```
var scryptEncoder = new ScryptEncoder(
    iterationCount: 65536,
    blockSize: 8,
    threadCount: 4);
```

It is also possible to provide a custom salt generator (the argument is adequately called saltGenerator), but usually this is not required.

Verifying a password provided upon login against a stored hash is rather trivial as well:

```
public void OnPostLogin()
{
    var scryptEncoder = new ScryptEncoder();
    var isValid = scryptEncoder.Compare(
        this.Password, this.HashToVerify);

    if (isValid)
    {
        Message = "Login successful";
    } else
    {
        Message = "Login failed";
    }
}
```

This time, there are no arguments required for the `ScriptEncoder` class, since all the hashing configuration options may be pulled from the hash itself.

8.2.5 *bcrypt*

Finally, let's have a look at an "oldie but goldie"—bcrypt was first unveiled in 1999 and has stood the test of time. This is pretty amazing given all the advances in computing power. For instance, `SHA1` is from 1995, and its use has basically been discouraged everywhere since 2017. There is a NuGet package called `BCrypt.Net-Next` that brings bcrypt support to .NET (if you want a signed package, use `BCrypt.Net-Next.StrongName`). Its source code is available from https://github.com/BcryptNet/bcrypt.net.

After installation of the package, hashing a password is essentially a one-liner. Note that the fully qualified method call would be `BCrypt.Net.BCrypt.HashPassword()`, so make sure to put the `using` within your current namespace, not outside of it:

```
...
namespace AspNetCoreSecurity.RazorSamples.Pages
{
    using BCrypt.Net;

    public class HashingModel : PageModel
    {

    ...

        public void OnPostRegister()
        {
            var hash = BCrypt.HashPassword(this.Password);
            var salt = string.Empty;

            this.HashToVerify = hash;
            this.SaltToVerify = salt;
            this.Message = "Hash created";
        }

    ...
    }
}
```

This code then generates a bcrypt hash with the default settings, which can look like this:

```
$2a$11$mxPcFdFcwKzn4Mv.11BaV.sOoGUaWCK.WdZZaEYQqP2wDwjMBvC.W
```

By now, you should know the drill: 2a is the identifier of the bcrypt hashing algorithm, and 11 is the cost factor (it corresponds to 2^{11}=2,048 iterations). OWASP recommends a minimum of 10 (1,024 iterations), so we are good. If you feel the need to increase the value, you can do so as follows:

```
var hash = BCrypt.HashPassword(
    this.Password,
    workFactor: 12);
```

The hash verification is done by the `BCrypt.Verify()` method:

```
public void OnPostLogin()
{
    var isValid = BCrypt.Verify(this.Password, this.HashToVerify);

    if (isValid)
    {
        Message = "Login successful";
    } else
    {
        Message = "Login failed";
    }
}
```

And that's it. Once you know how, securely creating a password hash and verifying it later is just a few lines of code. If you roll your own user management and login form, hashing is the best way to go. However, if you look at the ASP.NET Core templates, you will notice that they already use password hashing out of the box.

8.3   *Analyzing ASP.NET Core templates*

When creating an ASP.NET Core application based on the default template, one of the questions asked is whether you want to use authentication (figure 8.8).

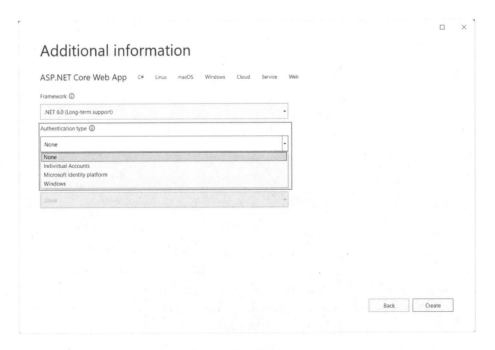

Figure 8.8   ASP.NET Core project creation in Visual Studio

NOTE When using another IDE, and/or using `dotnet new` to create a project based on the web template, use the `-au` option to configure the desired authentication type.

When choosing anything but None, the project will allow users to register and to log in. The URLs of these two pages end with `/Account/Register` and `/Account/Login`. Surprisingly, there are no associated Razor Pages in the project. The reason is that Microsoft is hiding the UI in a separate package. To take a look, go to Visual Studio's Project Explorer, right-click on the application, and select Add/New Scaffolded Item. Then you can pick the individual pages you would like to be added to the project (figure 8.9).

NOTE If you get an error message, try again—sometimes Visual Studio lags behind in the packages required for scaffolding. Also, you may want to manually install the `Microsoft.VisualStudio.Web.CodeGeneration.Utils` NuGet package to the project prior to scaffolding.

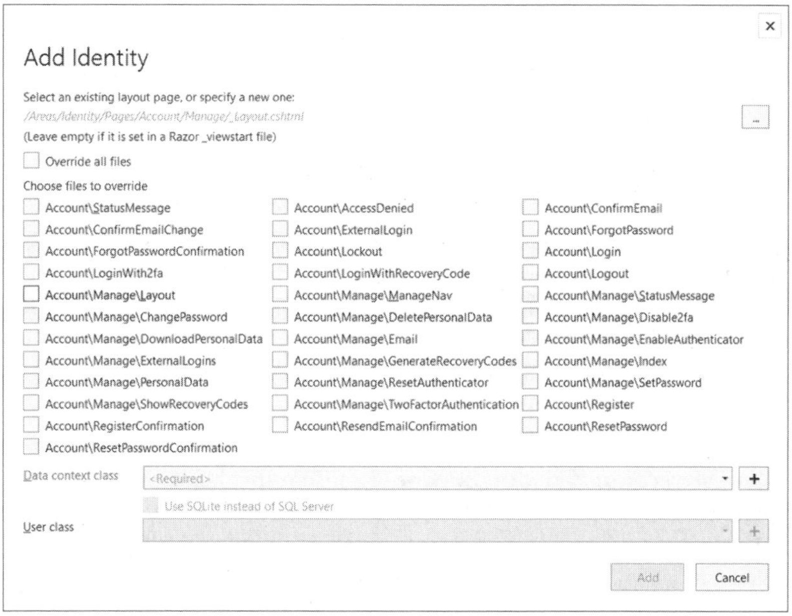

Figure 8.9   Adding account-related pages to the project

That's a lot of pages! We are only interested in *Account\Register* so far, but if you are curious, feel free to pick as many as you like. In the Data Context Class drop-down menu, pick the sole entry. Then the Areas/Identity/Pages/Account folder in the project will be filled with many new Razor Pages. We are especially interested in *Register .cshtml*, the registration page, and its associated model class, `Register.cshtml.cs`.

The latter file contains the `OnPostAsync()` method, which is executed if the registration form is submitted. The crucial lines of code are these two:

```
var user = new IdentityUser { UserName = Input.Email, Email = Input.Email };
var result = await _userManager.CreateAsync(user, Input.Password);
```

A new user is created, but the password is not part of the model. Instead, the `Create-Async()` method of the user manager receives the credentials as an additional argument. The implementation of this user manager is part of .NET, so looking at the source code is the best option here to understand what's going on. It is available at http://mng.bz/yvDp and looks like this (only showing the relevant parts, and the code is obviously subject to change):

```
public virtual async Task<IdentityResult> CreateAsync(TUser user, string
    password)
{
    var passwordStore = GetPasswordStore();
    var result = await UpdatePasswordHash(passwordStore, user, password);
    if (!result.Succeeded)
    {
        return result;
    }
    return await CreateAsync(user);
}
```

So before the user is created at the end of the method (by calling `CreateAsync()`, and just providing the user, sans the password), the password hash is updated. The method user, `UpdatePasswordHash()`, is implemented in the `PasswordHasher` class, with the source code available at http://mng.bz/M5KQ. If you glance over the source code, you can see that there are two versions of password hashing implemented: a v2, which uses `PBKDF2` with 1,000 iterations, and a v3, which uses 10,000 iterations (there are other subtle differences). It's good to know that ASP.NET Core is using a proven hashing algorithm. However, the iteration values are (currently) lower than what OWASP suggests.

The OWASP recommendation depends on the internal hashing algorithm used by the `PBKDF2` implementation. If `SHA256` is used (as v3 does), 310,000 iterations should be good. For `SHA1` (as v2 uses), an iteration count of 720,000 is the suggested setting.

Luckily, a simple addition to Program.cs can change the behavior of the `PBKDF2` hashing accordingly:

```
builder.Services.Configure<PasswordHasherOptions>(
    options => options.IterationCount = 310_000);
```

The password hasher may be swapped out against any other that implements the `IPasswordHasher` interface, which looks as follows:

```
public interface IPasswordHasher<TUser> where TUser : class
{
    string HashPassword(TUser user, string password);
    PasswordVerificationResult VerifyHashedPassword(TUser user,
    ➥string hashedPassword, string providedPassword);
}
```

That's pretty straightforward, so it is relatively easy to use other hashing algorithms, such as the alternatives just mentioned. But it's getting better: .NET security expert Scott Brady has created convenient NuGet packages for Argon2, bcrypt, and scrypt. With them, you can use a different hashing algorithm with minimal effort. Refer to http://mng.bz/aJzj, where you will find details about how to use the packages.

> **NOTE** We will thoroughly cover ASP.NET Core Identity—which is the base of the user manager, among many other things—in chapter 12.

Summary

Let's review what we have learned so far:

- An application does not need to know the passwords of its users; it only needs to be able to verify whether a password is correct.
- A hashing algorithm is a kind of one-way encryption and cannot be reversed.
- Hashing passwords with a secure algorithm like PBKDF2 allows password verification but prevents attackers from easily retrieving the password.
- ASP.NET Core supports PBKDF2 by default, but third-party libraries support alternatives like Argon2, bcrypt, and scrypt.
- The default settings of ASP.NET's password hashing need to be overridden for better security.
- The ASP.NET Core project templates use PBKDF2 password hashing by default but are also extensible to use other algorithms.

After all the coding, it's time to look at various configuration options that make our ASP.NET Core applications even more robust, starting with HTTP headers.

Part 4

Configuration

So far, most of the book has been rather code-centric, showcasing APIs and features of ASP.NET Core to mitigate many attacks. In this part of the book, however, configuration options are in the spotlight.

Chapter 9 introduces many HTTP headers that enable security features in modern browsers. Several of them are considered "quick wins": the security of a web application can be increased with very little effort. Chapter 10 discusses error handling, including best practices and how to create innocuous error pages that do not provide attackers with interesting bits of information. Chapter 11 then talks about logging in ASP.NET Core and a relatively unnoticed feature, health checks.

HTTP headers

MITRE Corporation, the well-known research facility doing major work for the US government, is the initiator and sponsor of the CVE Program (https://cve.org). Its goal is to identify and list common vulnerabilities, thus the name CVE: *Common Vulnerabilities and Exposures*. The website—www.cvedetails.com/, independent of MITRE and the CVE project, but reusing its classification scheme—provides a searchable list of all reported vulnerabilities in various software products. For instance, http://mng.bz/gwDe lists all security vulnerabilities from Microsoft's IIS (Internet Information Services), and http://mng.bz/e7j9 shows all security-related issues reported in ASP.NET Core (figure 9.1).

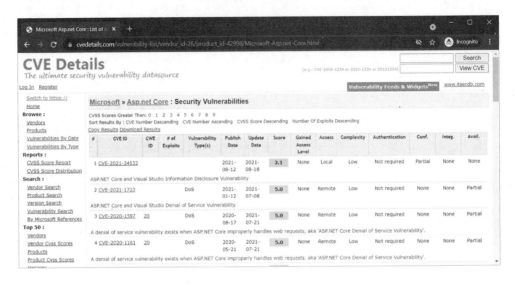

Figure 9.1   CVEs found in ASP.NET Core in the past

If you drill down in one specific CVE, you will find more details, including information about the version or patch in which the issue has been fixed.

Now take a closer look at the HTTP response headers an ASP.NET Core application sends to the client. Figure 9.2 shows a typical output of a site running on IIS.

Figure 9.2   HTTP headers returned by ASP.NET Core by default

As you can see, the data returned reveals the server software being used (`Server` header) and shows that ASP.NET (Core) is backing the application (`X-Powered-By` header), giving attackers potential pointers for targeted attacks.

NOTE The ASP.NET error page (when using legacy .NET Framework) even contained the version numbers of both the base framework and of ASP.NET. This is better now; even the developer error page of ASP.NET Core does not reveal any extra version information.

This chapter will cover how to make extra HTTP headers disappear to avoid information leakage as we have just discussed. Also, we will present HTTP headers that provide security functionality, either by protecting against a very specific attack or by mitigating other risks.

9.1 Hiding server information

Let's revisit figure 9.2 and take a closer look at the two specific HTTP headers that contain the revealing, not to say offending, information:

- `Server`—This standard HTTP header contains the server name and possibly also its version number.
- `X-Powered-By`—This nonstandard HTTP header contains the framework used; in previous versions of ASP.NET, it even included the specific .NET Framework version number.

Let's start with the server make and version number. Getting rid of them depends on the web server being used. Kestrel, the built-in .NET web server, can be configured in Program.cs; as part of this configuration, the server name and version can be dropped. The key is the `UseKestrel()` method of the `IWebHostBuilder` interface, which is usually available via the `builder.WebHost` property. The following code removes the `Server` HTTP header.

Listing 9.1 The default error page

```
var builder = WebApplication.CreateBuilder(args);

builder.WebHost.UseKestrel(options =>
{
    options.AddServerHeader = false;          ◁─┐ Removes Server
});                                             │ header

...
```

Setting the `AddServerHeader` property in the Kestrel options to `false` will skip the `Server` response header. When using IIS or IIS Express, things work differently. It's now a setting of the independent web server, not of the .NET application itself. IIS uses settings in the web.config file for several configuration options, including handling of HTTP headers. If your site does not have such a file yet, add it in the root folder (the Visual Studio file template for it is called *Web Configuration File*). There the `<system.webServer>` element may be used for specific IIS settings. The markup from the following listing sets the `removeServerHeader` attribute to remove the `Server` HTTP header.

Listing 9.2   Removing the Server HTTP header for IIS

```xml
<?xml version="1.0" encoding="utf-8"?>
<configuration>
    <system.webServer>
        <security>
            <requestFiltering removeServerHeader="true" />
        </security>
    </system.webServer>
</configuration>
```

Prevents the
Server header
from being sent

If you already have an existing web.config file in your project, just change it appropriately so that it contains the `<requestFiltering removeServerHeader="true" />` element. Note that this does not help with Kestrel, since in that case the `Server` header is added to the request pipeline too late.

The `X-Powered-By` HTTP header is sent only by IIS, not by Kestrel. It is not something ASP.NET actively uses, but rather is a setting created when ASP.NET Core is registered with IIS. Launch the IIS Manager, select the website that hosts the ASP.NET Core application in question, and open the HTTP Response Headers settings. It's likely that you'll now find the `X-Powered-By` header (figure 9.3). Go ahead and remove it.

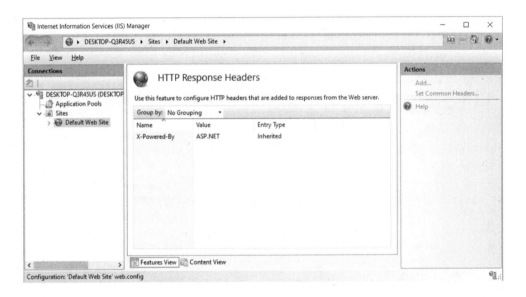

Figure 9.3   The `X-Powered-By` header is sent by default.

Alternatively, you can use web.config again. Since `X-Powered-By` is a custom header, it can be removed within the `<customHeaders>` element, as shown in the following listing.

Listing 9.3   Removing the X-Powered-By HTTP header via web.config

```xml
<?xml version="1.0" encoding="utf-8"?>
<configuration>
    <system.webServer>
        <security>
            <requestFiltering removeServerHeader="true" />
        </security>
        <httpProtocol>
            <customHeaders>
                <remove name="X-Powered-By" />
            </customHeaders>
        </httpProtocol>
    </system.webServer>
</configuration>
```

◁─┐ **Prevents the X-Powered-By header from being sent**

You can see the result in figure 9.4, where we look at the HTTP response headers in the browser's developer tools.

Both the `Server` and `X-Powered-By` HTTP headers are gone for good. So far, we have removed excessive HTTP headers to provide attackers less information about the system our web application is running on. Next, we will add extra HTTP headers to make the site even more secure.

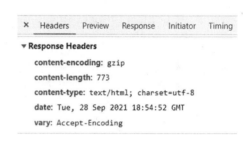

Figure 9.4   All revealing HTTP response headers are gone.

9.2   *Browser security headers*

When Internet Explorer 8 was released in March 2009, a paradigm shift took place. For the first time, a browser added security features, trying to prevent or at least mitigate attacks. In retrospect, IE8 wasn't a brilliant browser, but some of the features it introduced found their way into competing products, too.

Most of those security-related features came in the form of HTTP headers. The most notable one was `X-XSS-Protection`, which was used to configure the built-in cross-site scripting auditor. Chapter 2 already discussed this header and why all the browsers that adapted it have removed it by now.

Although that specific idea did not work out in the long run, the approach to use HTTP headers to enable security features has been a very good idea. Backward compatibility is not much of an issue, since older browsers just ignore headers they do not know. Most of the security features added via HTTP headers are defense-in-depth mechanisms, so it's also not a problem that older browsers will not receive that extra protection. Let's look at a variety of those headers.

9.2.1   *Referrer Policy*

The `Referer` (that's not a typo in this text, but was a typo in the original HTTP specification, which has been carried over since then due to backward-compatibility concerns) HTTP header contains the URL of the document that was loaded in the browser window or tab when the current HTTP request was made. When the user clicks a link, the URL of the current page will be put into that HTTP header. When an HTML page includes a reference to an image (`<img>` tag), the URL of the HTML page will be used.

This might pose a security risk, especially when doing a cross-site request. The URL may contain information that needs to be protected, such as "secret" endpoints or internal server names. The `Referer` header is sent automatically by web browsers, so it's not an application feature. To give developers control over when to send the header, and if so, whether to limit the information in it, Referrer Policy was created. It's been a W3C candidate recommendation since January 2017. As of the time of this writing, the specification (available at www.w3.org/TR/referrer-policy/) has still not made the final step toward being a final standard (W3C recommendation). However, all modern browsers—excluding Internet Explorer—do support this feature.

The central element of Referrer Policy is the `Referrer-Policy` HTTP header. Its value is the referrer policy that the browser should use for the current document. Table 9.1 contains a list of all available options.

Table 9.1   Available referrer policies

Policy name	Description
no-referrer	The `Referer` header will not be sent at all.
no-referrer-when-downgrade	The `Referer` header will only be sent if the current URL and the URL being navigated to both use HTTPS.
origin	The `Referer` header contains only the origin of the current page, plus a trailing slash (https://manning.com/, not https://manning.com).
origin-when-cross-origin	When doing a cross-origin request, the `Referer` header contains only the origin plus a trailing slash; the full URL is used otherwise.
same-origin	The `Referer` header will only be sent if the URL being navigated to has the same origin as the current URL.
strict-origin	The `Referer` header contains only the origin of the current page, plus a trailing slash. The header will only be sent if the current URL uses plain HTTP, or if both the current and target URLs use HTTPS.
strict-origin-when-cross-origin	The `Referer` header contains the full current URL for same-origin requests and the origin plus trailing slash for cross-origin requests (but in the latter case, only when the current URL uses HTTP, or both the current and target URL use HTTPS).
unsafe-url	The `Referer` header contains the URL of the current document, independent of whether the request is same-origin or cross-origin.

For a very long time, browsers defaulted to `unsafe-url`, filling the `Referer` header with the current URL every time. There were some security precautions in place—for instance, any credentials were stripped from the URL, and local URLs (file paths) were not allowed. Browsers that do support Referrer Policy first defaulted to `no-referrer-when-downgrade` to avoid leaking the referrer when switching from

HTTPS to HTTP. In November 2020, the specification was updated to make `strict-origin-when-cross-origin` the default, so only the origin will be sent when doing a cross-origin request, and only if it's not an HTTPS to HTTP request. All the current editors of the specification work for Google, so it is not surprising that Google Chrome and related browsers (Edge, Opera, etc.) changed their behavior accordingly. Chrome 85 was the first such release back in August 2020, even before the specification was altered. In March 2021, Firefox implemented the same behavior change (and later announced that less restricted policies will at a future point be ignored for cross-site requests). Safari's built-in Intelligent Tracking Prevention (ITP) feature automatically sends the origin in the `Referer` HTTP header when doing a cross-origin request, which corresponds to the `origin-when-cross-origin` setting.

To use Referrer Policy from an ASP.NET Core application, there are basically two options. If you are using IIS (and are certain that this will not change soon), you can add headers in web.config, as the following listing shows.

Listing 9.4 Adding the Referrer-Policy HTTP header via web.config

```xml
<?xml version="1.0" encoding="utf-8"?>
<configuration>
    <system.webServer>
        <httpProtocol>                                         Sends the Referrer-
            <customHeaders>                                    Policy HTTP header
                <add name="Referrer-Policy" value="no-referrer" />   ◁
            </customHeaders>
        </httpProtocol>
    </system.webServer>
</configuration>
```

The other option that then also works with the Kestrel web server would be code in the application that adds those headers. The easiest approach is to use a simple middleware in the `Program` class, which sets the header:

```csharp
app.Use(async (context, next) =>
{
    context.Response.Headers.Add(
        "Referrer-Policy", "no-referrer");          Adds the HTTP header
    await next.Invoke();                  ◁          Continues with the
});                                                  next middleware
```

Just make sure that you are using this code snippet before any other middleware that might cause a redirect; that redirect might then contain the `Referer` HTTP header with unwanted information. Figure 9.5 shows the result, using the `no-referrer` policy. The `Referer` HTTP header is not sent at all.

Figure 9.5 The `Referer` header is not sent, thanks to Referrer Policy.

It is, of course, also possible to set the HTTP header in an individual page:

```
HttpContext.Response.Headers.Add("Referrer-Policy", "no-referrer");
```

In most cases, the whole application will have the same set of security-related HTTP headers, so the global approach is usually the better idea.

9.2.2 *Feature and permissions policy*

Modern JavaScript code is very powerful. Thanks to APIs in current browsers, there are many features available to web applications these days. In the case of malicious code being injected, this might pose a bigger problem than just the existence of cross-site scripting alone. Of course, we did a lot in chapter 2 to make sure that XSS does not happen at all, but there's still room for improvement, and for another defense-in-depth mechanism.

With Feature Policy, the W3C tried to implement a standard that limits the use of browser features and APIs. The current, and final, version is available at www.w3.org/TR/2019/WD-feature-policy-1-20190416/. The URL already hints at the state of that document: WD for *working draft*. And although Feature Policy enjoyed very good browser support (basically everywhere except for Internet Explorer), the team behind the specification restarted their efforts and came up with Permissions Policy. The document available at www.w3.org/TR/permissions-policy/ is currently a working draft as well, but—unlike Feature Policy—is under active development.

The person responsible for the specification works at Google, which leads to an interesting situation: in Google Chrome 88 (released in December 2020), Permissions Policy was included, and all related browsers like Edge and Opera followed suit. Firefox and Safari, on the other hand, are still supporting only Feature Policy and are probably awaiting a stabilization of the standard before they proceed with implementing Permissions Policy.

The consequence for us is that we need to look at both. The intention is the same, but the syntax differs greatly. Feature Policy uses the `Feature-Policy` HTTP header, which contains a list of browser features and APIs as well as when the application is allowed to use them. For instance, the following header disabled the use of going full screen on the current page:

```
Feature-Policy: fullscreen 'none'
```

> **NOTE** Going full screen is not a security risk per se. It may be triggered only when a user performs an interaction such as a mouse button click, when an extra warning is displayed (including information on how to leave full-screen mode again), and when certain functionality such as keyboard input is disabled. Still, your website policy might be to prevent full screen because it might confuse users.

Let's imagine that you do want to allow going into full-screen mode, but only from the current origin and from another origin (which might be embedded into the page). Here is how that might look:

```
Feature-Policy: fullscreen 'self' https://example.com
```

You have already seen this kind of syntax in chapter 2 when discussing Content Security Policy (CSP), so everything is pretty self-explanatory. Permissions Policy, on the other hand, uses the `Permissions-Policy` HTTP header and a different syntax. Here are the two equivalents for the two preceding `Feature-Policy` headers:

```
Permissions-Policy: fullscreen=()
Permissions-Policy: fullscreen=(self "https://example.com")
```

You can set these headers exactly as before using a simple middleware, page-specific code, or, for IIS only, in web.config.

When using Google Chrome, there is a JavaScript API for access to Permission Policy directives. Curiously, the JavaScript object is (still) called `document.feature-Policy`, but might obviously change in the future.

A call to `document.featurePolicy.allowedFeatures()`, for instance, returns a list of all supported directives. Table 9.2 shows the full list of all (currently) available options a Windows version of Google Chrome offers. This shows how granular your control is over the individual features and APIs that JavaScript has access to.

Table 9.2 Available Permissions Policy directives

Directive name	Description
accelerometer	Accelerometer access
autoplay	Automatic playback of media
camera	Camera access
ch-device-memory	Access to amount of device RAM
ch-downlink	Access to client bandwidth
ch-dpr	Access to client device to pixel ratio (might be removed)
ch-ect	Access to client connection type
ch-lang	Access to client language
ch-prefers-color-scheme	Access to preferred client color scheme
ch-rtt	Access to client roundtrip time
ch-ua	Access to client user agent
ch-ua-arch	Access to client user agent's architecture
ch-ua-bitness	Access to client user agent bit value (32, 64)
ch-ua-full-version	Access to client user agent full version number
ch-ua-mobile	Access to whether client user agent is mobile or not
ch-ua-model	Access to client device model
ch-ua-platform	Access to client system platform

Table 9.2   Available Permissions Policy directives *(continued)*

Directive name	Description
`ch-ua-platform-version`	Access to client system platform version
`ch-ua-reduced`	Access to reduced client user agent information (to make fingerprinting harder)
`ch-viewport-width`	Access to client viewport width
`ch-width`	Access to client device width
`clipboard-read`	Read access to the clipboard
`clipboard-write`	Write access to the clipboard
`cross-origin-isolated`	Complete isolation from other origins
`display-capture`	Access to the Screen Capture API
`document-domain`	Access to the `document.domain` JavaScript property
`encrypted-media`	Access to the Encrypted Media Extension API
`fullscreen`	Full-screen mode access
`gyroscope`	Gyroscope access
`hid`	Access to the WebHID (Human Interface Device) API
`idle-detection`	Detect whether the client is idle
`magnetometer`	Magnetometer access
`microphone`	Microphone access
`midi`	Access to the Web MIDI API
`otp-credentials`	Access to the WebOTP (one-time password) API
`payment`	Access to the Payment API
`picture-in-picture`	PiP mode for videos
`publickey-credentials-get`	Public key access via Web Authentication API
`screen-wake-lock`	Access to the Screen Wake Lock API
`serial`	Serial port access
`sync-xhr`	Synchronous `XMLHttpRequest` calls
`usb`	Access to the WebUSB API
`xr-spatial-tracking`	Access to the WebXR device API

This list changes all the time. The W3C attempts to maintain an up-to-date list at http:/ /mng.bz/pOD5, but the truth is obviously what `document.featurePolicy .allowedFeatures()` returns.

9.2.3 Preventing content sniffing

The `Content-Type` HTTP header provides the browser with information about what type of resource is sent with an HTTP response: the MIME (Multipurpose Internet Mail Extensions, first introduced for email attachments) type. Here is an example that is used by ASP.NET Core for all HTML content:

```
Content-Type: text/html; charset=utf-8
```

Some older browsers (looking at some legacy Internet Explorer versions here) were notorious for the way that they sometimes ignored the content type value but tried to guess the actual file type instead. This could lead to some attack vectors. A scientific paper at http://mng.bz/OojK shows some interesting options, including a PostScript document containing a `<script>` tag, which is (unfortunately) interpreted by Internet Explorer as HTML, allowing cross-site scripting in the process.

> **NOTE** We do not present a full example, since you probably are not inclined to find a machine on which to install Internet Explorer 7. Attacks abusing content sniffing are extremely rare, but the mitigation—a simple HTTP header we will look at right now—is expected during security audits.

Luckily, modern browsers adhere to the MIME type, but just to be on the safe side, they explicitly forbid content sniffing (a better term for content guessing). The following HTTP header helps:

```
X-Content-Type-Options: nosniff
```

> **NOTE** This header was, along with some others, introduced in Internet Explorer 8 and then later adapted by the other major browsers.

As usual, set the header on a per-page basis, or (recommended) globally with middleware in Program.cs:

```
app.Use(async (context, next) =>
{
    context.Response.Headers.Add("X-Content-Type-Options", "nosniff");
    await next.Invoke();
});
```

If using IIS, you can use the following web.config setting:

```
<add name="X-Content-Type-Options" value="nosniff" />
```

9.2.4 Cross-origin policies

As we have already witnessed in chapter 4, cross-origin requests may lead to attack vectors. In those scenarios, additional (but still experimental) HTTP headers might provide additional protection.

First of all, the `Cross-Origin-Embedder-Policy` header prevents the current document from loading any cross-origin resources that explicitly opt in to that. There are two ways this HTTP header may be used:

```
Cross-Origin-Embedder-Policy: unsafe-none
Cross-Origin-Embedder-Policy: require-corp
```

The first option is the default behavior; there are no additional limits on loading cross-origin resources. When using the `require-corp` value, though, things change. Then, one of these three prerequisites must be met to load a cross-origin resource:

- The resource must use CORS and appropriately set the `Access-Control-Allow-Origin` HTTP header (see chapter 4 for details).
- The HTML attribute `crossorigin` must be present when loading the resource.
- The resource must use the `Cross-Origin-Resource-Policy` header to explicitly allow the resource being loaded. Possible values are `same-site` (same site only), `same-origin` (same origin only), and `cross-origin` (cross-origin requests are allowed).

A related HTTP header is `Cross-Origin-Opener-Policy`. It isolates the current document in case it was opened in a pop-up window. The following three values are supported:

- `same-origin`—Isolate the document from other origins.
- `same-origin-allow-popups`—Isolate the document, with the exception of pop-ups within the same origin that do not set the `Cross-Origin-Opener-Policy-Header` (or use `unsafe-none`, the next option).
- `unsafe-none`—No isolation, which is the default value.

> **NOTE**   Due to the length and similarity of those headers, acronyms are commonly used. In the order of appearance, this section mentioned `Cross-Origin-Embedder-Policy` (COEP), `Access-Control-Allow-Origin` (ACAO), `Cross-Origin-Resource-Policy` (CORP), and `Cross-Origin-Opener-Policy` (COOP).

As usual, you may set these headers in an ASP.NET Core application via middleware or IIS's web.config file.

9.2.5   *Further headers*

New security headers are sporadically added to browsers, and some are deprecated and eventually vanish. An interesting service that tests for the presence of certain headers is https://securityheaders.com. It scans a website for security-related HTTP headers and provides a grade, depending on how many of the expected headers have been detected. Figure 9.6 shows the result for https://manning.com.

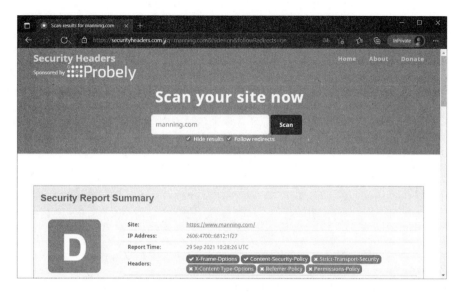

Figure 9.6 Some security headers are being sent, and some aren't.

Not all headers were found, but that's not automatically a critical issue. Not all websites require all headers for decent security. Also, it's not always feasible to implement headers that only enjoy partial support in browsers (yet). For instance, the aforementioned service expected the presence of the `Permissions-Policy` HTTP header before that feature was released in the stable Google Chrome channel. It's a good indication to identify additional headers to consider and is well-suited for a management summary when the results are good, but it is usually not a reason to take immediate action. Even microsoft.com only gets a C.

Throughout this book, we have already covered several other HTTP headers that provide security features; they are shown here for sake of completeness:

- `Content-Security-Policy` *and* `X-XSS-Protection` *headers*—Prevent cross-site scripting (chapter 2)
- `Strict-Transport-Security` *header and the* `HttpOnly` *and* `secure` *cookie flags*—Help prevent session attacks (chapter 3)
- `SameSite` *cookie flag and the* `X-FRAME-OPTIONS` *header*—Prevent cross-site request forgery and protect from clickjacking, respectively (chapter 4)

Set security headers with NWebsec

Using middleware—as simple as it is—to set HTTP headers might look a little bit clumsy. A popular third-party project, NWebsec, may help. The NuGet package `NWeb-sec.AspNetCore.Middleware` (http://mng.bz/8MEZ) provides a few middleware

(continued)

options that are ready to be added to the request pipeline. Here are a few of the methods provided—you'll certainly be able to identify which header they send:

```
UseCsp()
UseCspReportOnly()
UseHsts()
UseReferrerPolicy()
UseXContentTypeOptions()
UseXfo()
UseXXssProtection()
```

This might facilitate applying those security headers to a site. Another project with the same goal is the `NetEscapades.AspNetCore.SecurityHeaders` NuGet package by Andrew Lock (http://mng.bz/YGMo).

Summary

Let's review what you have learned so far:

- ASP.NET Core sends out revealing HTTP headers, telling attackers which framework and web server are used, sometimes including version information.
- Revealing HTTP headers can be removed with simple configuration settings.
- HTTP headers may restrict the way HTTP referrers are handled and which browser features are available to JavaScript code.
- Content type sniffing may open up attack vectors and can be deactivated with an HTTP header.
- For cross-origin requests, HTTP headers may limit which resources may be loaded.

This chapter started with leaking information in HTTP headers. Another source for information leakage is improper error handling, which will be discussed in the following chapter.

Error handling

10

This chapter covers

- Learning how ASP.NET Core handles uncaught exceptions
- Knowing when to use the developer exception page
- Setting up a custom error page
- Displaying error messages specific to the HTTP status code
- Formatting errors within an API

In 2018, health care and health IT news portal Healthcare Dive reported about a white paper by security company Zingbox, which analyzed medical IoT devices (http://mng.bz/aJem). They specifically looked at the error messages displayed on those devices. As they found out, the following information was included on several devices:

- Database names and usernames
- File paths on the server

189

- Source code filenames and the names of classes, methods, and parameters
- Source code line numbers
- Full-stack traces
- And more

Error messages may be crucial during development. On a production system, they may have an entirely different impact—that is, telling attackers intimate details about the system and software. With our ASP.NET Core applications, we need to, and can, make this better.

10.1 Error pages for web applications

If the type of web server, application framework, or database is known, attacks can be much more targeted. Errors will eventually occur in a web application, and they need to be properly handled. For the end user, however, no valuable information must be given, since that might provide inside knowledge to facilitate attacks. This is especially true when the error is an unhandled server exception that the user can't fix anyway. That's why we look at ASP.NET Core error-handling options and available features.

Admittedly, the default settings of ASP.NET Core web applications—including Web API and Blazor—are pretty decent. Here is a snippet from the `Configure()` method within the Startup.cs file when using a .NET version prior to 6 (from .NET 6 onward, the developer exception page is not activated by default any longer, and all code has been moved to the Program.cs file):

```
if (env.IsDevelopment())
{
    app.UseDeveloperExceptionPage();
}
else
{
    app.UseExceptionHandler("/Error");
...
}
```

If the system is running in development mode—chapter 7 described how this is determined—then a developer exception page is displayed whenever an unhandled exception occurs (courtesy of the `UseDeveloperExceptionPage()` method). Otherwise, a custom exception handler with the URL `/Error` is being used. Let's start with the exception page first, which is shown in figure 10.1.

The exception page contains a wealth of information, including

- The exception error message
- A complete stack trace, including the offending line of code
- Information about the HTTP request, including query parameters (depending on the HTTP method), cookies, and all other HTTP headers
- Routing information (in our case, this reveals the name of the base view)

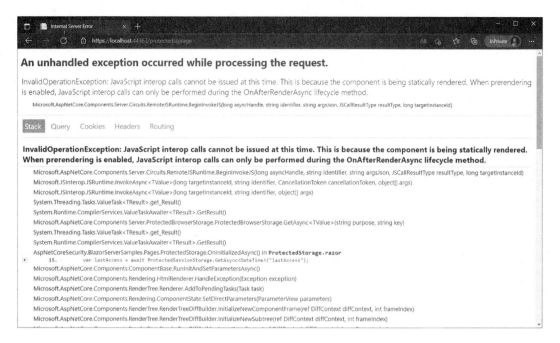

Figure 10.1 The built-in developer exception page

As helpful as all this information is, it is obvious that no one else—especially not attackers—should ever get access to it. The `env.IsDevelopment()` condition from the template will guarantee that, unless you set the `DOTNET_ENVIRONMENT` or `ASPN-ETCORE_ENVIRONMENT` environment variables on your production system to `Devel-opment` (who would ever want to do that?). Depending on your level of paranoia, you might even remove that code. Without the developer exception page, the server will just return an HTTP error (usually HTTP status code 500, Internal Server Error). Browsers then may display a blank page, or a "pretty" error message, as shown in figure 10.2.

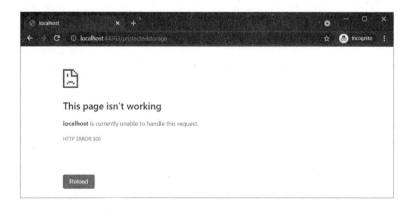

**Figure 10.2
No developer error
page, no useful
information**

That browser-generated error message is not really helpful to anyone, including legitimate users. Therefore, proper error handling should be used.

10.1.1 Custom error pages

This may be achieved by using a specific error handler. The `UseException-Handler()` method activates middleware that ensures that no unhandled exceptions are displayed. Instead, the web application displays a specific error view. The URL of that view is the argument for the `UseExceptionHandler()` call:

```
app.UseExceptionHandler("/Error");
```

> **WARNING**   Make sure that you load this middleware before any other request-handling one so that the exception is handled early enough. This also applies to the other middleware described in this chapter.

It is important to note that the client is not redirected to that error page—the URL would change then, and a reload would just refresh the error page, not the original page. Instead, the content of the exception handler URL is returned, using the original URL of the page where the error was thrown.

> **NOTE**   You can also generate the error page's markup directly in the `Use-ExceptionHandler()` call via a lambda function. It would probably make sense to use a specific file for that, as shown here.

When using the standard .NET application templates, the error page will already have been generated. When using ASP.NET Core MVC, the associated file is /View/Shared/Error.cshtml; for Razor Pages and Blazor applications, the error page is in /Pages/Error.cshtml. The following listing shows the MVC version, but the differences compared to the other options are negligible.

Listing 10.1   The default error page

```
@model ErrorViewModel
@{
    ViewData["Title"] = "Error";
}

<h1 class="text-danger">Error.</h1>                     Displays generic
<h2 class="text-danger">                                error message
  An error occurred while processing your request.</h2>
</h2>

@if (Model?.ShowRequestId ?? false)
{
    <p>
        <strong>Request ID:</strong>            Shows
        <code>@Model?.RequestId</code>          request ID
    </p>
}
                                  Shows general information about
<h3>Development Mode</h3>         additional options in development mode
<p>
```

```
    Swapping to <strong>Development</strong> environment will display more
    detailed information about the error that occurred.
</p>
<p>
    <strong>The Development environment shouldn't be enabled for deployed
    applications.</strong>
    It can result in displaying sensitive information from exceptions to
    end users.
    For local debugging, enable the <strong>Development</strong>
    environment by setting the <strong>ASPNETCORE_ENVIRONMENT</strong>
    environment variable to <strong>Development</strong>
    and restarting the app.
</p>
```

You can see how the error page looks in figure 10.3.

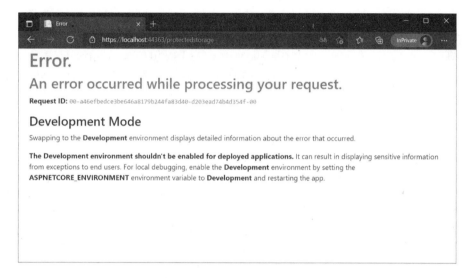

Figure 10.3   The error page when the application is not in development mode

Users see only a very generic error message ("An error occurred while processing your request"), without any additional information (you can still deduce that ASP.NET Core was involved, though). If a request ID is available, it will be shown. This request ID is generated as follows:

```
Activity.Current?.Id ?? HttpContext.TraceIdentifier
```

Displaying such an ID does not leak sensitive information, since the ID itself does not contain any valuable information. The benefit is that if the application is logging additional exception details, this request ID might also be logged along with it. Then users might send a support request, stating detailed information about how to reproduce the error and providing the request ID. Thus, it might be easier to find out the root of the problem by combining the user report with the information logged on the server.

> **NOTE** Personally, I'd get rid of the information about the development mode (the <h3> element and the two paragraphs that follow it) first, since it does not provide any value, except for making some attackers curious.

The error-handling page gets access to the exception information by using the `IExceptionPathHandlerFeature` interface from the `Microsoft.AspNetCore.Diagnostics` namespace. It can be used in `OnGet()` for Razor Pages and Blazor applications and in the action method for the error page in MVC applications (the template uses the `Error()` method in the `HomeController` class). This code snippet shows how it works:

```
var exceptionData = HttpContext.Features.Get<IExceptionHandlerPathFeature>();
```

The `exceptionData` variable has two relevant properties:

- `Error`—The original exception
- `Path`—The original path as a string

This information may be used both for proper logging (see chapter 11 for how to do this) and for handling specific errors differently. For instance, exceptions occurring in a restricted area of the web application might trigger a different kind of error page than unhandled errors in the public area.

It is also possible to implement specific error pages depending on the HTTP status code the server sends to the client.

10.1.2 Status code error pages

We have already seen that some browsers autogenerate "smart" error pages for certain HTTP status codes. The attempt is laudable, since not everyone knows what HTTP 404 or HTTP 500 means. Yet it does make sense to specifically control what users are seeing. Generating the error pages ourselves maintains a common UI for all parts of our web application.

ASP.NET Core comes with another piece of middleware that decides which error page to use depending on the HTTP status code. This applies whenever an HTTP status code that suggests that an error occurred will be returned—basically, that means a value between 400 and 599. This call in Program.cs activates the middleware:

```
app.UseStatusCodePagesWithReExecute("/Error/{0}");
```

The argument to that method call is the pattern for the URL of the error page. The HTTP status code is used where the `{0}` placeholder is. In the case of HTTP 404 (file not found), the content of /Error/404 is returned to the user. The HTTP status code is still 404, though.

Let's assume we create a page called *404.cshtml* and place it in our application so that it would be accessible via /Error/404. With the aforementioned call to `UseStatusCodePagesWithReExecute()`, requesting a resource that does not exist would lead to a result similar to figure 10.4.

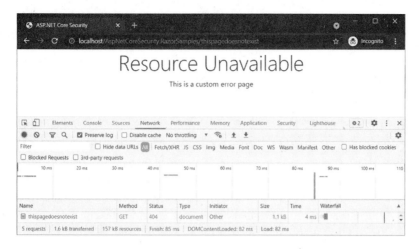

Figure 10.4 Displaying a custom error page

Note the URL trying to load a file that most certainly does not exist. The server responds with our custom error page. As you can see in the browser developer tools, the HTTP status code is still, correctly, `404`.

If you want to actually redirect to the associated error page, use the `UseStatus-CodePagesWithRedirects()` method instead:

```
app.UseStatusCodePagesWithRedirects("/Error/{0}");
```

The different behavior can be seen in figure 10.5. Accessing the URL that yields the error leads to an `HTTP 302` redirect to the status-code-specific error page. That error page is then returned with HTTP status code `200 OK`.

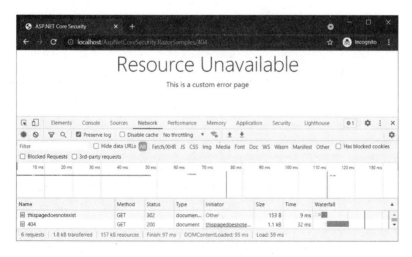

Figure 10.5 The application redirects to the error page.

NOTE There is one more piece of middleware for status codes—
`UseStatusCodePages()`. Those "pages" basically return the status code and
name as text, so they are rarely used.

The same advice applies to APIs as well; however, an error "page" is not always what
we want.

10.2   *Handling errors in APIs*

Perhaps surprisingly, the `UseDeveloperExceptionPage()` method also works for
APIs. When requesting an API resource in the web browser, the exception page
appears as it does with regular ASP.NET Core applications. When using another client
(which sends a different HTTP `Accept` header that does not contain `text/html`,
such as `*/*`), the server returns data as shown in figure 10.6. The stack trace with the
exception information is returned as plain text.

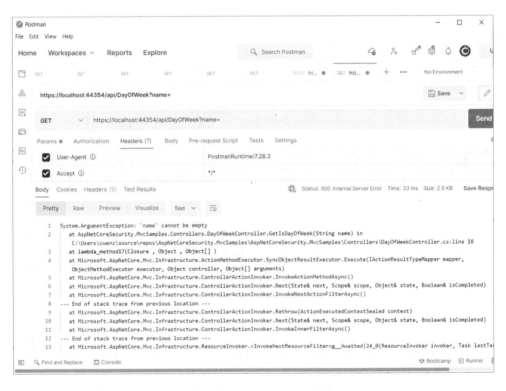

Figure 10.6   Postman requests the API with `Accept: */*`, and the server returns plain text.

For production purposes, a less detailed output of errors is required. Since RESTful
APIs rely on HTTP status codes anyway, returning `404`, `500`, and other error states is
usually "good enough." Yet, the IETF has proposed a standard for a format for error

details for APIs. It was assigned RFC 7807 and is available at https://datatracker .ietf.org/doc/html/rfc7807. The idea is to include some error details in the payload of the HTTP response in a predictable format. Here is a typical output according to that RFC:

```
{
    "type": "https://tools.ietf.org/html/rfc7231          Points to the error status
    #section-6.6.1",                                      in the HTTP specification
    "title": "An error occurred while processing          Displays
    your request.",                                       Error title
    "status": 500,                                         Shows HTTP
    "traceId": "00-486e3f8ca16f1c49a444390706029d28-       status code
[CA]ff3d9cf43f42d04c-00"                    Shows
}                                           trace ID
```

ASP.NET Core Web API comes with built-in support for this standard. The `ControllerBase` class, where API controllers derive from, contains the `Problem()` method, which returns a correctly formatted response according to RFC 7807. The minimal error controller in the following listing shows a bare-bones but effective implementation for a suitable error page.

Listing 10.2   API error page according to RFC 7807

```
using Microsoft.AspNetCore.Mvc;

namespace AspNetCoreSecurity.MvcSamples.Controllers
{
    [Route("[controller]")]
    [ApiController]
    public class ApiErrorController : ControllerBase
    {
        public IActionResult Error() => Problem();
    }
}
```

The API method in the controller just returns the result of a call to `Controller-Base.Problem()`. All that remains to be done is to set up that endpoint as the "error page," similarly to before. This happens, as usual, in Program.cs:

```
app.UseExceptionHandler("/apierror");
```

To test this new behavior, we use the simple API controller from the next listing.

Listing 10.3   An API controller that may throw an exception

```
using Microsoft.AspNetCore.Mvc;

namespace AspNetCoreSecurity.MvcSamples.Controllers
{
    [Route("api/[controller]")]
    [ApiController]
```

```
public class DayOfWeekController : ControllerBase
{
    private string[] _daysOfWeek = new[] {
        "Sunday",
        "Monday",
        "Tuesday",
        "Wednesday",
        "Thursday",
        "Friday",
        "Saturday"
    };

    public bool GetIsDayOfWeek(string name)
    {
        if (string.IsNullOrEmpty(name))
        {
            throw new ArgumentException(
                "`name` cannot be empty");          ◁── Throws an exception if the
        }                                                Name parameter is empty
        return _daysOfWeek.Contains(name);
    }
}
}
```

Calling that API endpoint without the `name` parameter (or with an empty string) triggers an `ArgumentException`. This exception is uncaught and will result in HTTP status `500`. Thanks to our configuration, the error page kicks in, as figure 10.7 shows.

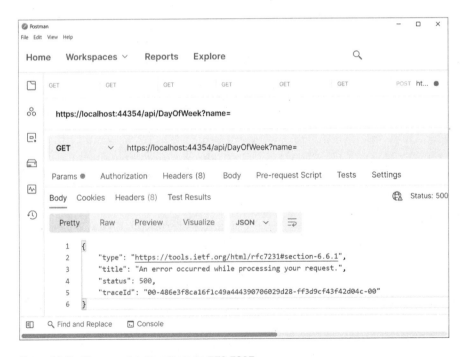

Figure 10.7   The error details adhere to RFC 7807.

The basic information about the error—its type, status code, and a trace ID—is returned as JSON.

> **NOTE** As we saw earlier in this chapter, the modular nature of ASP.NET Core allows us to inject our own logic into the `UseExceptionHandler()` call. For an API, this includes setting the proper HTTP status code and defining the exact data being returned.

Summary

Let's review what we have learned so far:

- Sending detailed error information might provide an attacker with valuable inside information, allowing more targeted (and successful) attacks.
- The developer exception page from ASP.NET Core is strictly applicable in a development environment only, preventing information leakage on the production system.
- A custom error handler defines both the behavior and the UI of an error page, should an unhandled exception occur. This allows proper error handling on the server and a "friendly" error page for users.
- ASP.NET Core can automatically display or redirect to error pages, depending on the HTTP status code that the server responds with.
- ASP.NET Core Web APIs support developer exception pages as well—in text form, if the client requires it.
- RFC 7807 defines a format for API exceptions, which is supported by ASP.NET Core Web API out of the box.

We have now made sure that our users do not receive any excessive information about issues that happen on the server. In the next chapter, we will switch sides and help developers get to the root of any issues by logging data and performing automated health checks.

Logging and health checks

This chapter covers

- Logging within web applications and using monitoring
- Learning how ASP.NET Core health checks work
- Adding a UI to display the application state, based on the health checks
- Introducing the ASP.NET Core logging system
- Identifying which target systems can be used for log entries

So far, this book has attempted to make sure that an application is secure and that all attacks are futile. In theory, our websites are now in good shape. But, as the famous saying goes, "in theory there is no difference between theory and practice, while in practice there is" (incorrectly attributed to various sources, but Benjamin Brewster coined that first in 1882: https://quoteinvestigator.com/2018/04/14/theory/). Something will always go wrong eventually, and the application needs to be prepared for that. Note that this is the first chapter in the book that does not start with a specific attack or case study. Instead, the topics covered here are an important ingredient of a holistic security strategy, without specific attacks assigned to them. This trend will continue throughout the remainder of the book.

There are two ingredients to being prepared in case of an application failure: monitoring needs to be in place to find out if something went wrong, and the application needs to log everything that might be useful later to find out what happened. ASP.NET Core offers two options out of the box: ASP.NET Core health checks as an API to facilitate application monitoring, and a robust logging infrastructure in ASP.NET Core (actually in .NET) itself. This helps to mitigate the two associated risks: not noticing that something went wrong and not being able to find out why.

11.1 Health checks

ASP.NET Core health checks are HTTP (or, better, HTTPS) endpoints that provide the health status of a web application. They can be periodically polled to find out whether the application still works within the defined parameters and to take appropriate action if it doesn't. Unfortunately, this does not all happen automatically; the health checks need to be configured properly to deliver any value.

Setting up health checks in an ASP.NET Core application consists of several steps. First, the health checks middleware needs to be registered; then we need to implement the individual health checks.

11.1.1 Health check setup

First of all, the NuGet package `Microsoft.AspNetCore.Diagnostics.Health-Checks` needs to be installed into the application. The starting point for code is the `Program` class where the services are configured. We are using the project template with Razor Pages, but it would be no different with MVC. There, the `AddHealth-Checks()` method registers the heath check middleware with the application. In the same class, you can provide an endpoint for all the health checks (which are yet to be implemented!). Use the `MapHealthChecks()` method within a call to `Use-Endpoints()`:

```
using Microsoft.AspNetCore.Diagnostics.HealthChecks;

var builder = WebApplication.CreateBuilder(args);

builder.Services.AddHealthChecks();          ◁──┐ Loads the
builder.Services.AddRazorPages();                │ middleware

var app = builder.Build();

...

app.UseEndpoints(endpoints =>
{
    endpoints.MapRazorPages();                    │ Defines the health
    endpoints.MapHealthChecks("/health");   ◁──┘ checks API endpoint
});

app.Run();
```

The `MapHealthChecks()` method expects the URI from which the health status of the application may be retrieved. `/health` is a common name, but you may choose whatever you deem viable. Loading that endpoint in the browser leads to the result shown in figure 11.1.

Figure 11.1   **The application is (still) in a healthy state.**

The application is in a healthy state! Time to celebrate? Not yet—we haven't implemented any *actual* health checks yet. By default, the application is considered healthy.

The return value of the call to `services.AddHealthChecks()` is of type `IHealthChecksBuilder`. This already suggests that we may use a fluent API to add several health checks. And this is exactly what the `AddCheck()` method does. We basically need two arguments: the name of the check and its implementation. The return value of the latter needs to be of the type `HealthCheckResult` (also defined in `Microsoft.Extensions.Diagnostics.HealthChecks`). This is a struct that supports three methods:

- `Healthy()`—The application works as expected.
- `Degraded()`—The application does not work as expected but is still in a usable state.
- `Unhealthy()`—The application does not work as expected.

Note that the return values created by these three methods do not have any functional consequences but provide a very useful categorization. Here is a simple implementation that sets a different health status each second:

```
builder.Services
    .AddHealthChecks()
    .AddCheck("Changing health states", () =>
    {
        return (DateTime.Now.Second % 3) switch
        {
            0 => HealthCheckResult.Healthy(),
            1 => HealthCheckResult.Degraded(),
            _ => HealthCheckResult.Unhealthy(),
        };
    });
```

If the second value of the current time is 0, 3, 6, and so on, the application is returning the `Healthy` state; for 1, 4, 7, . . . , `Degraded` will be used. In all other cases, an Unhealthy state is reported. When reloading the health check endpoint, you should now see a different result every second—for instance, the Degraded one, as in figure 11.2.

Figure 11.2   The application is now (temporarily) Degraded.

It does not seem wise to put implementation details such as health check logic into the Program class, though. A better place for that is in a class of its own. All health checks need to implement the IHealthCheck interface, which contains exactly one method:

```
public Task<HealthCheckResult> CheckHealthAsync(HealthCheckContext context,
➥CancellationToken cancellationToken = default)
```

The following listing shows the refactored implementation of the previous health check. Basically, the health check implementation was moved to a new class.

Listing 11.1   A health check in its own class

```
using Microsoft.Extensions.Diagnostics.HealthChecks;

namespace AspNetCoreSecurity.RazorSamples.Classes
{
    public class ChangingHealthStates : IHealthCheck
    {
        public Task<HealthCheckResult> CheckHealthAsync(HealthCheckContext-
        ➥context, CancellationToken cancellationToken = default)
        {
            return (DateTime.Now.Second % 3) switch
            {
                0 => Task.FromResult(HealthCheckResult.Healthy()),
                1 => Task.FromResult(HealthCheckResult.Degraded()),
                _ => Task.FromResult(HealthCheckResult.Unhealthy()),
            };
        }
    }
}
```

The only actual code change was to add Task.FromResult() due to the asynchronous nature of the interface's method.

Back in the `Program` class, the new health check class (here: `ChangingHealth-States`) can be added to the list of health checks as follows:

```
builder.Services
    .AddHealthChecks()
    .AddCheck<ChangingHealthStates>("Changing health states");
```

The `AddCheck()` call supports three extra parameters:

- `failureStatus`—The status to use when there is a failure in the health check itself. The enum `HealthStatus` contains the three possible values, `Healthy`, `Degraded`, and `Unhealthy`.
- `tags`—A list of strings that serve as tags for the health checks. Those strings are arbitrary but may be later used to group health checks; for instance, API-related health checks versus web application–related ones.
- `timeout`—This `TimeSpan` value sets the amount of time to wait for the health check's result before failure is assumed.

If you are using more than one health check, the worst result of all individual health checks is used (`Unhealthy` is worse than `Degraded` is worse than `Healthy`). The health check endpoint therefore returns only one value. Consider these three health checks:

```
builder.Services
    .AddHealthChecks()
    .AddCheck("good", () => HealthCheckResult.Healthy())
    .AddCheck("so-so", () => HealthCheckResult.Degraded())
    .AddCheck("bad", () => HealthCheckResult.Unhealthy());
```

The string returned from the health check endpoint will always be `Unhealthy`, since this is the worst individual check result.

11.1.2 *Advanced heath checks*

All the existing health checks are pretty dumb—they just return a result independent of the actual state of the application. It's obvious what needs to happen: the concrete health check implementation needs to verify the health of the site. For common scenarios, though, several helper packages exist. Just search for "HealthCheck" in Visual Studio's NuGet package manager (figure 11.3), or scan NuGet for packages starting with `AspNetCore.HealthChecks`.

> **NOTE** The namespace does *not* start with `Microsoft`, so these are third-party contributions, not supported by Microsoft.

The screenshot shows a sample of the available options, but as you can see, there is support for both specific databases (such as MongoDB) and for other specific use cases (like URIs). Table 11.1 shows a few of the most popular options (by number of downloads at the time of this writing).

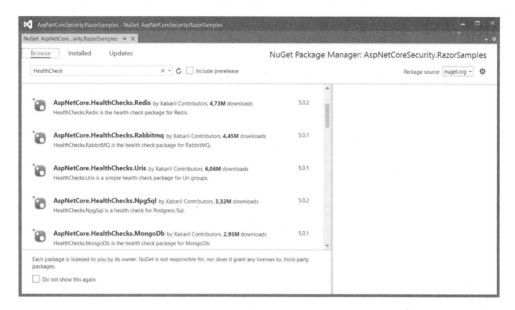

Figure 11.3   Some of the many health checks already implemented

Table 11.1   Selection of health check packages

Package name within the `AspNetCore.HealthChecks` namespace	Description
SqlServer	Microsoft SQL Server database
Uris	URIs
Redis	Redis in-memory database
Rabbitmq	RabbitMQ message broker
NpgSql	PostgreSQL database
MogoDb	MongoDB database

As mentioned, these are community efforts, not official Microsoft initiatives. The GitHub repository at http://mng.bz/gw0v hosts close to 50 different health checks; the list at http://mng.bz/e7GV gives you a good overview. Let's try one of those options.

The `AspNetCore.Diagnostics.HealthChecks.Uris` package checks whether a URI, or a group of URIs, still responds. If there's a response, by default, it needs to have an HTTP status code between 200 and 299. The library waits up to 10 seconds for a result, so it might make sense to decrease this value. This is how it's done:

```
services
    .AddHealthChecks()
    .AddUrlGroup(
        new Uri("https://www.manning.com/"),        ◁──┐   Shows the URI
        timeout: TimeSpan.FromSeconds(3)),                  or URIs to check
        tags: new string[] { "URIs" });       ◁──┐      ◁──┐  Decreases the timeout
                                                              value to three seconds
                      Using a tag is optional.
```

Typically, this health check returns `Healthy`, since the Manning website is up and running 24/7. When you are testing the ASP.NET Core application locally and then cut your internet connection, you will get `Unhealthy`.

11.1.3 *Formatting the output*

Remember the three available `HealthCheckResult` methods—`Healthy()`, `Degraded()`, and `Unhealthy()`? They accept two optional arguments: an error description and additional data in the form of a dictionary. As of now, this extra information is not used, and neither is the list of tags that we may have assigned to some of the health checks. We are about to change that, starting with the tags.

When setting up the health check API endpoints, we can provide a predicate that lets us filter health checks by their tags or any other criteria. The setting is, aptly, called `Predicate`. The following setting creates the */health-uris* endpoint, which contains only health checks that have a tag that includes `"URIs"`:

```
endpoints.MapHealthChecks(
    "/health-uris",
    new HealthCheckOptions()
    {
        Predicate = (item) => item.Tags.Contains("URIs")
    });
```

> **TIP** An easy way to provide an endpoint that does not run any health checks but can still be used to find out whether the actual application is running is by using this predicate: `_ => false`.

But what about the other health check metadata, like the error description? It could be used to display more information for administrators about what went wrong, perhaps presented via a dashboard. ASP.NET Core offers functionality out of the box here. This is not provided by Microsoft, though, but by the same team that was also responsible for the additional health checks listed in this section.

11.1.4 *Health checks UI*

To add a dashboard for ASP.NET Core health checks, you need to install at least two of the following three NuGet packages to get a UI running in no time:

- `AspNetCore.HealthChecks.UI`—A package that displays the health check information

- AspNetCore.HealthChecks.UI.Client—Abstractions that the UI is relying upon
- AspNetCore.HealthChecks.UI.InMemory.Storage—In-memory database support for storing health check information

The last package is not mandatory; any database store may be used. With the in-memory provider, the installation and configuration efforts are almost zero.

Then, two steps similar to those for adding health check support apply. First, add the health checks UI middleware in the ConfigureServices() method, and configure it to use in-memory storage:

```
services
    .AddHealthChecksUI()
    .AddInMemoryStorage();
```

Then, in the Configure() method, register the health checks UI:

```
app.UseEndpoints(endpoints =>
{
...
    endpoints.MapHealthChecksUI();
});
```

You will notice that no additional configuration has been used. But where does the UI get all the information from? So far, all HTTP endpoints have returned only a simple string with the absolute health state for the application.

It turns out that there are two extra steps required. First of all, we need to create an endpoint the UI may use. This endpoint must return all data about all the health checks. Within a MapHealthChecks() call, you may use the ResponseWriter option to provide code that then converts the health check information into a format of your choosing. The health check UI already comes with such a helper class that generates exactly the format required. It is called UIResponseWriter.WriteHealthCheckUIResponse and comes from the AspNetCore.HealthChecks.UI.Client package. Here is how you can set up this new endpoint:

```
endpoints.MapHealthChecks(
    "/health-ui",              ◁──┐ Shows the
    new HealthCheckOptions()      │ endpoint URI
    {
        ResponseWriter =
        ⟹UIResponseWriter.WriteHealthCheckUIResponse,   ◁──┐ Makes sure that the correct
        Predicate = _ => true                              │ format is generated
    });
```

The predicate _ => true ensures that all health checks are used. Feel free to alter that if you only want to have select health checks appear in the UI. The following listing shows the full Program class with all relevant health check code in bold.

Listing 11.2   Setting up health checks and the health checks UI

```
using AspNetCoreSecurity.RazorSamples.Classes;
using HealthChecks.UI.Client;
using Microsoft.AspNetCore.Diagnostics.HealthChecks;

var builder = WebApplication.CreateBuilder(args);

builder.Services
    .AddHealthChecks()
    .AddCheck<ChangingHealthStates>("Changing health states")
    .AddUrlGroup(
        new Uri("https://www.manning.com/"),
        tags: new string[] { "URIs" },
        timeout: TimeSpan.FromSeconds(3));
builder.Services
    .AddHealthChecksUI()
    .AddInMemoryStorage();

builder.Services.AddRazorPages();

var app = builder.Build();

if (!app.Environment.IsDevelopment())
{
    app.UseExceptionHandler("/Error");
    app.UseHsts();
}

app.UseHttpsRedirection();
app.UseStaticFiles();

app.UseRouting();

app.UseAuthorization();

app.UseEndpoints(endpoints =>
{
    endpoints.MapRazorPages();
    endpoints.MapHealthChecks("/health");
    endpoints.MapHealthChecks(
        "/health-ui",
        new HealthCheckOptions()
        {
            ResponseWriter = UIResponseWriter.WriteHealthCheckUIResponse,
            Predicate = _ => true
        });
    endpoints.MapHealthChecks(
        "/health-uris",
        new HealthCheckOptions()
        {
            Predicate = (item) => item.Tags.Contains("URIs")
        });
```

```
    endpoints.MapHealthChecksUI();
});

app.Run();
```

If you call the new endpoint in your browser (we were using */health-ui*, but you may change that if needed), the output may look like this (formatted for legibility):

```
{
    "status": "Unhealthy",
    "totalDuration": "00:00:01.1661514",
    "entries": {
        "Changing health states": {              ◁──┐ Results from the time-
            "data": {},                               dependent health check
            "duration": "00:00:00.0007781",
            "status": "Unhealthy",
            "tags": []
        },                                        ┌─ Results from the
        "uri-group": {                        ◁──┘  URI health check
            "data": {},
            "duration": "00:00:01.1606426",
            "status": "Healthy",
            "tags": [
                "URIs"
            ]
        }
    }
}
```

As you can see, all the check's information shows up. Had we set the additional data property for the health check, those values would be part of the output as well.

The stage is set for the health checks UI, but it still doesn't know which endpoint to use. We could use configuration options when calling `MapHealthChecksUI()`, but a more scalable approach is to use a configuration setting. We will use appsettings.json for that task, and you may use different versions of that file for different target systems, as chapter 7 covered in depth. In that file, add configuration settings in this fashion:

```
{
...
  "HealthChecksUI": {
    "HealthChecks": [
      {                                           ┌─ Shows the title of the health
        "Name": "Razor Site Health Checks",   ◁──┘  checks to be displayed in the UI
        "Uri":  "https://localhost:5001/health-ui"  ◁──┐ Shows the URI of
      }                                                 the new endpoint
    ]
  }
}
```

In the different system-specific appsettings.json files, you can alter the URI for the health check endpoint accordingly. And that's it—by default, the health check UI is using */healthchecks-ui* as the endpoint name. Calling that URI in the browser leads to a result similar to that shown in figure 11.4.

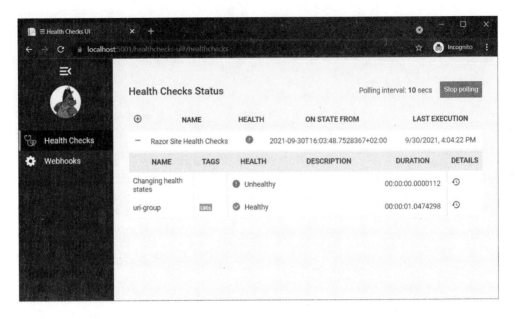

Figure 11.4   The health checks UI in action

Securing health check endpoints

So far, the health check endpoints may be accessed by anyone; that also includes the health checks UI. It makes perfect sense to limit the availability of that information.

One approach is to provide a list of allowed hosts where the endpoints are available. You could greenlight certain systems, blocking all others. The `RequireHost()` method does exactly that:

```
endpoints
    .MapHealthChecks("/health")
    .RequireHost("example.com");
```

When you do want health checks on publicly accessible websites—and chances are that you do—then using the standard ASP.NET Core authentication middleware is the easiest solution:

```
endpoints
    .MapHealthChecks("/health")
    .RequireAuthorization();
```

We can now query our application as to whether it is running as expected (depending on what we are testing within the health checks). But once something goes wrong, we need to be able to dig and retrace what happened. Logging is the first step toward that goal.

11.2 Logging

The default ASP.NET Core templates include logging out of the box, even if it might not be obvious at first sight. The call to `Host.CreateDefaultBuilder()` in the `Program` class sets up some useful standard behavior, such as loading the appropriate appsettings.json files (see chapter 7 for detailed coverage). In addition, it also loads several logging providers, which are then directly available within the application:

- `Console`—For logging to the console window
- `Debug`—For logging to the debug output window, or */var/log/syslog* on macOS and Linux (some distributions use */var/log/message*)
- `EventSource`—For logging to an event source
- `EventLog`—For logging into the Windows event log (which makes this functionality OS-dependent)

11.2.1 Creating log entries

The main interface to use for logging is `ILogger<T>`, which looks like this:

```
public interface ILogger<out TCategoryName> : ILogger
{
    IDisposable BeginScope<TState>(TState state);

    bool IsEnabled(LogLevel logLevel);

    void Log<TState>(LogLevel logLevel, EventId eventId,
        TState state, Exception exception,
        Func<TState, Exception, string> formatter);
}
```

Begins a logical scope

Indicates whether a given log level is enabled

Creates a log entry

The main method, of course, is `Log()`, which can be used to create a log entry.

The `ILogger` interface can be made available to a Razor Page's code or to an MVC action method via dependency injection. The non-empty ASP.NET Core templates already contain a sample implementation for that. Here is an excerpt from the `IndexModel` class that comes with the ASP.NET Core Web App template and is used for the `Index` Razor Page:

```
using Microsoft.AspNetCore.Mvc.RazorPages;

namespace AspNetCoreSecurity.RazorSamples.Pages
{
    public class IndexModel : PageModel
    {
        private readonly ILogger<IndexModel> _logger;

        public IndexModel(ILogger<IndexModel> logger)
        {
```

This is the class variable holding the ILogger reference.

Shows the constructor injection

```
        _logger = logger;            ◁─── Stores the ILogger reference
    }                                     in the class variable

...

    }
}
```

The ASP.NET Core Web App (Model-View-Controller) template puts similar code in the `HomeController` class:

```
using Microsoft.AspNetCore.Mvc;

namespace AspNetCoreSecurity.MvcSamples.Controllers
{                                                            Shows the class
    public class HomeController : Controller                 variable holding the
    {                                                        ILogger reference
        private readonly ILogger<HomeController> _logger;    ◁───

        public HomeController(ILogger<HomeController> logger)
        {
            _logger = logger;            ◁─── Stores the ILogger reference
        }                                     in the class variable

...

    }
}
```

Shows the constructor injection → points to constructor

NOTE You don't have the luxury of "works by default" within a class library. You need to add the `Microsoft.Extensions.Logging` NuGet package first.

You will have already noticed the `Log()` method as part of the `ILogger` interface. Let's go through the method parameters one by one:

- `logLevel`—The log level to use
- `eventId`—The ID of the event being logged
- `state`—The value being logged
- `exception`—The associated exception for the log entry
- `formatter`—The formatting function using the state and exception values

There are many more extension methods for `ILogger` (see https://docs.microsoft.com/en-us/dotnet/api/microsoft.extensions.logging.ilogger-1 for a complete list); some even add signatures to `Log()`. The `message` argument that contains the log message, including placeholders, is frequently used. Those placeholders are then replaced with the data from the `args` argument. The following listing shows an exemplary call in the `OnGet()` method of a Razor Page.

Listing 11.3 Logging in a Razor Page

```
using Microsoft.AspNetCore.Mvc.RazorPages;

namespace AspNetCoreSecurity.RazorSamples.Pages
{
```

```
public class LoggingModel : PageModel
{
    private readonly ILogger<LoggingModel> _logger;

    public LoggingModel(ILogger<LoggingModel> logger)
    {
        _logger = logger;
    }

    public void OnGet()
    {
        _logger.Log(
            logLevel: LogLevel.Information,
            message: "Calling OnGet method in {0}",
            args: new string[] { HttpContext.Request.Path });
    }
}
```

Figure 11.5 shows that the log entry shows up when running the application in debug mode and navigating to the Razor Page.

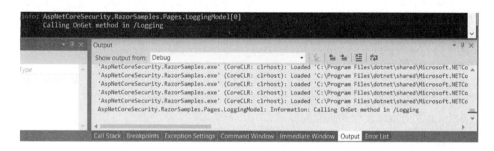

Figure 11.5   **The log entry appears in the console window (top) and debug window (bottom).**

We were using Kestrel, so the console window is up and also gets the log entry. Since we are in debug mode, Visual Studio receives the same message in the output window (this obviously also applies to Visual Studio Code and third-party IDEs).

11.2.2 *Log levels*

The log entry in listing 11.3 uses the Information log level. There are six more. Table 11.2 contains a complete list.

Table 11.2   **Available log level**

Numeric value	Log level name
0	Trace
1	Debug
2	Information

Table 11.2   Available log level *(continued)*

Numeric value	Log level name
3	Warning
4	Error
5	Critical
6	None

Note that there is no functional consequence of choosing one log level (except for log level None, where nothing will be logged). However, the order of log levels is important. To avoid too much noise in the logs, but also to facilitate drilling down to the important bits, using appropriate levels is key. The appsettings.json file from the ASP.NET Core application templates implements default log levels, as the following listing shows.

Listing 11.4   Log level configuration in the application settings

```
{
  "Logging": {
    "LogLevel": {
      "Default": "Information",
      "Microsoft.AspNetCore": "Warning"
    }
  }
}
```

Everything within the Microsoft.AspNetCore namespace will be logged in case of Warnings only (probably assuming that nothing is wrong with ASP.NET Core itself, at least in theory). For our own code, the default behavior is to also log everything with log level Information and upward.

> **TIP**   Remember that you can provide different appsettings.json files for different environments (see chapter 7). You may want to consider logging differently in production than on the development system, for instance.

To save some typing when logging often, there are a few extension methods that have the log level in their names. Admittedly, you lose less than a dozen keystrokes, but it might make the code easier to read. Here are the options:

- LogTrace()
- LogDebug()
- LogInformation()
- LogWarning()
- LogError()
- LogCritical()

Every log level except None is catered for.

11.2.3 Log scopes

The more you log, the more valuable information you will store, but the harder it will be to find it. One way to group log entries is to use scopes. The ILogger interface provides the BeginScope() method for that. It starts a scope, and we can provide a name for it. The next listing uses a request ID for that. Since BeginScope() returns IDisposable, a using statement will be used.

Listing 11.5 Using a log scope

```
using Microsoft.AspNetCore.Mvc.RazorPages;
using System.Diagnostics;

namespace AspNetCoreSecurity.RazorSamples.Pages
{
    public class LoggingModel : PageModel
    {
        private readonly ILogger<LoggingModel> _logger;

        public LoggingModel(ILogger<LoggingModel> logger)
        {
            _logger = logger;
        }

        public void OnGet()
        {
            var requestId = Activity.Current?.Id ?? HttpContext.TraceIdentifier;

            using (_logger.BeginScope("Request {0}", new string[] { requestId }))
            {
                _logger.Log(
                    logLevel: LogLevel.Information,
                    message: "Calling OnGet method in {0}",
                    args: new string[] { HttpContext.Request.Path });

                // ...

                _logger.Log(
                    logLevel: LogLevel.Information,
                    message: "Reaching the end of OnGet method in {0}",
                    args: new string[] { HttpContext.Request.Path });
            }
        }
    }
}
```

All log entries created within that scope are grouped within it. By default, you do not see this in the log entries; it first needs to be configured. Of all the built-in logging providers, only the Console provider supports this feature. The following listing shows what you need to add to the appsettings.json file.

Listing 11.6   Log scope configuration in the application settings

```
{
  "Logging": {
    "LogLevel": {
      "Default": "Information",
      "Microsoft.AspNetCore": "Warning"
    },
    "Console": {
        "IncludeScopes":  true
    }
  }
}
```

Setting `IncludeScopes` to `true` does the trick. Then scoped log entries in the console are prefixed with information about the scope, including our chosen request ID. Figure 11.6 shows what that will look like.

Figure 11.6   Logging with scopes (see the last two entries)

Third-party logging providers

The built-in logging providers of ASP.NET Core, enabled by `CreateDefault-Builder()`, only bring you so far. There are other options, some coming from .NET and from Microsoft, and some originating from third parties. Here are a few options worth looking at.

Three Azure-related logging providers are available in ASP.NET Core: `Application-Insights`, `AzureAppServicesBlob`, and `AzureAppServicesFile`. To activate them, add them to the logging system right after the `CreateDefault-Builder()` call:

```
.ConfigureLogging(builder => builder.AddAzureWebAppDiagnostics())
```

Probably the most popular third-party logging library is Serilog (https://serilog.net/). The main NuGet package is aptly called `Serilog`. A NuGet search for "Serilog" returns literally hundreds of related packages, including sinks (log targets) for almost any format and system. The sink packages start with `Serilog.Sinks` and cover logging to files, various databases, email, other software like Slack, and more.

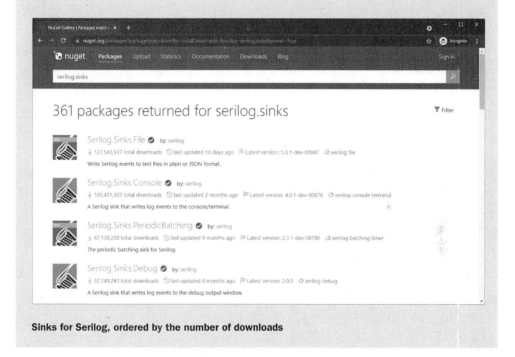

Sinks for Serilog, ordered by the number of downloads

Summary

Let's review what we have learned so far:

- ASP.NET Core health checks provide a mechanism to verify the "health" of an application.
- HTTP endpoints return the application's health status.
- A third-party project provides a UI to display health check information, with minimal configuration.
- Logging to various sinks works out of the box in ASP.NET Core applications.

- Third-party logging libraries provide turnkey solutions for logging to any imaginable target.

This book will continue with a central topic for many applications: proper authentication for regular websites, single-page applications, and APIs.

Part 5

Authentication and authorization

For many websites, users need to be able to log in, and the application needs to decide whether or not users are allowed to perform an action. This gets more complicated when using the same login provider for various sites (single sign-on) or when working with APIs or single-page applications (SPAs).

Chapter 12 introduces ASP.NET Core Identity, the built-in system in ASP.NET Core that allows users to register, sign in and out, and more. In chapter 13, different protocols and standards for security APIs and SPAs are discussed, explained, and implemented.

Securing web applications with ASP.NET Core Identity

This chapter covers

- Using ASP.NET Core Identity for authentication and authorization
- Using scaffolding to tweak the ASP.NET Core Identity UI
- Configuring password options
- Implementing two-factor authentication
- Allowing users to log into an application with a third-party account

At the end of 2011, Microsoft released the MS11-100 security advisory (which basically means number 100 in 2011, which is quite a lot, actually). The title of the document, available at http://mng.bz/pOXK, sounds pretty dramatic: "Vulnerabilities in .NET Framework Could Allow Elevation of Privilege." And, indeed, it was dramatic. In early October of that year, security researchers found a security vulnerability in the built-in ASP.NET user management features. Basically, it was possible to log into an application as an arbitrary user.

The security researchers' writeup (http://mng.bz/44RR) is an interesting read. According to their description of events, six weeks after reporting the vulnerability, they asked Microsoft for a status update; according to the case manager, an update was expected in February or March, so 4 to 6 months after reporting the issue.

Luckily, someone escalated the vulnerability to the right set of people, and Microsoft released an out-of-bands update to ASP.NET as part of MS11-100 and made the then-lead of the ASP.NET team, Scott Guthrie (now executive VP of the Cloud and AI group at Microsoft) write a blog post (http://mng.bz/OoWw) urging his readers to install the patch.

This was not the first time that a patch for .NET or ASP.NET had to be released on a day other than "Patch Tuesday" (which is the second Tuesday each month and the day Microsoft routinely rolls out updates). In September 2010, something similar happened: a severe security vulnerability was found, patched (as Guthrie said then: after working through the weekend), and blogged about at http://mng.bz/YGvz.

I'm not telling this story to make fun of the security record of .NET or ASP.NET. To the contrary, ASP.NET Core especially has had an excellent track record so far (fingers crossed!), and its open source approach to developing makes it easier for more eyes to have a good look at the code's security. The example from 2011 teaches another highly important lesson: issues, once they get reported, get fixed. The internet is full of stories where custom implementations of security features like authentication, session management, or password storage get hacked because they are just not on par with industry standards. And even though ASP.NET messed up once or twice in the past, the technology is under constant scrutiny. So instead of arguing, "I'll roll my own security, because I do not trust the thousands of people developing .NET," you should embrace the de facto standards provided by the framework, and this also includes user management.

The story from 2011 referred to ASP.NET Web Forms, and we are working with something entirely different this time. Still, ASP.NET Core comes with a built-in system for user management: ASP.NET Core Identity (sometimes just referred to as Identity). This chapter will get you started and will show you the most important of the available features and how to tweak them. The goal is not to provide a complete coverage of everything in ASP.NET Core Identity (this might be a task for another book), but to tell you enough for you to be able to use it and to understand how it works and why it is considered secure.

12.1 ASP.NET Core Identity setup

When creating a new ASP.NET Core project, some of the ASP.NET Core Identity features are already built in—if you create the project correctly. The easiest way to do that is to use Visual Studio. Creating a new ASP.NET Core web application, whether you use Razor Pages or MVC, gives you the Authentication Type option as part of the wizard, shown in figure 12.1.

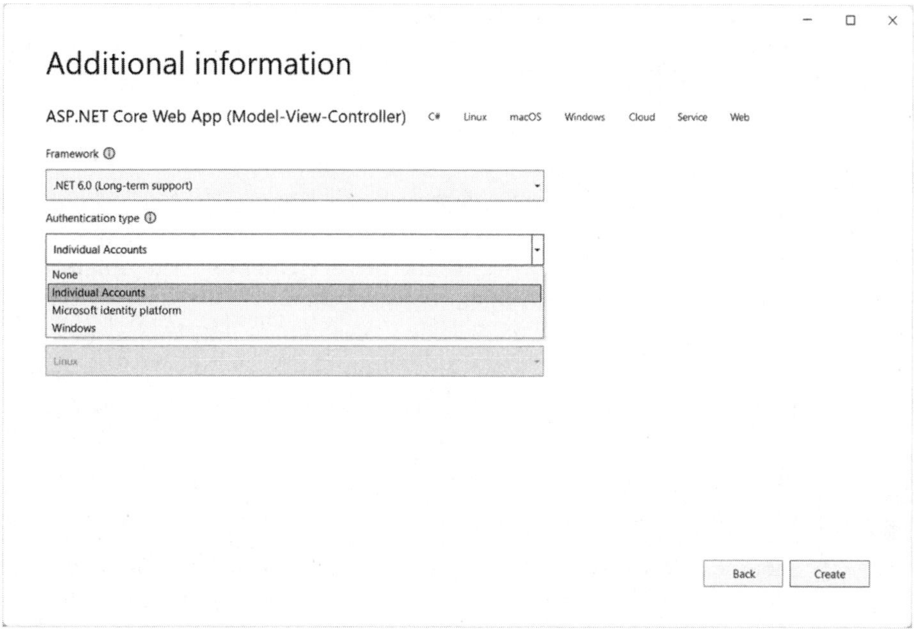

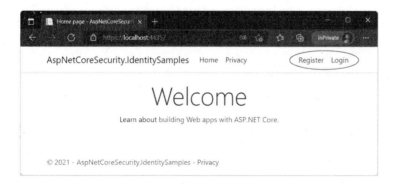

Figure 12.1   Choosing the authentication type in the Visual Studio project creation wizard

If you pick the Individual Accounts option, the application will come with user management out of the box. Launching the application will lead to a home page that looks like the one in figure 12.2. Notice the Register and Login links in the top right corner.

Figure 12.2   The application generated by the template offers registration and login features.

With no additional configuration or code, you can register new users for the application and then log in with those credentials.

   NOTE   If you are using Visual Studio Code or any other IDE, you can still get access to those features—just create the web application using the dotnet

CLI tool. The command `dotnet new webapp --auth Individual -o NameOfApp` does the trick (you can also use `mvc` instead of `webapp` to use MVC instead of Razor Pages).

If you look at the project, you might wonder how that is even possible. The URL of the registration page, for instance, looks similar to https://localhost:12345/Identity/ Account/Register, but there is no view or Razor Page called that. The pages and the implementation logic are "hidden" in the form of a Razor class library. The user data is stored in a LocalDB database within the project; the project template automatically sets that up, including Entity Framework migrations.

But no worries; you can look at the implementation and change every detail of it. The easiest way to get started is to use scaffolding to add the hidden content to the application. In order to do so, right-click the web application project in Visual Studio's Solution Explorer, and choose the Add/New Scaffolded Item option. Choose the Identity option, and wait a few seconds for Visual Studio to initialize code generation in the background.

TIP   If you receive an error message, just click the Add button again, and it will likely work (it's a common bug that seems to pop up from time to time).

The next and final step of the wizard is shown in figure 12.3: you get a list of all the available pages that may be scaffolded.

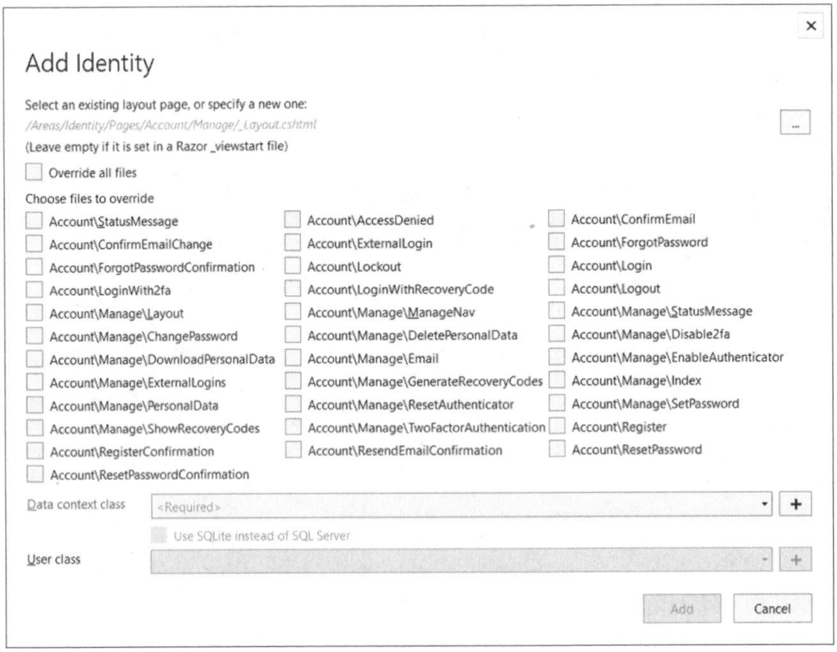

Figure 12.3   Select which views or pages to generate.

It's a long list, and you probably only want to generate those pages that you want to change—for instance, to amend the layout. The Override All Files checkbox activates all the pages, which will lead to generating all of them.

You are also required to pick a data context class. Select one that's already part of the application, or create a new data context. This is used so that the application knows where to store and retrieve user management data. If you already have a class that represents a user in the application, you may provide it in the wizard as well. This step is not mandatory, however.

After a short while, Visual Studio has generated all the required files, so you can now see exactly what the default implementation looks like. Figure 12.4 shows the result of that process in a Razor Pages application; the outcome looks very similar for ASP.NET Core MVC.

The Areas\Identity\Pages\Account folder is filled with over a dozen Razor Pages (most with an associated page class); the Areas\Identity\Pages\Account\Manage folder (not expanded in figure 12.4) contains a similar number of files.

Figure 12.4   The Solution Explorer after scaffolding

Identity scaffolding with the CLI

The scaffolding process is very convenient when using Visual Studio, but a bit more cumbersome when relying on the terminal. Here is what you need to do to get everything up and running. First of all, install the following NuGet packages to your project (using `dotnet add package`):

- `Microsoft.AspNetCore.Identity.EntityFrameworkCore`
- `Microsoft.AspNetCore.Identity.UI`
- `Microsoft.EntityFrameworkCore.SqlServer`
- `Microsoft.EntityFrameworkCore.Tools`
- `Microsoft.VisualStudio.Web.CodeGeneration.Design`
- `Microsoft.EntityFrameworkCore.Design`

Then install the ASP.NET Core code generation tool:

```
dotnet tool install -g dotnet-aspnet-codegenerator
```

(continued)

Finally, run the scaffolding tool. Make sure that you are in the project folder, and run either the `dotnet-aspnet-codegenerator` tool or `dotnet aspnet-codegenerator`. Using `identity -h` as an argument gives you all available options, and `dotnet aspnet-codegenerator identity -lf` provides a list of all files that may be generated. You may then choose what will be scaffolded.

Time to look what the template has to offer! We will use the Razor Pages template, but you will also be able to follow along when using an MVC application, since the base concepts will be the same (just some filenames or URLs may differ).

12.2   *ASP.NET Core Identity fundamentals*

The first place to look for configuration options is in Program.cs (or, when using the configuration pattern from .NET versions prior to 6, Startup.cs). A database context is set up so that ASP.NET Core Identity may store users and other information. The vital setting to add Identity to the project looks like this:

```
builder.Services.AddDefaultIdentity<IdentityUser>(options =>
    options.SignIn.RequireConfirmedAccount = true)
  .AddEntityFrameworkStores<ApplicationDbContext>();
```

The code may look a bit different in your project, especially if you have created classes for the users and for the database context, but in essence, this sets up the Identity system. The code also shows how to set options: just provide them in the lambda expression within the call to the `AddDefaultIdentity()` method (we will look at other configuration options later in this chapter).

Every page in the application contains the Registration and Login links. After logging into the application (and, of course, registering a user first), a Manage and a Logout link appear. This must have been defined in the main template, the Pages\Shared_Layout.cshtml file. We find a reference to a partial called _Login-Partial there:

```
<partial name="_LoginPartial" />
```

The file _LoginPartial.cshtml resides in the same folder and has the following structure:

```
@using Microsoft.AspNetCore.Identity
@inject SignInManager<IdentityUser> SignInManager

@if (SignInManager.IsSignedIn(User))
{
    // Manage/Logout links
}
else
{
    // Register/Login links
}
```

The `SignInManager` that is automatically inserted here via dependency injection provides helper functionality, such as whether a user is logged in. The `User` property contains the current user, if any. The `SignInManager` class also handles logging the user in and out and issues the authentication cookie that is used by ASP.NET Core to recognize the user.

Let's look at the registration page first, *Register.cshtml.* It first and foremost contains a form with an email and a password field. Upon form submission, the `OnPostAsync()` method in the Register.cshtml.cs file is called. The code looks like this (edited and shortened a bit, by removing error handling, comments, logging, and external logins):

```
public async Task<IActionResult> OnPostAsync(string returnUrl = null)
{
    returnUrl ??= Url.Content("~/");
    if (ModelState.IsValid)
    {
        var user = new IdentityUser {
        ➥UserName = Input.Email, Email = Input.Email };       Tries to create
        var result = await _userManager.CreateAsync(         the user
        ➥user, Input.Password);
        if (result.Succeeded)
        {
            var code = await _userManager
            ➥.GenerateEmailConfirmationTokenAsync(user);
            code = WebEncoders.Base64UrlEncode(Encoding.UTF8.GetBytes(code));
            var callbackUrl = Url.Page(
                "/Account/ConfirmEmail",
                pageHandler: null,
                values: new { area = "Identity", userId = user.Id, code = code,
                ➥returnUrl = returnUrl },
                protocol: Request.Scheme);

            await _emailSender.SendEmailAsync(Input.Email,
            ➥"Confirm your email",
                $"Please confirm your account by
                ➥<a href='{HtmlEncoder.Default.Encode(callbackUrl)}'>
                ➥clicking here</a>.");

            if (_userManager.Options.SignIn
            ➥.RequireConfirmedAccount)
            {
                return RedirectToPage(
                ➥"RegisterConfirmation", new {
                ➥email = Input.Email, returnUrl = returnUrl });
            }
            else
            {
                await _signInManager.SignInAsync(
                ➥user, isPersistent: false);
                return LocalRedirect(returnUrl);
            }
        }
    }
    return Page();
}
```

Generates a confirmation token (opt-in) → (points to the `GenerateEmailConfirmationTokenAsync` block)

Sends an opt-in email to confirm the email address (points to the `SendEmailAsync` block)

If a confirmed account is required to sign in, this redirects to the confirmation page. (points to the `RedirectToPage` block)

If no confirmed account is required to sign in, then sign in the user. (points to the `SignInAsync` / `LocalRedirect` block)

There is quite a lot going on in this code, so let's look at everything that happens. First, the code instantiates the `IdentityUser` class, which is the default class to represent a user within ASP.NET Core Identity, with the username and email address.

> **TIP**   If you have chosen a custom user class in the wizard, that's the one that will be used. This enables you to use custom properties for the user (e.g., first name and last name). If you choose to implement that at a later stage, create a new class for your user, inheriting from `IdentityUser`, and replace `IdentityUser` with your new class wherever you find it in the scaffolded code.

The `CreateAsync()` method of the dependency-injected `UserManager` class then attempts to create the user. If that succeeds, the `UserManager` instance then generates a one-time token that will be used to confirm the account—a typical opt-in mechanism. The `GenerateEmailConfirmationTokenAsync()` method, using the previously created `IdentityUser` as an argument, takes care of that. This token is then sent to the provided email address, linking back to the */Account/ConfirmEmail* page (which we will look at in a moment).

By default, the confirmation email functionality is disabled, since email server setups can greatly differ: SMTP, SendGrid, Graph API, and many others. Instead, the RegistrationConfirmation.cshtml.cs file sets the `DisplayConfirmAccountLink` variable to `true`. This means that the confirmation email is not sent; instead, the confirmation link is directly shown after registration. This is, of course, no viable option for a production system—since it allows users to register without validating their email addresses—so this offending line of code needs to be removed:

```
DisplayConfirmAccountLink = true;
```

In order to be able to send an email, ASP.NET Core Identity expects a service fulfilling the `IEmailSender` interface (which is defined in the `Microsoft.AspNetCore` `.Identity.UI.Services` namespace). The class needs to implement the `SendEmailAsync()` method. The implementation details depend on how you want to send the email, but the following listing shows code that uses SMTP, and .NET's `SmtpClient` class. The SmtpClient instance will send the email to the provided recipient.

Listing 12.1   The SMTP email service

```
using Microsoft.AspNetCore.Identity.UI.Services;
using System.Net.Mail;

namespace AspNetCoreSecurity.IdentitySamples.Classes
{
    public class SmtpEmailSender : IEmailSender      ← Implements the
    {                                                  IEmailSender interface
```

```
public Task SendEmailAsync(string email, string subject,
    string htmlMessage)
{
    var smtpClient = new SmtpClient
    {
        Port = 25,
        Host = "localhost",
        DeliveryMethod =
            SmtpDeliveryMethod.Network,
        UseDefaultCredentials = false
    };

    return smtpClient.SendMailAsync(
        "website@localhost", email,
        subject, htmlMessage);
}
}
}
```

Shows the SMTP configuration options

Sends the email

NOTE You will notice that there are some hardcoded values in the code. In a real-world application, these settings will certainly be put into a configuration file (see chapter 7).

In order to make this class available to the ASP.NET Core Identity system, it needs to be registered as a service. Add the following call to Program.cs:

```
builder.Services.AddTransient<IEmailSender, SmtpEmailSender>();
```

After these steps, the confirmation email is sent properly. For convenient local testing, I often use the smtp4dev fake SMTP email server from https://github.com/rnwood/smtp4dev. It comes in the form of a .NET tool and can be installed from the command line as follows:

```
dotnet tool install -g Rnwood.Smtp4dev
```

This installs the smtp4dev executable on the system. When you run it, there are now both an SMTP server available on port 25 and a web UI on ports 5000 (HTTP) and 5001 (HTTPS). Figure 12.5 shows this web interface with a confirmation email coming from ASP.NET Core Identity; the link URL looks like this (the code URL parameter is the token):

```
https://localhost:12345/Identity/Account/
    ConfirmEmail?userId=92c7a...&code=Q2ZESj...&returnUrl=%2F
```

The standard template requires that this confirmation link actually be called. Remember the configuration setting from earlier in this chapter?

```
services.AddDefaultIdentity<IdentityUser>(options =>
    options.SignIn.RequireConfirmedAccount = true)
```

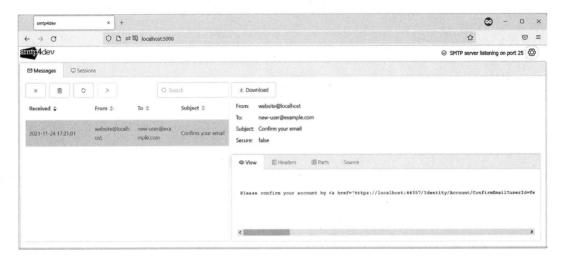

Figure 12.5   The opt-in email with the confirmation link

Setting `SignIn.RequireConfirmedAccount` to `false` would log the user in right after registration. Otherwise, the ConfirmEmail.cshtml page calls the `UserManager`'s `ConfirmEmailAsync()` method, which then verifies whether the code in the confirmation URL is correct. If so, the user is considered confirmed.

The next page to analyze is *Login.cshtml*, which contains a simple HTML form to log in the user. The actual login takes place in the Login.cshtml.cs file and looks like this (once again edited to show just the vital components):

```
public async Task<IActionResult> OnPostAsync(string returnUrl = null)
{
    returnUrl ??= Url.Content("~/");          ◁── Determines the URL to
                                                  redirect to after login
    if (ModelState.IsValid)
    {
        var result = await _signInManager.PasswordSignInAsync(
        ➥Input.Email, Input.Password,
        ➥Input.RememberMe, lockoutOnFailure: false);    ◁── Shows the login using
        if (result.Succeeded)                               the SignInManager
        {
            return LocalRedirect(returnUrl);    ◁── Redirects to the URL
        }                                           determined earlier
    }

    return Page();
}
```

The logic of how to determine whether a username/password combination is correct or not happens in the `SignInManager` instance. This allows ASP.NET Core Identity to support a variety of different database schemes and authentication mechanisms.

The `PasswordSignInAsync()` method not only validates the credentials provided, but also persists the logged-in state of the user (if signing in is successful). By default, a cookie is used for that.

> **NOTE** Logging out works in a similar fashion; this time, the `SignOut-Async()` method of the `SignInManager` instance is used after doing a `POST` request to make CSRF harder (see chapter 4).

Once a user is logged in, the `HttpContext`'s `User` property (which is of type `ClaimsPrincipal`) is populated with the user. `User.Identity` then contains the identity information of the user, including their username (`User.Identity.Name`). This is output in the LoginPartial.cshtml template in the link to the user management page:

```
<a class="nav-link text-dark" asp-area="Identity" asp-page="/Account/Manage/
    Index" title="Manage">Hello @User.Identity?.Name!</a>
```

Being able to log in users is certainly nice, but the most common use case is to provide registered users access to some resources that anonymous users do not have. As you have previously seen, a call to `SignInManager.IsSignedIn(User)` determines whether a user is currently logged in, but this looks like a cumbersome approach to protect individual pages from anonymous access. Instead, it is usually much more convenient to just configure this behavior. The `[Authorize]` attribute, when applied to a Razor Page class, a controller class, or a controller method, protects the associated page or view(s).

> **NOTE** You cannot apply `[Authorize]` to individual Razor Page class methods like `OnGet()` or `OnPost()`. If you want to handle different HTTP methods differently, it's better to use the MVC framework. You may also use the `[AllowAnonymous]` attribute to grant anonymous access to a resource (consider an MVC controller with the `[Authorize]` attribute, where one individual view will be open to anyone). Even if your whole site is protected from unauthorized access, the login page should be available to all.

The next listing shows a simple page that outputs the logged in user's name (similar to before), and listing 12.3 shows the associated page class that protects the resource.

Listing 12.2 The protected page

```
@page
@model AspNetCoreSecurity.IdentitySamples.Pages.ProtectedModel
@{
    ViewData["Title"] = "Protected page";
}

<div class="text-center">
    <h1 class="display-4">Welcome, @User.Identity?.Name</h1>
</div>
```

Listing 12.3   The page class, protecting the page

```
using Microsoft.AspNetCore.Authorization;
using Microsoft.AspNetCore.Mvc.RazorPages;

namespace AspNetCoreSecurity.IdentitySamples.Pages
{
    [Authorize]
    public class ProtectedModel : PageModel
    {
        public void OnGet()
        {
        }
    }
}
```

If no user is logged in, trying to access the protected page (in our example, */Protected*) immediately leads to a redirect URL with the following pattern:

```
https://localhost:12345/Identity/Account/Login?ReturnUrl=%2FProtected
```

The `ReturnUrl` query string parameter contains the URL we actually wanted to load. This makes sure that after login, the application can redirect us back to the original target page. There are two more pieces required to complete the puzzle and make all of this work:

- ASP.NET Core's authentication middleware, among other things, reads out the authentication cookie created after logging in, updates the `User` object, and creates the `ClaimsPrincipal`.
- ASP.NET Core's authorization middleware authorizes the user to access a resource, which the `[Authorize]` attribute relies on.

The relevant calls can be found in the Program.cs file:

```
app.UseAuthentication();
app.UseAuthorization();
```

> **WARNING**   These two calls must be in precisely the order shown (first `Use-Authentication()`, then `UseAuthorization()`). At least the latter must come after a call to `UseRouting()` (to have access to routing information), and both need to happen before `UseEndpoints()` calls (to authenticate prior to endpoint access).

It is also possible to use role-based authorization. Users may have an arbitrary number of roles, and access may be granted only if the user holds at least one fitting role. In order to do so, the `[Authorize]` attribute may be changed like this:

```
[Authorize(Roles="Administrator,Supervisor")]
```

The class responsible for managing roles is `RoleManager`, but it is not injected by default (not all applications need roles). In order to get access to that class, the ASP.NET Core Identity middleware needs to be configured appropriately:

```
builder.Services.AddDefaultIdentity<IdentityUser>(options =>
    options.SignIn.RequireConfirmedAccount = true)
  .AddRoles<IdentityRole>()
  .AddEntityFrameworkStores<ApplicationDbContext>();
```

> **NOTE** The `RoleManager` class is used to create roles. Applying a role to or removing a role from a user is done by the `UserManager` class.

But how does all of this work? The magic lies primarily in the `UserManager` and `SignInManager` implementations that ship with ASP.NET Core. Figure 12.6 shows the database schema that is generated.

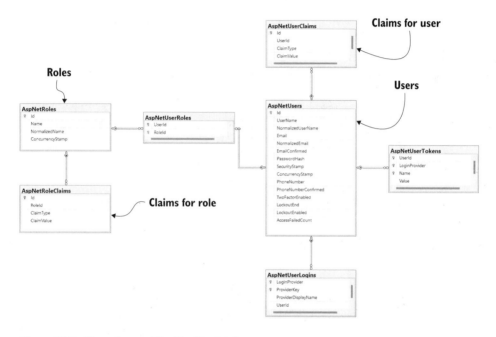

Figure 12.6   **The schema of the Identity database**

Several of the database tables directly map to data and features we have discussed so far:

- `AspNetUsers` contains the users.
- `AspNetRoles` holds all user roles, and `AspNetUserRoles` stores which users hold which roles.
- For users and roles, `AspNetUserClaims` and `AspNetRoleClaims` contain associated claims

Obviously, the database schema follows the best practices from chapter 8. There is no database column for the password; instead, a hash is stored, making a data leak a little bit less catastrophic.

> **NOTE**   If you are curious, the default implementation for password hashing is in this file: http://mng.bz/GEDD. For .NET 6, the hashing algorithm is PBKDF2 with 10,000 iterations. Chapter 8 describes how you can increase this value.

For many common scenarios, this database structure works really well. As soon as you want extra features not covered by the built-in implementation, you can get them just by using the available interfaces.

Instead of doing that, however, let's look at more built-in features that do require some extra configuration.

12.3   Advanced ASP.NET Core Identity features

So far, most of the implementation has been scaffolded for us (which is actually a pretty good starting point). There are many ways to tweak what we have and to explore and implement additional features.

12.3.1   Password options

When registering at the web application, chances are that your first pick of password was rejected. Figure 12.7 shows the associated error message. By default, the password has to meet these criteria:

- At least six characters long
- At least one lowercase letter
- At least one uppercase letter
- At least one digit
- At least one nonalphanumeric character

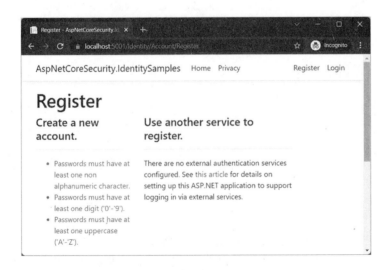

Figure 12.7   The password is not strong enough.

We've already discussed password requirements in chapter 8, arguing that the length of the password is paramount, much more important than whether or not there is a special character in it. Since 2020, NIST has recommended that passwords should be at least eight characters long, and no complexity requirements (uppercase/lowercase letter, digits, special characters) should be used. If we want to apply this rule to our applications, we can configure that in Program.cs when setting the Identity options.

Here are the default settings that include the complexity requirements:

```
services.AddDefaultIdentity<IdentityUser>(options => {
    options.SignIn.RequireConfirmedAccount = true;

    options.Password.RequireDigit = true;
    options.Password.RequiredLength = 6;
    options.Password.RequiredUniqueChars = 1;
    options.Password.RequireLowercase = true;
    options.Password.RequireNonAlphanumeric = true;
    options.Password.RequireUppercase = true;
});
```

The password must contain at least one digit.

The password must be at least six characters long.

The password must contain at least one lowercase letter.

The password must contain at least one character (self-evident).

The password must contain at least one nonalphanumeric character.

The password must contain at least one uppercase letter.

> **NOTE** The `RequiredUniqueChars` option has an effect only for values greater than 1. For instance, if set to 2, the password needs to consist of at least two *different* characters.

If you want to set a minimum password length of eight characters, at least six of which have to be different, and no other restrictions should apply, you can use these settings:

```
services.AddDefaultIdentity<IdentityUser>(options => {
    options.SignIn.RequireConfirmedAccount = true;

    options.Password.RequireDigit = false;
    options.Password.RequiredLength = 8;
    options.Password.RequiredUniqueChars = 6;
    options.Password.RequireLowercase = false;
    options.Password.RequireNonAlphanumeric = false;
    options.Password.RequireUppercase = false;
});
```

There is no setting for maximum password length. And, truth to be told, since passwords must be hashed anyway, there should be no such restriction. The template does limit the password length, but at least to a sensible maximum of 100 characters. This setting is hidden in the `RegistrationModel` (Registration.cshtml.cs file) by using the `[StringLength]` attribute (see chapter 5 for more information). Here is the complete class:

```
public class InputModel
{
    [Required]
    [EmailAddress]
    [Display(Name = "Email")]
    public string Email { get; set; }
```

```
[Required]
[StringLength(100, ErrorMessage =
➡ "The {0} must be at least {2} and at max
➡ {1} characters long.", MinimumLength = 6)]
[DataType(DataType.Password)]
[Display(Name = "Password")]
public string Password { get; set; }


[DataType(DataType.Password)]
[Display(Name = "Confirm password")]
[Compare("Password", ErrorMessage = "The password and confirmation
  password do not match.")]
public string ConfirmPassword { get; set; }
}
```

12.3.2 Cookie options

After successfully authenticating a user, an authentication cookie will be set with a long, impossible-to-guess value. Figure 12.8 shows how this may look like.

Figure 12.8   **The ASP.NET Core authentication cookie with the default settings**

The following cookie settings can be detected by looking at the figure:

- The cookie is called `AspNetCore.Identity.Application`.
- The `HttpOnly` and `secure` flags are set (the latter one only when HTTPS is being used).
- The `SameSite` mode is `Lax`.
- The cookie expires when the browser is closed, so no explicit expiration date is set.

All of these settings—and more!—may be changed in Program.cs by calling the `ConfigureApplicationCookie()` method. Figure 12.9 shows the cookie after applying these settings:

```
Builder.Services.ConfigureApplicationCookie(options =>
    {                                                         ┐ Shows the
                                                              ┘ cookie name
        options.Cookie.Name = "MyAuthenticationCookie";    ◄─┘
        options.Cookie.HttpOnly = true;                         ┐ Shows
        options.Cookie.SecurePolicy = CookieSecurePolicy.Always;  ◄─┘ Secure flag
```

Displays the
HttpOnly flag └─►

Figure 12.9 **The ASP.NET Core authentication cookie with the updated settings**

All the configuration updates are reflected in the cookie, except for the expiration date, which is stored in the payload of the cookie. Two new cookies were created, `ai_user` and `ai_session`, and they implement the expiration window.

12.3.3 *Locking out users*

Punishing users for failed password attempts is a measure with side effects. Temporarily locking out users after a number of incorrect passwords may prevent brute-forcing passwords, but is also an easy mechanism to, well, prevent users from legitimately accessing a web application. If the attacker knows their victim's username, it's easy to lock them out if the application supports that. There are three lockout settings that ASP.NET Core Identity supports:

- `MaxFailedAccessAttempts`—The number of failed login attempts before an account is locked; defaults to five
- `DefaultLockoutTimeSpan`—How long users are locked out of the application; defaults to 5 minutes
- `AllowedForNewUsers`—Whether new users may also be locked out (before even logging in once); defaults to `true`

These options may be applied when calling `AddDefaultIdentity()`; the default values are explicitly set in the following code snippet:

```
services.AddDefaultIdentity<IdentityUser>(options => {
    ...
    options.Lockout.MaxFailedAccessAttempts = 5;
    options.Lockout.DefaultLockoutTimeSpan = TimeSpan.FromMinutes(5);
    options.Lockout.AllowedForNewUsers = true;
});
```

When logging in, using the `SignInManager`'s `PasswordSignInAsync()` method, you can overwrite the locking behavior. One scenario would be that you prioritize usability over security and do not want users to get locked out if someone else knows their username and just randomly tries out passwords. The scaffolded template actually does that by using the following call in the Login.cshtml.cs file:

```
var result = await _signInManager.PasswordSignInAsync(Input.Email,
    ↪Input.Password, Input.RememberMe, lockoutOnFailure: false);
```

12.3.4 *Working with claims*

We have used the term *claims* before in this chapter, albeit only briefly. We saw that `User` is of type `ClaimsPrincipal`, and we also noticed the `AspNetUserClaims` and `AspNetRoleClaims` tables in the automatically created database schema. What exactly is a claim? In the context of ASP.NET Core Identity, a claim is basically a piece of information about a user. Claims were first somewhat standardized in the web services era in the 2000s, when SOAP was still extremely popular, and RESTful APIs using JSON were uncommon, to say the least. The OASIS Open initiative (www.oasis -open.org/) was a joint venture of several organizations (including Microsoft) and tried to set standards for web services. Some of the approaches back then are still in use today, as you will see shortly.

We will add a UI to display the user's claims has and integrate the UI into the already scaffolded application, within the Areas\Identity\Pages\Account\Manage folder. The `User` object has a `Claims` property, which we iterate over and output all contents. The following listing shows how that is done in the newly created Claims.cshtml file.

Listing 12.4 Listing all claims

```
@page
@{
    ViewData["Title"] = "Claims";
    ViewData["ActivePage"] = ManageNavPages.Claims;
}

<h4>@ViewData["Title"]</h4>

<div class="row">
    <div class="col-md-6">
        <p>Here is a list of your claims:</p>
        <p>
            <ul>
                @{
                    foreach (var claim in User.Claims)
                    {
                        <li>@claim.Type: @claim.Value</li>
                    }
                }
            </ul>
        </p>
    </div>
</div>
```

Each claim has a `Type` and `Value` property, which the preceding code outputs in a list. There are two more steps required to make that page appear in the account management UI. First, add two new entries to the `ManageNavPages` class:

```
using Microsoft.AspNetCore.Mvc.Rendering;

namespace
AspNetCoreSecurity.IdentitySamples.Areas.Identity.Pages.Account.Manage
{
    public static class ManageNavPages
    {
...
        public static string Claims => "Claims";
...
        public static string ClaimsNavClass(ViewContext viewContext) =>
        PageNavClass(viewContext, Claims);
...
    }
}
```

Finally, add a new navigation link to the `<ul>` list in the _ManageNav.cshtml file:

```
<li class="nav-item"><a class="nav-link
    @ManageNavPages.ClaimsNavClass(ViewContext)" id="claims" asp-page="./
    Claims">Claims</a></li>
```

The claims page now shows up in the navigation and is also accessible via its direct URL, https://localhost:12345/Identity/Account/Manage/Claims (using your local port number, of course). Figure 12.10 shows a typical output.

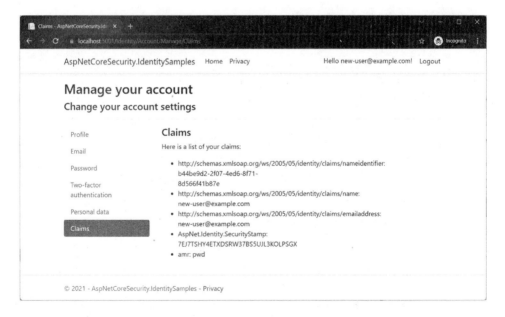

Figure 12.10 All of the user's claims

The user we are logged in with currently has five claims:

- A name identifier (basically the user's unique ID).
- A name (in our case, the email address, since the registration form did not ask for more information).
- An email address.
- A security stamp (which is basically a fingerprint of the user's credentials and changes once the password is updated). This is specific to ASP.NET Core Identity.
- The authentication method used (amr stands for *authentication methods references*); pwd obviously means *password.*

The UserManager class provides a variety of helper methods to handle claims for a given user:

- AddClaimAsync(user, claim)—Adds a new claim to a user
- AddClaimsAsync(user, listOfClaims)—Adds several new claims to a user
- GetClaimsAsync(user)—Retrieves all of a user's claims
- GetUsersForClaimAsync(claim)—Retrieves all users who have a given claim
- RemoveClaimAsync(user, claim)—Removes a claim from a user
- RemoveClaimsAsync(user, listOfClaims)—Removes several claims from a user
- ReplaceClaimAsync(user, oldClaim, newClaim)—Replaces one claim for a user with another one

---

Authorization with claims

Instead of role-based authentication, you could also determine the claims a user has and then decide which of the contents of the current page the user is allowed to see, if any. Policies make that relatively easy. Call AddAuthorization() in Program.cs, set up policies there, and provide the claim that must be present so that the policy is met. Here is how that will look:

```
builder.Services.AddAuthorization(options => {
    options.AddPolicy(
        "ManningAuthors",
        policy => policy.RequireClaim("Publisher", "Manning"));
});
```

Then provide the policy name in the [Authorize] attribute like this:

```
[Authorize(Policy = "ManningAuthors")]
public class ProtectedManningModel : PageModel
```

Both role-based authorization and claims-based authorization have their place. A claim is information about the user, whereas a role is more of a category for users sharing certain security privileges. Choose what suits your application model best. Mike Brind's *ASP.NET Core Razor Pages in Action* (Manning, 2022) covers this in more depth, including code examples.

12.3.5   *Two-factor authentication*

One of the most secure approaches to preventing account theft is to add a second factor to logging in. The process is called *two-factor authentication* (2FA). The second factor (the password being the first one) is often a one-time code, either in a text message or in one of the authenticator apps (those from Google and Microsoft are the most commonly used ones). If the mobile device with the authenticator app stops working, previously generated recovery codes grant a "back door" to the system, allowing login and, for instance, configuring another device.

Conveniently, the scaffolded ASP.NET Core Identity app is already prepared for 2FA, so we can look at the implementation and see how that works and what can be configured. The two-factor authentication section of the management UI (https:// localhost:12345/Identity/Account/Manage/TwoFactorAuthentication), shown in figure 12.11, helps set everything up.

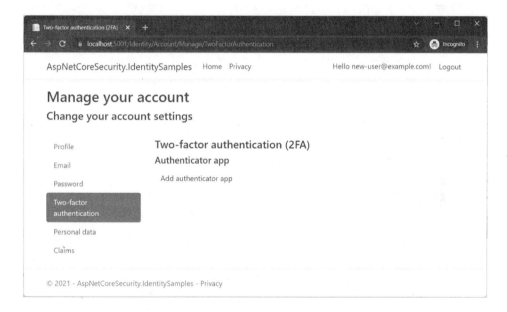

Figure 12.11   The two-factor authentication settings page

But before you attempt to configure the authenticator app, let's first tweak the application a little (which will then make 2FA setup a little bit easier). We need to include a QR code generation library that does not ship as part of the scaffolded templates. The ASP.NET Core team recommends QRCode.js by Shim Sangmin. The code is available on GitHub at https://github.com/davidshimjs/qrcodejs. The code was last updated in 2015, but it still works well (you might still consider scouting for a library that is actively maintained). Also, the library is trivially accessible; you just download one JavaScript file and you're ready to go, without any package management requirements.

A ZIP package with the QR code library is available at http://mng.bz/z4z1. In that archive, find the qrcode.min.js file and copy it to the wwwroot\js folder of the web application. In the same folder, create a file called enableAuthenticator.js with the following content.

Listing 12.5   JavaScript code to create a QR code for authenticator

```
$(function() {
    new QRCode(                          ⟵─ Creates a new
        $("#qrCode")[0],                      QR code
        {                            ⟵─ Provides placeholder where
            text: $("#qrCodeData").data("url"),   the QR code will appear
            width: 150,           ⟵─ Retrieves the URL encoded
            height: 150               in the QR code from the
        });                           qrCodeData HTML element
});
```

This code snippet creates a QR code in a placeholder on the page (with the ID qrCodeData). Include both JavaScript files in the Scripts section of the *EnableAuthenticator.cshtml* page (in the Areas\Identity\Pages\Account\Manage folder):

```
@section Scripts {
    <partial name="_ValidationScriptsPartial" />
    <script src="~/js/qrcode.min.js"></script>
    <script src="~/js/enableAuthenticator.js"></script>
}
```

Make sure that you first load the QR code library, then the custom. Next, locate the following markup in the CSHTML page:

```
<div class="alert alert-info">Learn how to <a href="https://go.microsoft.com/
    fwlink/?Linkid=852423">enable QR code generation</a>.</div>
```

You have already learned how to enable QR code generation, so just remove this <div> element. If you refresh the page, you will see something very similar to figure 12.12.

Use an authenticator app—the most common choices are the ones from Microsoft and Google—and scan the QR code. You will then have an entry in that app for the application and see a time-based one-time password (also called TOTP) that changes every 30 seconds or so (figure 12.13).

> **NOTE**   If you are not happy with the application name shown in the authenticator app, go to the EnableAuthenticator.cshtml.cs file and look for the GenerateQrCodeUri() method. There, you will easily see the string that also shows up in the authenticator app. Change it at will.

Make sure that you type in the current TOTP into the text field on the 2FA page of the application, and click the Verify button. If the TOTP is correct, 2FA is correctly set up. You will also get ten recovery codes that allow you to log into the application even without the device with the authenticator app—but only once per code.

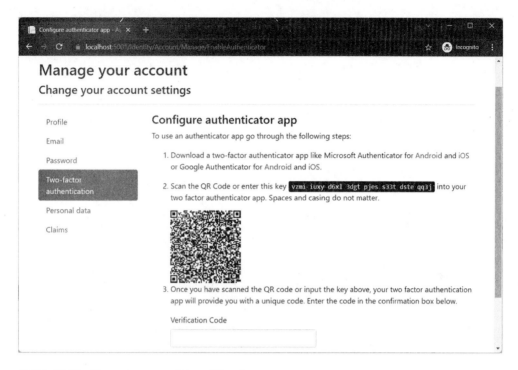

Figure 12.12 The page now contains a QR code.

Figure 12.13 The authenticator app shows a TOTP for the web application.

Next time you try to log in with your username and password, you will be prompted to enter a one-time code from the authenticator app (figure 12.14). You can also click the "You can log in with a recovery code" link and "waste" one of your ten lifelines.

This was pretty seamless to set up, but which APIs were doing the heavy lifting in the background? Spoiler: the UserManager and SignInManager classes contain all we need. The former class takes care of setting up 2FA, and the latter one is used when logging in.

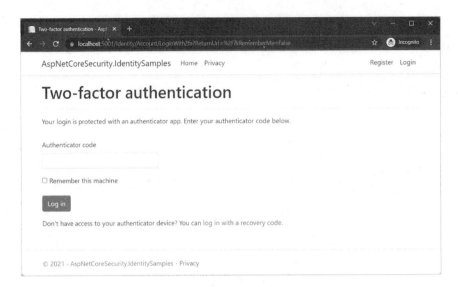

Figure 12.14   Two-factor authentication requires a TOTP to log in.

Let's start with the registration process. The following methods set up the user appropriately:

- `SetTwoFactorEnabledAsync(user, true)`—Enables 2FA for a given user
- `GenerateNewTwoFactorRecoveryCodesAsync(user, count)`—Generates count new recovery codes
- `GetAuthenticatorKeyAsync(user)`—Creates the key used in the authenticator app (the QR code creation will not be covered here)

On the login page (*Login.cshtml.cs*), after validating the credentials, the `SignIn-Manager` class determines whether the user has 2FA enabled. If so, the return value of the `PasswordSignInAsync()` has the `RequiresTwoFactor` property set to `true`. In that case, a redirection to *LoginWith2fa.cshtml* takes place:

```
var result = await _signInManager.PasswordSignInAsync(Input.Email,
Input.Password,
Input.RememberMe, lockoutOnFailure: false);
...
if (result.RequiresTwoFactor)
{
    return RedirectToPage("./LoginWith2fa", new { ReturnUrl = returnUrl,
    RememberMe = Input.RememberMe });
}
```

On that page, the user is prompted to enter the TOTP code the authenticator app is currently displaying. The validation of that code is very easy because the `Sign-InManager` class has all we need. First, the user currently trying to sign in is determined (this is made possible courtesy of a temporary cookie):

```
var user = await _signInManager.GetTwoFactorAuthenticationUserAsync();
```

Then the `TwoFactorAuthenticatorSignInAsync()` validates the authenticator code:

```
var result = await
    _signInManager.TwoFactorAuthenticatorSignInAsync(authenticatorCode,
    rememberMe, Input.RememberMachine);
```

Note that this method does not require the `user` object, because the identity is read from the temporary cookie from earlier. If the user wants to use their recovery codes, they can go to the *LoginWithRecoveryCode.cshtml* page. The page model class again refers the heavy lifting to the `SignInManager`. First, the code validates whether there's really a user trying to sign in:

```
var user = await _signInManager.GetTwoFactorAuthenticationUserAsync();
```

Next, the user-provided recovery code is validated with the aptly named `TwoFactor-RecoveryCodeSignInAsync()` method:

```
var result = await
    _signInManager.TwoFactorRecoveryCodeSignInAsync(recoveryCode);
```

It looks like magic, and the inner workings are not really trivial, but ASP.NET Core Identity comes with an almost ready-to-use solution.

> **NOTE** Since this chapter mentioned text messages as an alternative mechanism for the second factor, the ASP.NET Core documentation has detailed instructions for several SMS services at http://mng.bz/06BJ.

12.3.6 *Authenticating with external providers*

A study claims that the average user has about 100 passwords (see http://mng.bz/KxdX). For some, logging into a third-party application using one of their existing accounts from Google, Facebook, Twitter, Apple, or others is an attractive proposition. Chapter 13 will show more details about this scenario when covering OAuth and OpenID Connect, the standard used for this functionality. But since we already have a scaffolded app and ASP.NET Core Identity supports third-party authentication services, we can take a look.

The implementation details vary between providers, but the usual steps are along the following lines:

1 Install a NuGet package specific to the authentication provider.
2 Register an application with the provider, which should give you app credentials (usually an ID and a secret token).
3 Store those credentials in the ASP.NET Core app, and let the NuGet package and ASP.NET Core Identity do their magic.

As an example, we are using Microsoft accounts for authentication. An application in Microsoft Azure's cloud will serve as the link between our application and the

Microsoft accounts. Be aware that costs may incur for setting up this app. Go to the "App registrations" section in Azure, either by using the search bar on top or by trying this direct link (which obviously is subject to change): https://portal.azure.com/ #blade/Microsoft_AAD_RegisteredApps/ApplicationsListBlade. Click the New Registration link, and register a new application. Figure 12.15 shows the form where you can enter the app details.

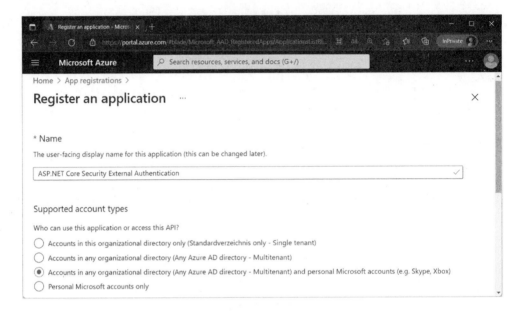

Figure 12.15   Registering an application in Microsoft Azure

Provide a name for the application, and choose the "Accounts in any organizational directory (Any Azure AD directory - Multitenant) and personal Microsoft accounts (e.g., Skype, Xbox)" option. In the "Redirect URI" section, enter a URL consisting of the root of your web application, concatenated with */signin-microsoft*. For our sample application, this results in https://localhost:5001/signin-microsoft, but make sure you use the address of your server. The `signin-microsoft` endpoint does not exist yet; the NuGet package will register it later.

Click Register, and on the page that follows, write down the application ID shown (a long GUID). Then search for the Certificates & Secrets link in the navigation bar on the left-hand side. Click that element, and create a new client secret (you only have to fill out the description). Afterward, you will see something like figure 12.16. The secret value (labeled "Value") is relevant for the next steps, not the GUID labeled "Secret ID.0"

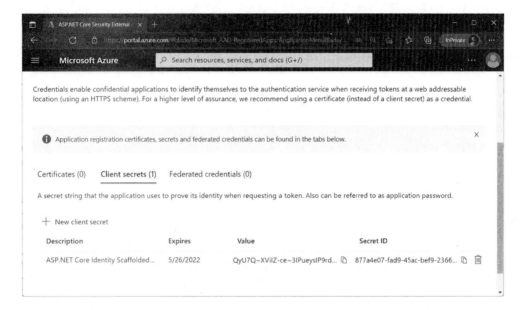

Figure 12.16 The client secret has been created.

Back in the web application, add the application ID from Azure and the secret value to the appsettings.json configuration file (or use some of the other options for storing secrets from chapter 7). The structure and names for those configuration options are arbitrary as long as you use the same approach when reading out this information later:

```
{
  "MicrosoftAuthentication": {
    "AppID": "212ff228-effd-4111-8118-878ade97abad",
    "Secret": "QyU7Q~XViIZ-ce~3IPueysIP9rdZJ_zUjiem~"
  },
  ...
}
```

Now it's time to install the NuGet package that communicates with the Azure app. It is called `Microsoft.AspNetCore.Authentication.MicrosoftAccount`; use the version matching your .NET version.

In Program.cs, look for the `AddAuthentication()` call; if it's not there, add it. The NuGet package defined an extension method called `AddMicrosoftAccount()`. Provide the configuration options from the apsettings.json file in the following fashion:

```
builder.Services.AddAuthentication()
    .AddMicrosoftAccount(options =>
    {
        options.ClientId =
    builder.Configuration["MicrosoftAuthentication:AppID"];
        options.ClientSecret =
    builder.Configuration["MicrosoftAuthentication:Secret"];
    });
```

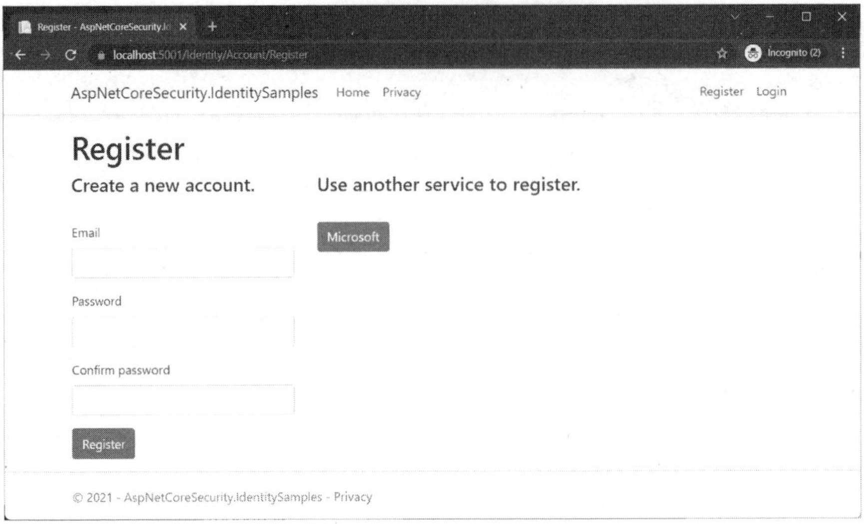

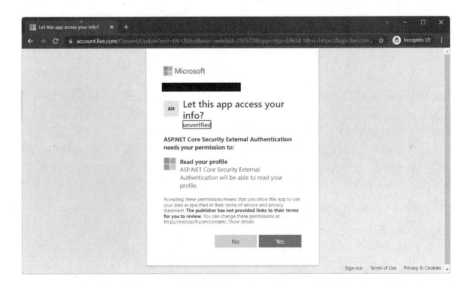

Figure 12.17   The user may now log in with a Microsoft account.

When you launch the application again and try to register an account, you will see that a Microsoft option has appeared (figure 12.17).

When you choose that option, you will be redirected to a Microsoft account login screen. After logging in, you need to give your consent for the application to receive your personal information (basically, the email address). Figure 12.18 shows that screen.

Figure 12.18   The web application wants to access Microsoft account data.

Once you agree, you will be redirected back to the application, where you may need to confirm your email address, and then you will be ready to use the application with a Microsoft account. You can then log into the web app using that account.

From a code perspective, the effort to implement this is quite limited, since the NuGet package takes care of most of the work. In the application itself, the first step is to call the `SignInManager`'s `GetExternalAuthenticationSchemesAsync()` method, which returns all external authentication services registered with the application. The login page uses that to decide which external authentication links to show (remember, figure 12.17 showed a link labeled "Microsoft"). Clicking that link sends an HTTP POST request to the *ExternalLogin.cshtml* page. Here, a redirect to the third-party authentication service's login page is triggered:

Creates the URL the external authentication services redirect back to

```
public IActionResult OnPost(string provider, string returnUrl = null)
{
    var redirectUrl = Url.Page("./ExternalLogin",
    ➥pageHandler: "Callback", values: new { returnUrl });
    var properties = _signInManager.ConfigureExternalAuthenticationProperties
    ➥(provider, redirectUrl);
    return new ChallengeResult(provider, properties);
}
```

Determines provider-specific properties

Prompts the provider to execute a redirect to the third-party site

In the `Callback` method (which kicks in once the third-party authentication site redirects back to the application), the central line of code is once again a call to the `SignInManager`:

```
var result = await
    _signInManager.ExternalLoginSignInAsync(info.LoginProvider,
    info.ProviderKey, isPersistent: false, bypassTwoFactor : true);
```

The `ExternalLoginSignInAsync()` method parses the data coming from the authentication service and can then decide whether the login was successful or not. If the user registers with the external account for the first time, they must register for a local account first (which will then be linked to the external account). Otherwise, the user will have immediate access to the application.

This was just one of over a dozen possible authentication services, but no matter which one you are using, ASP.NET Core Identity's provider model does not require any major code changes to make that work, as long as there's a NuGet package. You can find many more options at http://mng.bz/06BJ. The `aspnet-contrib` project contains many more NuGet packages for external authentication ready to be used in an ASP.NET Core app. Just search for "owners:aspnet-contrib title:OAuth" at http://mng.bz/j26a. As of the time of writing, there were over 80 matches.

Other types of authentication

Using individual user accounts is the most common authentication type for publicly available web applications. There are other options, too, especially for intranet and extranet applications. Here are a few alternative approaches as well as where to find more information on how to use them:

- Windows authentication (http://mng.bz/Wxmg)
- WS-Federation (http://mng.bz/8M8K)
- Certificate authentication (http://mng.bz/EWjq)

Summary

Let's review what we have learned so far:

- ASP.NET Core Identity is an API that can handle all aspects of user management and sign-in management.
- ASP.NET Core comes with a full implementation for user self-management and sign-in management, but you can implement your own.
- Via scaffolding, you can make both the UI and the logic of ASP.NET Core Identity features visible.
- By default, passwords are stored securely (with a hash, using the best practices from chapter 8).
- The [Authorize] attribute can be used to prevent unauthenticated users accessing pages of the web application.
- Resource access may also be limited to certain roles, also using [Authorize].
- Claims are name-value pairs containing information about a user. They may also be used for authorization.
- After a configurable number of failed logins, an account can be locked for a certain amount of time.
- ASP.NET Core Identity supports two-factor authentication (2FA). With little extra effort, the application can generate QR codes that facilitate onboarding of authenticator apps.
- With the aid of specific NuGet packages, users can also register and authenticate with the web application using a third-party account from sites such as Facebook, Google, or Microsoft.

Sign-in management and user management are things that don't always require a custom implementation from scratch—no need to reinvent the wheel every time. ASP.NET Core Identity provides everything required to allow users to log into an application and can be configured and extended to a great degree. For single-page applications (SPAs), some extra work is required. Chapter 13 has all the details.

Securing APIs and
single page applications

Chapter 12 explained ASP.NET Core Identity, which includes full user and sign-in management. This works really well for traditional, page-based web applications. The server issues an authentication cookie, which is automatically returned to the server with each subsequent HTTP request—that's just how cookies work. For APIs or single-page applications (SPAs), this approach is still viable, but rather uncommon. Let's take an API, for instance. It may have clients that are not web browsers (e.g., console applications, desktop applications, or other servers) and as such might not even support cookies. Things get even more complicated if the server doing the authentication (e.g., validating credentials) is different from the one doing the authorization. One server cannot reliably issue cookies for another server, and `SameSite` cookie settings make things even harder.

This chapter will describe several approaches to provide solid authentication and authorization solutions for APIs and SPAs. We will use tokens and look at standards for single sign-on scenarios. Everything will be implemented for ASP.NET Core, relying on .NET features and reliable third-party packages with an excellent track record.

One important note: the main goal of this chapter is to give you an excellent understanding of the security aspects involved and to provide relevant code samples in ASP.NET Core. This chapter will not be able to detail all features available or every third-party library or product. We have selected those which a great user base and an excellent reputation. There are always other options, of course, but we are basically talking about implementation details here. The general approaches are more or less the same, independent of the software components used.

13.1 Securing APIs with tokens

Many applications work with claims—information about users (see also chapter 12, where this concept was first explained). An example of a claim could be the name of the user, their email address, or just the information that they are "currently logged in as a user with administrative privileges." So, how about storing claims in a kind of token and sending that to an API endpoint? In theory, that sounds like a good idea, but to make it work in practice, some additional concerns need to be handled. For example, can you ensure that no one forges a token or tampers with the data in it? A signature would be a good idea, one that only the server that issues the token can verify.

As usual when talking about common security-related problems, researchers and industry practitioners have already found a solution that we can piggyback on. The most common token format for web applications is JWT (JSON Web Token; often pronounced "jot"). The IETF lists JWT as a "proposed standard" under RFC 7519 (https://datatracker.ietf.org/doc/html/rfc7519). A JWT represents a list of claims and uses the JSON syntax. The data in the JSON structure can be signed or encrypted to enable verification and privacy of such a token.

With regard to claims, the JWT token may contain an arbitrary number of them with arbitrary names (as long as there's no collision). However, there are a few registered claim names that are defined in the standard (and commonly used in practice). All of these claims are optional:

- `iss`—The issuer of the JWT
- `sub`—The subject of the JWT (e.g., the username or user ID)
- `aud`—The audience of the JWT, or the intended recipient of the JWT
- `exp`—The expiration date and time of the JWT
- `nbf`—The start time of the JWT validity ("not before")
- `iat`—The issue date and time of the JWT ("issued at")
- `jti`—The JWT ID

Let's add JWT support to the application from chapter 12 (where we scaffolded ASP.NET Core Identity). This is a bare-bones approach to demonstrate vital concepts (using OAuth, as described later in this chapter, is the preferred option). Still, the implementation requires quite a lot of additions, which we will describe step by step:

1 Add an API to the web application.
2 Add the JWT middleware to the application.
3 Implement a login API endpoint that returns a token.
4 Add another API endpoint that accepts the JWT token.

The sample code from chapter 12 uses Razor Pages and is not prepared for API controllers. This requires supplements to Program.cs. In addition to the `AddRazor-Pages()` call that's already there, the `AddControllers()` method is required:

```
builder.Services.AddRazorPages();
builder.Services.AddControllers();
```

The call to `MapRazorPages()` sets up the default routing for the application. We should do the same for API controllers. The `MapControllers()` method does the trick:

```
app.UseEndpoints(endpoints =>
{
    endpoints.MapRazorPages();
    endpoints.MapControllers();
});
```

We now have all we need to create a new API controller and will call it `TokenAuth-Controller`. This will be the base structure of that controller, which will contain two endpoints—one for login and one for retrieving data:

```
using Microsoft.AspNetCore.Mvc;
using static
➡AspNetCoreSecurity.IdentitySamples.Areas.Identity.Pages.Account.LoginModel;

namespace AspNetCoreSecurity.IdentitySamples.Controllers
{
    [Route("api/[controller]")]
    [ApiController]
    public class TokenAuthController : ControllerBase
    {
        [HttpPost]
        [Route("login")]
        public async Task<IActionResult> Login(          │ Login endpoint (HTTP POST,
        ➡[FromBody] InputModel model)           ⊲──┘ /api/tokenauth/login)
        {
        }

        [Route("data")]                                   │ Data endpoint (HTTP GET,
        public IActionResult Data()     ⊲──┘ /api/tokenauth/data)
        {
        }
    }
}
```

Note how the `Login()` method is reusing the `InputModel` class that was scaffolded by ASP.NET Core Identity (it basically contains a username, a password, and the Boolean "remember me" value).

Next, JWT support is added to the application. .NET comes with a suitable implementation. The `Microsoft.AspNetCore.Authentication.JwtBearer` NuGet package provides a middleware that will later help the application accept the token in a specific way (more about that soon). Why do we start with that package? Because it comes with several other dependencies, as figure 13.1 shows.

Figure 13.1
**The `Microsoft.AspNetCore`
`.Authentication.JwtBearer`
dependencies**

The `System.IdentityModel.Tokens.Jwt` package, for instance, does not just allow parsing of JWT tokens, but it also creates them. And that's what the application needs to do next. First, the `UserManager` and `IConfiguration` classes are made available to the controller class via dependency injection:

```
private readonly IConfiguration _configuration;
private readonly UserManager<IdentityUser> userManager;

public TokenAuthController(UserManager<IdentityUser> userManager,
    IConfiguration configuration)
{
    this.userManager = userManager;
    _configuration = configuration;
}
```

We will also need a secret—a password or passphrase—that will be stored in appsettings.json (or, alternatively, in another secure location; see chapter 7 for options). We will use a symmetric key here for the sake of simplicity:

```
{
  "JWT": {
    "Key": "correct horse battery staple"
  },
  ...
}
```

The name and the value are arbitrary, but make sure that you apply all changes here to the rest of the code as well. With this passphrase, the JWT signature will be created and will later be validated.

Next, remember the signature of the Login() method:

```
public async Task<IActionResult> Login([FromBody] InputModel model) {}
```

The InputModel class will contain a username and password, which will be validated first, courtesy of the injected UserManager class:

```
var user = await userManager.FindByNameAsync(model.Email);
if (user == null || !await userManager.CheckPasswordAsync(user,
    model.Password))
{
    return Unauthorized();
}
```

The FindByNameAsync() method first checks whether the user exists (remember that the scaffolded ASP.NET Core Identity template uses the user's email address as their username). Then the CheckPasswordAsync() method validates the password. If it's incorrect, the API endpoint immediately returns HTTP 401–Unauthorized. Otherwise, the code may proceed.

Since we want to store claims in the token, we start collecting our information. The JwtRegisteredClaimNames enumeration contains the registered claim names from the JWT standard, as well as a few others (such as email). We will set that claim, as well as the sub (subject) and jti (JWT ID):

```
var authClaims = new List<Claim>
{
    new Claim(JwtRegisteredClaimNames.Sub, user.UserName),
    new Claim(JwtRegisteredClaimNames.Email, user.Email),
    new Claim(JwtRegisteredClaimNames.Jti, Guid.NewGuid().ToString())
};
```

If the user has roles, we can create claims for those roles as well:

```
var roles = await userManager.GetRolesAsync(user);
foreach (var role in roles)
{
    authClaims.Add(
        new Claim(ClaimTypes.Role, role));
}
```

NOTE The sample application does not use roles (yet), so be aware that you will not see any (yet).

We are almost done! All that's left is issuing the token. This requires a few classes, starting with `SecurityTokenDescriptor`, which basically describes the token. We set three properties: the list of claims, the token's expiration date (we use 10 minutes from now), and the signature, which in turn uses the passphrase from our appsettings .json file:

```
var tokenDescriptor = new SecurityTokenDescriptor()
{
    Subject = new ClaimsIdentity(authClaims),
    Expires = DateTime.Now.AddMinutes(10),
    SigningCredentials = new SigningCredentials(
        key, SecurityAlgorithms.HmacSha512Signature)
};
```

> **TIP** You can also set the token's issuer and audience here (and validate it later). We will take a shortcut here, skip those two values for now, and skip validating them.

To finally create the token, a `JwtSecurityTokenHandler` comes into play:

```
var tokenHandler = new JwtSecurityTokenHandler();
var token = tokenHandler.CreateToken(tokenDescriptor);
```

The API endpoint returns this token (as a Base64-encoded string, thanks to the token handler's `CreateToken()` method), along with its expiration date, which is optional here but may be useful for some client applications:

```
return Ok(new
{
    token = tokenHandler.WriteToken(token),
    expires = token.ValidTo
});
```

An excellent tool for testing APIs is the Postman application that we used in chapter 10 (available at https://www.postman.com/downloads/ as a desktop app for Windows, macOS, and Linux, and as an in-browser tool). Postman is not a hard requirement—any other tool that allows creating HTTP requests is just fine.

In Postman (or the tool of your choice), configure an HTTP POST request to the login endpoint—in our setup, the URL is https://localhost:5001/api/tokenauth/login, but this may vary on your system. In the Headers tab, add the `Content-Type` header and set it to `application/json`. Then, in the Body tab, set the input type to `raw`, and provide the email address and password of a user that already exists in the application. Here is an example, but you obviously need to use credentials you have previously used when registering that user in your application:

```
{
    "Email": "new-user@example.com",
    "Password": "Secret+123"
}
```

Sending that request should lead to output similar to figure 13.2.

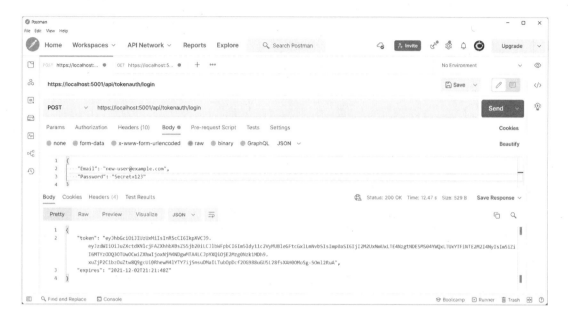

Figure 13.2 **The login endpoint returns a JSON Web Token.**

The token is a pretty long string. If you look at it closely (or, even better, create your own token), you will see that it's actually three strings, separated by dots. They contain these three pieces of information:

- A header with information about the token type (spoiler: JWT) and the algorithm used for the signature
- The actual payload (the claims, as well as metadata such as creation and expiration dates)
- A signature

The token itself is hard to decipher, unless you are fluent in Base64 (just kidding), but can easily be deconstructed. A very convenient way is by using the online tool from https://jwt.ms, which decodes JWT tokens (figure 13.3).

In the payload section, you can make out the email address (aka username), the GUID that serves as the JWT ID, and the start, expiration, and creation timestamps of the token.

> **WARNING** A real token may grant access to a secured web application, so it is not a good idea to paste it into a web application you do not know.

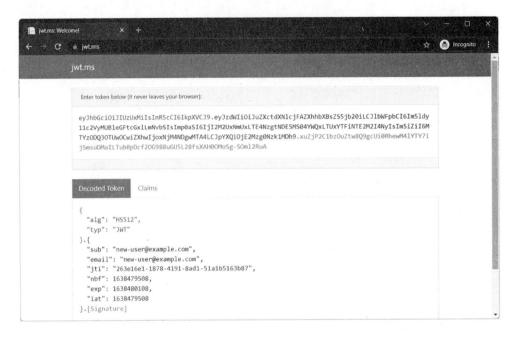

Figure 13.3   Decoding the JWT

We finally reveal why the `Microsoft.AspNetCore.Authentication.JwtBearer` NuGet package was added to the project: not only will JWTs be used, but so will so-called bearer tokens (their background will be covered later in this chapter; it is not important at the moment). They basically work like this—the HTTP header contains an HTTP header and value that looks similar to this:

```
Authorization: Bearer this-is-the-token
```

More configuration is required so that this works in the ASP.NET Core application. The Program.cs file already has an `AddAuthorization()` call. The middleware supporting JWT bearer tokens needs to be added afterward and needs to be configured properly:

```
builder.Services.AddAuthentication()          Adds the                    Loads the
    .AddJwtBearer(options =>        ◄──┘        middleware          passphrase from the
    {                                                             application settings
        var key = new SymmetricSecurityKey(
            Encoding.UTF8.GetBytes(builder.Configuration["JWT:Key"]));

        options.SaveToken = true;
        options.RequireHttpsMetadata = false;       Sets JWT behavior options
        options.TokenValidationParameters =
            new TokenValidationParameters()       ◄──┐  Sets token
        {                                             validation options
            ValidateAudience = false,
            ValidateIssuer = false,
```

```
                IssuerSigningKey = key
            };
    })
```

There is quite a bit happening in this brief code snippet. When the JWT bearer middleware is added, a few options are set:

- `SaveToken`—The token will be stored in the `AuthenticationProperties`.
- `RequireHttpsMetadata`—If set to `false`, the application works with plain HTTP as well, which might be useful for some testing scenarios but should be avoided on production systems, of course.

The `TokenValidationParameters()` class then configures the key used for the signature—the application is using the one from the appsettings.json file, which was also the one used when creating the token. Since the issuer and audience of the JWT were not set, these two values cannot be validated, so `ValidateIssuer` and `ValidateAudience` are set to `false`.

It's time to enter the final stage of the implementation: creating the secured endpoint. The actual logic within the method is pretty straightforward and returns all current claims:

```
[Route("data")]
public IActionResult Data()
{
    var user = User.Identity as ClaimsIdentity;
    var claims = new Dictionary<string, string>();
    foreach (var claim in user?.Claims ?? Array.Empty<Claim>())
    {
        claims.Add(claim.Type, claim.Value);
    }
    return Ok(claims);
}
```

The code accesses the `User.Identity` property and casts it to `ClaimsIdentity` to be able to access all the claims, and then iterates over them. But how can we make sure that only authenticated users may access this endpoint so that `User.Identity` is properly set?

The [Authorize] attribute might come to mind. We just have to configure it so that the application knows that a JWT bearer token is expected (and not, for instance, the cookie-based authentication from chapter 12). Here is how this may be achieved:

```
[Authorize(AuthenticationSchemes = JwtBearerDefaults.AuthenticationScheme)]
[Route("data")]
public IActionResult Data()
{
...
}
```

Protecting the API required several steps. On the positive side, if you have executed those steps once, you can apply those experiences to all other applications that follow.

Let's reiterate what we have done by looking once again at the code of the API controller.

Listing 13.1   The protected API controller

```
using Microsoft.AspNetCore.Authentication.JwtBearer;
using Microsoft.AspNetCore.Authorization;
using Microsoft.AspNetCore.Identity;
using Microsoft.AspNetCore.Mvc;
using Microsoft.IdentityModel.Tokens;
using System.IdentityModel.Tokens.Jwt;
using System.Security.Claims;
using System.Text;
using static
➡AspNetCoreSecurity.IdentitySamples.Areas.Identity.Pages.Account.LoginModel;

namespace AspNetCoreSecurity.IdentitySamples.Controllers
{
    [Route("api/[controller]")]
    [ApiController]
    public class TokenAuthController : ControllerBase
    {
        private readonly IConfiguration _configuration;
        private readonly UserManager<IdentityUser> userManager;

        public TokenAuthController(
                UserManager<IdentityUser> userManager,
                ➡IConfiguration configuration)
        {
            this.userManager = userManager;
            _configuration = configuration;
        }

        [HttpPost]
        [Route("login")]
        public async Task<IActionResult> Login(
            [FromBody] InputModel model)
        {
            var user = await userManager.FindByNameAsync(model.Email);
            if (user == null ||
                !await userManager.CheckPasswordAsync(
                    user, model.Password))
            {
                return Unauthorized();
            }
            var authClaims = new List<Claim>
            {
                new Claim(JwtRegisteredClaimNames.Sub, user.UserName),
                new Claim(JwtRegisteredClaimNames.Email, user.Email),
                new Claim(JwtRegisteredClaimNames.Jti,
                ➡Guid.NewGuid().ToString())
            };

            var roles = await userManager.GetRolesAsync(user);
```

Shows the class constructor with dependency injection

The login endpoint verifies credentials and issues the JSON Web Token.

```
        foreach (var role in roles)
        {
            authClaims.Add(
                new Claim(ClaimTypes.Role, role));
        }

        var key = new SymmetricSecurityKey(Encoding.UTF8.GetBytes
        ➥(_configuration["JWT:Key"]));

        var tokenDescriptor = new SecurityTokenDescriptor()
        {
            Subject = new ClaimsIdentity(authClaims),
            Expires = DateTime.Now.AddMinutes(10),
            SigningCredentials = new SigningCredentials(
                key, SecurityAlgorithms.HmacSha512Signature)
        };

        var tokenHandler = new JwtSecurityTokenHandler();
        var token = tokenHandler.CreateToken(tokenDescriptor);

        return Ok(new
        {
            token = tokenHandler.WriteToken(token),
            expires = token.ValidTo
        });
    }

    [Authorize(AuthenticationSchemes =
    ➥JwtBearerDefaults.AuthenticationScheme)]
    [Route("data")]
    public IActionResult Data()
    {
        var user = User.Identity as ClaimsIdentity;
        var claims = new Dictionary<string, string>();
        foreach (var claim in user?.Claims ?? Array.Empty<Claim>())
        {
            claims.Add(claim.Type, claim.Value);
        }
        return Ok(claims);
    }
  }
}
```

This is the protected endpoint, expecting a bearer token.

The login endpoint verifies the email address and password provided and issues a JWT with several claims when correct. When this token is sent to the protected data endpoint, the API returns a list of all claims in the token.

Back to Postman (or the HTTP request tool of your choice). Create an HTTP GET request to the data endpoint. The URL will be https://localhost:5001/api/token auth/data or similar. Switch to the Authorization tab, change the authorization type to Bearer Token, and paste the JWT. If it's correct, you will get a result similar to that shown in figure 13.4.

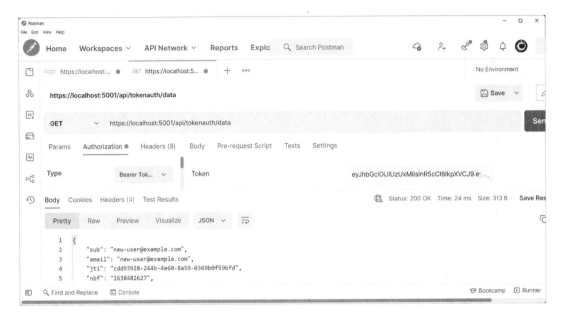

Figure 13.4   The token is valid, and the endpoint returns data.

The claims from the token are returned, proving that the application accepted the JWT. When sending an invalid token (this category also includes expired ones), the API returns `HTTP 401 Unauthorized`.

This works well, but the approach has flaws. If the client is a regular web browser, it needs to store the token somewhere, which opens up potential security risks such as token theft (similar to session hijacking from chapter 3) and more. In a nutshell: don't use it. Instead, let's look at established standards that can help here.

13.2 *OAuth and OpenID Connect*

We will be describing OAuth and OpenID Connect (OIDC), two standards or protocols that are related, yet a bit different. After a brief description of what these two terms are all about, we will look at use cases and, of course, ASP.NET Core implementations for them.

13.2.1 *OAuth vs. OpenID Connect*

The main idea behind OAuth is that users want to give web applications (and other apps as well, but we focus on web technologies here) a way to grant them access to their data, but without providing them with their credentials. Instead of having two parties involved, a client and a server, there is now a third protagonist: an authorization server. The new piece of the puzzle can authenticate the user and issue a token, which is then accepted by the web application. JSON Web Tokens come in handy here, but OAuth does a bit more. It is essentially a framework that allows a delegated access to a resource, providing different mechanisms for issuing and using the token (so-called flows—we will cover several of them shortly).

Logging into a web application with a third-party account (as shown in chapter 12—using the Microsoft account there) uses exactly this approach: the third-party site accepts credentials and issues the token, and the actual web application grants access based on the token alone, without knowing the user's password for the external service. When you can sign into several applications with the same set of credentials (and a central external login service), you are talking about *single sign-on*. Figure 13.5 shows how an authorization server comes into play in a simplified diagram.

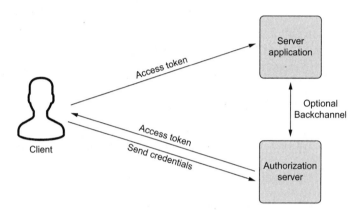

Figure 13.5   Using an authorization server

OAuth 1.0 became IETF RFC 5849 in 2010, and OAuth 2.0 followed two years later, in the form of several individual RFCs. The two most common ones are RFC 6749 for the standard itself (https://datatracker.ietf.org/doc/html/rfc6749) and RFC 6750 for bearer-token handling (https://datatracker.ietf.org/doc/html/rfc6750). At the time of this writing, OAuth 2.1 is in the works (the latest version is at https://datatracker .ietf.org/doc/html/draft-ietf-oauth-v2-1-04), merging several RFCs into one. These RFCs include the 6749 and 6750, as well as additional OAuth-related RFCs created afterward.

A common misconception is that OAuth is an authentication framework—it only handles access token requests. Since authentication is a related topic when authorization is required, many different flavors exist as to how to handle identity. Enter OpenID Connect 1.0 (OIDC 1.0), a layer on top of OAuth 2.0, described at the OpenID Foundation website at https://openid.net/connect/. Whereas OAuth is working with access tokens ("What is the user allowed to access?"), OIDC uses identity tokens ("Who is the user?").

Feel free to look closely at the specifications for these protocols. But then follow the recommendation already given in this book: don't roll your own security; use vetted, high-quality libraries and products to implement. For signing in with the external service in chapter 12, ASP.NET Core Identity provided all we needed. For implementing an authorization server or identity server, we need to use third-party tools. The OpenID website has a list of all certified OpenID Connect implementations (https://openid.net/developers/certified/), which means that those libraries and servers have passed an official test suite and should be reliable to use. As always, verify the license terms for whatever you are using, since this may change after this book is published. OIDC sits on top of OAuth 2.0, so let's go back to the latter and discuss the different available flows.

13.2.2 OAuth flows

The OAuth 2.0 framework defines several flows for different scenarios. Let's look at a few of them and see when when (or whether!) to use them!

For years, the most widely used flow for SPAs was probably *implicit flow* or *implicit grant*, defined in section 4.2 of OAuth 2.0, which basically gave JavaScript a simple API to retrieve a token from an authorization server via a URL. Figure 13.6 shows the process.

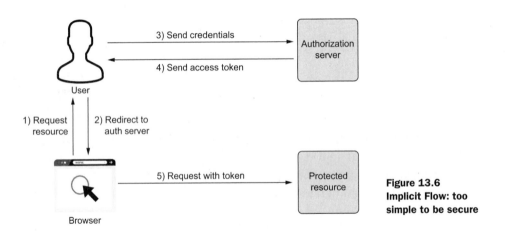

**Figure 13.6
Implicit Flow: too
simple to be secure**

The client would send a request to the authorization server asking for a token. The server would usually show a login form, accept credentials, and—if valid—generate a token. This token would be appended to a callback URL so that JavaScript could read this information and then use the token on any subsequent requests to an API, for instance. At first this sounds like a good and intuitive idea, but beware: usage of this flow is discouraged. The tokens are part of the URL and thus might leak via a variety of ways:

- `Referer` HTTP header
- Browser history
- Logs
- Proxy servers

Another flow that's part of OAuth 2.0 but should not be used is *password flow*, or the *password grant*. You directly send credentials to the authorization server, which not only teaches users to type in their credentials anywhere (and desensitizes them to phishing attacks), but it just does not work with 2FA and other advanced scenarios.

The *authorization code flow* (or *authorization code grant*) from section 4.1 of OAuth 2.0 tries to provide a more secure approach than the implicit flow by first receiving an authorization code from the authorization server and then using that code to retrieve an access token for the actual application. Figure 13.7 shows this concept in more detail.

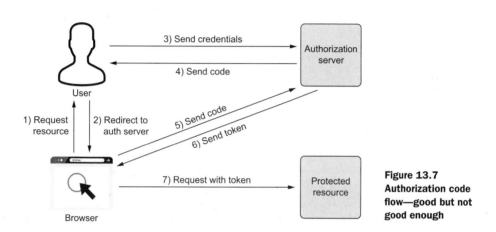

Figure 13.7 Authorization code flow—good but not good enough

The client application requests the authorization code from the authorization server and will probably be prompted with a login screen. After entering (correct) credentials, the authorization server redirects the browser to a URL where the authorization code is appended. With this authorization code, a second call to the authorization server will return an access token. This works pretty well in practice, but there are several potential attack vectors:

- The authorization code might leak via the `Referer` HTTP header, an open network, or other means.
- The web application might have an open redirect (an endpoint that redirects to an arbitrary URL), so the attacker could use that to redirect the authorization code to an endpoint of their choosing.
- A specific attack called *authorization code injection* or *replay attack* tries to inject an authorization code into a victim's client. When the client then retrieves an access token based on the stolen authorization code, the attacker can do the same and potentially impersonate their victim. The attack uses a comparable approach to cross-site request forgery (CSRF), discussed in chapter 4.

There is a better alternative: authorization code + PKCE (Proof Key for Code Exchange; pronounced "pixie"). Figure 13.8 shows that this approach adds an additional secret to the flow.

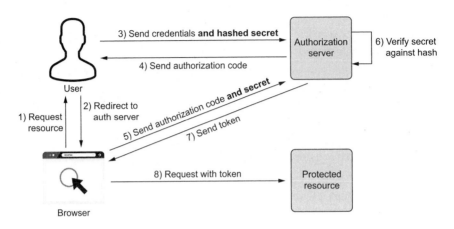

Figure 13.8 Authorization code flow with PKCE

The client first generates a secret and sends that (or, to be precise, its hash) to the authorization server when requesting the authorization code. Then, when exchanging the code with an access token, the client secret is sent alongside that request. That way, the authorization server knows exactly whether the same user sent both requests. Also, an attacker stealing the authorization code cannot use it because they do not know the secret. Even eavesdropping on both the authorization code request and response does not work, since the attacker then only knows the hash of the secret, not the secret itself. The latter is required to retrieve an access token, though.

> **NOTE** To prevent CSRF attack vectors, the request for the authorization code can also contain secret information (think of an anti-CSRF token). Only if the authorization server returns this value can the client be sure that the code has not been tampered with.

There is one more flow worth noting, the *client credentials flow*. Here, the client sends a secret to the authorization server and retrieves an access token. This is obviously only used for machine-to-machine communication.

With all the theory now out of the way, it's time to secure ASP.NET Core applications with OAuth 2.0 and OpenID Connect!

13.3 *Securing applications*

When the ASP.NET Core application is the consumer of a protected API or service, the framework comes with everything required out of the box. However, an identity server is not part of the package—third-party support is required here. Let's look at a few widely used options.

13.3.1 *Third-party tools*

There are several services and products to choose from: some free, some commercial, and some in the middle. The options provided here are not an exhaustive list but should give you a good idea of how to evaluate and use them in your own projects.

OpenIddict (https://documentation.openiddict.com/), the self-proclaimed "OpenID Connect stack you'll be addicted to," is an open source OpenID Connect server by Kévin Chalet. It works with ASP.NET Core and even supports ASP.NET 4.x. The associated GitHub page (https://github.com/openiddict) contains repositories for the server code, samples, and documentation. The OpenID Connect module of CMS, Orchard Core (https://orchardcore.net/), is based on OpenIddict and is ready to use.

While OpenIddict is free and has a specific feature set, Auth0 (https://auth0.com) is probably on the opposite side of the spectrum. This commercial offering (which also has a free tier) provides a full platform for identity, including single sign-on, multifactor authentication, social identity providers, and more. In 2021, Auth0 was acquired by Okta (https://www.okta.com) and turned into a product unit.

The best-known identity server back when ASP.NET was still a thing, and also for ASP.NET Core, is aptly called IdentityServer. Created by Dominick Baier and Brock Allen, it is an OpenID Connect and OAuth 2.0 framework—not a turnkey solution, but a highly flexible set of components that can be used to implement any kind of identity solution for ASP.NET Core. IdentityServer was so popular that Microsoft mentions the product in their documentation and ships IdentityServer templates with Visual Studio.

However, there were some changes when .NET 5 came out, and they continue to impact .NET 6 (and future versions) as well. The IdentityServer authors found out that running the open source project was not sustainable, so in 2020, they founded a product company called Duende Software (https://duendesoftware.com) to be able to continue working on the product. This also changed the license for the software. The source code and issue tracker are still available transparently and openly on GitHub, but depending on the size of the company, a license fee is required. The IdentityServer pricing page (http://mng.bz/Qv76) will have the most up-to-date information. IdentityServer is free for development and testing (so basically, non-production environments), as is a Community Edition for smaller companies or for individuals.

To give you a good assessment of how you can implement OAuth and OpenID Connect in your ASP.NET Core application, we use IdentityServer for the sample code, in part due to the good templates that ship with Visual Studio or can be installed separately. They will get you up and running in no time, with relatively little extra work to be done.

At the time of this writing, IdentityServer 6 was the latest stable version. We expect the source code to be upward-compatible and will update the code examples online if there are any breaking changes.

Before we proceed, it's a good idea to install the IdentityServer templates. Run the following command:

```
dotnet new --install Duende.IdentityServer.Templates
```

This will add six new templates, as figure 13.9 shows.

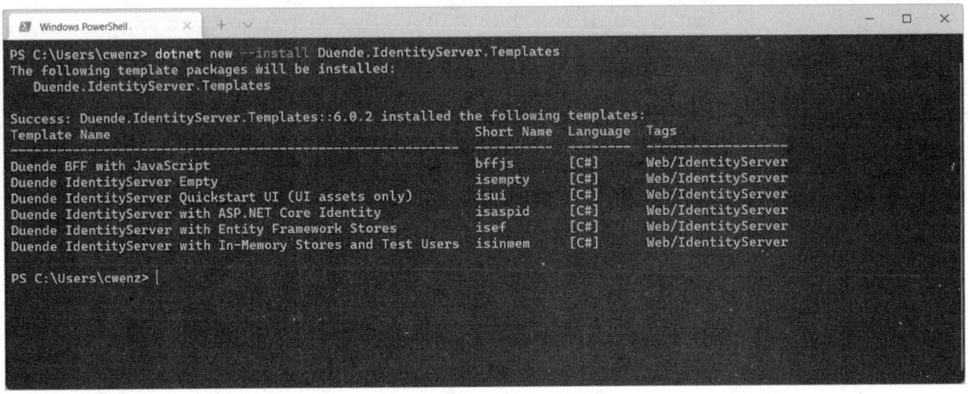

Figure 13.9   Installing IdentityServer templates via the command line

If you are using Visual Studio, you will then see some of those IdentityServer templates, as shown in figure 13.10 (look for "Duende" if you don't see them right away). These serve as a good starting point for the next examples.

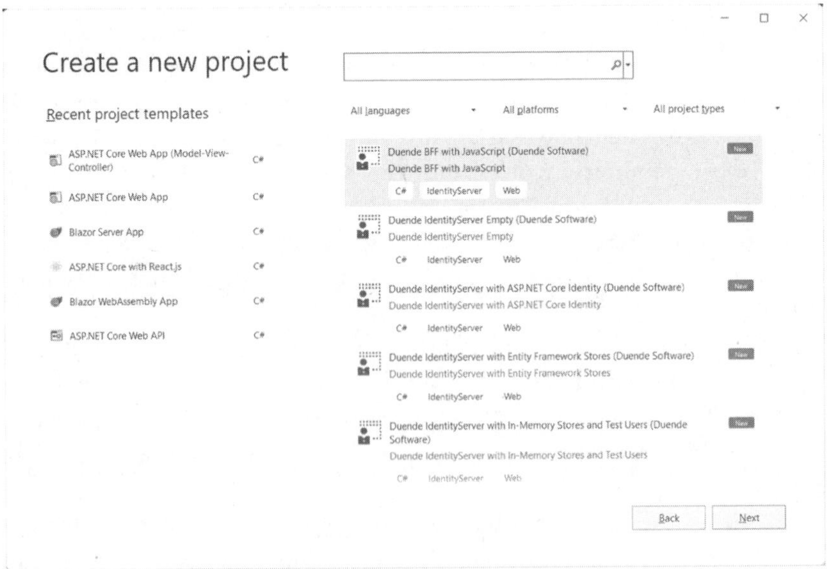

Figure 13.10   IdentityServer templates in Visual Studio

We will use the Duende IdentityServer Empty project to implement one instance of IdentityServer. Then we will add several clients to the solution, showcasing various OAuth and OpenID Connect approaches.

> **NOTE** When starting the IdentityServer project, the browser will try to load https://localhost:5001 and will show HTTP 404—File Not Found. This is expected, since we do not have a UI for IdentityServer—yet.

13.3.2 Client credentials

The first resource we would like to protect using IdentityServer is an API that is called from another application (think of a website where the backend calls the API, or a Blazor Server application). In that case, using client credentials is a good mechanism, since the communication takes place on the server and is usually at less risk than when a web browser is handling secrets.

Make sure you have created a new solution based on the Duende IdentityServer Empty project template (when using the CLI, the template name is `isempty`). Add a new project to the current solution, and pick the ASP.NET Core Web API template. Uncheck the Use Controllers checkbox so that you are using a minimal API; you also do not need OpenAPI support.

One important piece of housekeeping comes first. The IdentityServer project uses 5001 as the HTTPS port when using Kestrel (and we will not be using IIS or IIS Express here). The API will have another, random HTTPS port. For the sake of simplicity, we will assign specific ports for the API. In the Properties\launchsettings.json file, search for the line that looks like this:

```
"applicationUrl": "https://localhost:7051;http://localhost:5051",
```

Change it to use the following port:

```
"applicationUrl": "https://localhost:5011",
```

When you want to use different ports on your system, just make sure that you replace 5001 and 5011 (and the ports in the following code samples) with your ports for the IdentityServer instance and the API.

The API template already comes with the usual random temperature-generating code. Since the project is using a minimal API, the whole implementation resides in Program.cs (look for the `app.MapGet("/weatherforecast")` call). This serves as a good starting point. To protect the API endpoint, add the `[Authorize]` tag to this method call:

```
app.MapGet("/weatherforecast", [Authorize] () => { ... }
```

> **NOTE** You could also add `.RequireAuthorization()` directly after the call to `.MapGet()`, which would have the same effect.

Now it's time to add the `Microsoft.AspNetCore.Authentication.JwtBearer` NuGet package that we have used before, including all of its dependencies. This allows us to set up the JWT handling in Program.cs. Add the code printed in bold:

```
var builder = WebApplication.CreateBuilder(args);

// Add services to the container.
builder.Services.AddControllers();
builder.Services.AddAuthentication("Bearer")
    .AddJwtBearer("Bearer", options =>
    {                                                          ┐ Displays the
        options.Authority = "https://localhost:5001";    ◁─┘ IdentityServer URL
        options.TokenValidationParameters = new TokenValidationParameters()
        {
            ValidateAudience = false    ◁─┐ Skips audience validation
        };                                └ (we will not use this)
    });

var app = builder.Build();
```

We will use a bearer token again, and IdentityServer running at https://localhost:5001 serves as the authority to issue that token.

To finish our additions to the API's Program.cs file, we will need to configure the HTTP pipeline a little more by adding authentication and authorization support, for instance. The following listing shows the complete code for that file, with remaining additions marked in bold.

Listing 13.2   The protected minimal API

```
using Microsoft.AspNetCore.Authorization;
using Microsoft.IdentityModel.Tokens;

var builder = WebApplication.CreateBuilder(args);

// Add services to the container.                      Configures
builder.Services.AddControllers();                     authentication and the
builder.Services.AddAuthentication("Bearer")    ◁─┐ bearer token handling
    .AddJwtBearer("Bearer", options =>
    {
        options.Authority = "https://localhost:5001";
        options.TokenValidationParameters = new TokenValidationParameters()
        {
            ValidateAudience = false
        };
    });

var app = builder.Build();

// Configure the HTTP request pipeline.

app.UseHttpsRedirection();
app.UseRouting();
app.UseAuthentication();
app.UseAuthorization();

app.UseEndpoints(endpoints =>
{
```

```
    endpoints.MapControllers();
});

var summaries = new[]
{
    "Freezing", "Bracing", "Chilly", "Cool", "Mild", "Warm", "Balmy", "Hot",
    ➥"Sweltering", "Scorching"
};

app.MapGet("/weatherforecast", [Authorize] () =>
{
    var forecast = Enumerable.Range(1, 5).Select(index =>
      new WeatherForecast
      (
          DateTime.Now.AddDays(index),
          Random.Shared.Next(-20, 55),
          summaries[Random.Shared.Next(summaries.Length)]
      ))
        .ToArray();
    return forecast;
});

app.Run();

internal record WeatherForecast(DateTime Date, int TemperatureC, string?
➥Summary)
{
    public int TemperatureF => 32 + (int)(TemperatureC / 0.5556);
}
```

Implements the
API endpoint

Calling https://localhost:5011/weatherforecast returns exactly what is expected now—HTTP 401–Unauthorized. Time to build a client for machine-to-machine communication that receives a token and can properly call the API!

For the sake of simplicity, we will create a console client in the current solution for this; of course, you could also implement a, say, WinForms or web application where the server issues HTTP requests, using the patterns detailed here. The console client will need to do two things:

- Receive a valid token from IdentityServer
- Use that token to be authorized when calling the API

First, the IdentityModel NuGet package needs to be added to that console application; a using statement makes one of its namespaces available to the code in Program.cs:

```
using IdentityModel.Client;
```

We will use the HttpClient class twice: once to call IdentityServer and once to call the API. We commence with the former to retrieve the token. The instance of Identity-Server provides a "discovery document" with information about its configuration. You can look at it yourself by loading the https://localhost:5001/.well-known/openid -configuration URL in the browser. The IdentityModel package can read the information from there to know exactly what to do when; for instance, requesting an access token. The following code shows how this works (for the sake of simplicity, the secret is directly within the code and not externalized):

```
var tokenClient = new HttpClient();                            Retrieves discovery
                                                                       document
var doc = await tokenClient.GetDiscoveryDocumentAsync(
    "https://localhost:5001");
var token = await tokenClient.RequestClientCredentialsTokenAsync(    Requests
    new ClientCredentialsTokenRequest                                token
    {
        Address = doc.TokenEndpoint,
        ClientId = "api-client",                               Configures
        ClientSecret = "correct horse battery staple",         token request
        Scope = "api"
    });
```

The `GetDiscoveryDocumentAsync()` method retrieves, well, the discovery document. This document contains, among other things, the URL of the endpoint to request the access token from (`TokenEndpoint` property). The `RequestClient-CredentialsTokenAsync()` method then issues a request for such a token by using client credentials. These client credentials are configured in the `Client-CredentialsTokenRequest` instance. Three pieces of information help identify the client and the request:

- The client ID, identifying the client.
- The client secret (sent in cleartext but stored as an SHA-256 hash on the server). The server can authorize the request based on that.
- The scope of access requested by the client. When working with a more complex application, we might define different scopes (the client may request read access and write access, and there could be different scopes for that). In our application, there is just one uniform scope for API access, called `api`.

The `AccessToken` property of the awaited `RequestClientCredentialsToken-Async()` return value contains the access token. This may then be used to call the API, using the second `HttpClient`:

```
var apiClient = new HttpClient();                      Sets the bearer token
apiClient.SetBearerToken(token.AccessToken);           for the HTTP request

var response = await apiClient.GetAsync(               Calls the API endpoint
    "https://localhost:5011/weatherforecast");
var data = await response.Content.ReadAsStringAsync();
Console.WriteLine(data);
```

After setting the access token as a bearer token (with the `SetBearerToken()` method), the console application may directly call the API. Well, almost. So far, IdentityServer does not know anything about the console client, the client secret, or the `api` scope. All of this needs to be configured. The IdentityServer project template already created the Config class in the Config.cs file. This class contains, among others, two properties: ApiScopes and Clients. Update them so that the api scope and the new client are known to IdentityServer:

```
using Duende.IdentityServer;
using Duende.IdentityServer.Models;
using System.Collections.Generic;

namespace AspNetCoreSecurity.IdentityServer
{
    public static class Config
    {
...
        public static IEnumerable<ApiScope> ApiScopes =>
            new ApiScope[]
            {
                new ApiScope("api", "API")        ⊲─┤ Defines scope
            };

        public static IEnumerable<Client> Clients =>
            new Client[]
            {
                new Client()        ⊲─┤ Defines client
                {
                    ClientId = "api-client",
                    ClientSecrets =
                    {
                        new Secret("correct horse battery staple".Sha256())
                    },
                    AllowedScopes = { "api" },
                    AllowedGrantTypes = GrantTypes.ClientCredentials
                }
            };
    }
}
```

Note how the client definition mirrors the setting we've previously added to the console client—the client ID, the client secret, and the scope.

One final step remains: the API needs to enforce the policy—so far, it is only requiring authentication, so any access token will do. In Program.cs, add a call to AddAuthorization(), and add the policy that contains a claim for the api scope:

```
builder.Services.AddAuthorization(options =>    ⊲─┘ Configures authorization
{
    options.AddPolicy("ApiScopePolicy", policy =>    ⊲─┤ Adds a policy for the API
    {
        policy.RequireAuthenticatedUser();    ⊲─┐ Users need to be authenticated.
        policy.RequireClaim("scope", "api");    ⊲─┘ The api scope needs to be present.
    });
});
```

Finally, enforce this policy for all API endpoints by extending the `MapControllers()` call:

```
app.UseEndpoints(endpoints =>
{
    endpoints.MapControllers()
        .RequireAuthorization("ApiScopePolicy");
});
```

You can now run the IdentityServer, API, and console apps at the same time (Visual Studio allows setting several startup projects at once). See figure 13.11 for a possible output—the console application does receive a return value from the API, proving that authentication and authorization work as expected.

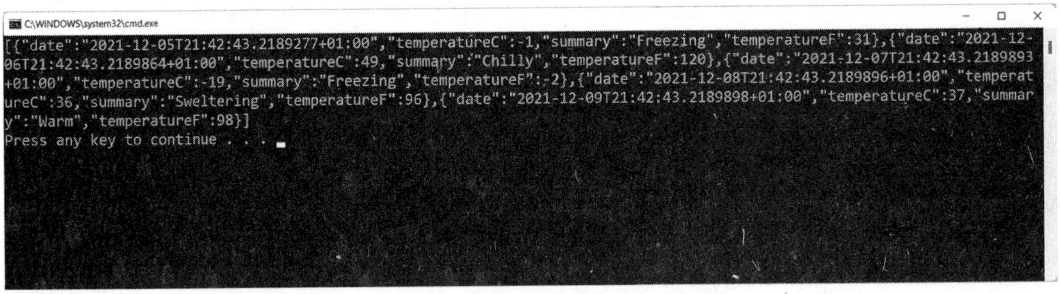

Figure 13.11 The console app authenticates against IdentityServer and calls the API.

13.3.3 *Authorization code + PKCE*

For browser applications, the authorization code + PKCE flow is arguably the best choice. With IdentityServer, it can be set up relatively easily (and with most alternative projects as well). We will add a project based on the ASP.NET Core Web App template to the solution, so Razor Pages will be used. No need to pick an authentication type in the project-creation wizard—that's IdentityServer's job now. First, go to the Properties \launchSettings.json file, and change the randomly assigned ports for the application to use only a specific one for HTTPS, 5021:

```
{
...
  "profiles": {
    "AspNetCoreSecurity.RazorPagesUI": {
      "commandName": "Project",
      "dotnetRunMessages": true,
      "launchBrowser": true,
      "applicationUrl": "https://localhost:5021",
...
    },
...
}
```

Next, add the `Microsoft.AspNetCore.Authentication.OpenIdConnect` NuGet package to the application, which implements OpenID Connect functionality. This allows us to configure authentication in the project's `Program` class. We basically want to do three things:

- Set configuration to use OpenID Connect for authentication against Identity-Server and to use cookies in the web application.
- Configure OpenID Connect so that it matches the IdentityServer configuration.
- Configure the application so that only authorized users may have access to it.

The following listing shows the complete code of Program.cs after implementing this, with additions in bold.

Listing 13.3   The protected Razor Pages application

```csharp
using System.IdentityModel.Tokens.Jwt;

var builder = WebApplication.CreateBuilder(args);

// Add services to the container.
builder.Services.AddAuthentication(options =>
{
    options.DefaultScheme = "Cookies";
    options.DefaultChallengeScheme = "oidc";
})
    .AddCookie("Cookies")
    .AddOpenIdConnect("oidc", options =>
    {
        options.Authority = "https://localhost:5001";
        options.ClientId = "web";
        options.ClientSecret = "correct horse battery staple";
        options.ResponseType = "code";
        options.ResponseMode = "query";
        options.SaveTokens = true;
        options.Scope.Add("profile");
        options.GetClaimsFromUserInfoEndpoint = true;
        options.MapInboundClaims = false;
    });
builder.Services.AddRazorPages();

var app = builder.Build();

// Configure the HTTP request pipeline.
if (!app.Environment.IsDevelopment())
{
    app.UseExceptionHandler("/Error");
    app.UseHsts();
}

app.UseHttpsRedirection();
app.UseStaticFiles();
app.UseRouting();
app.UseAuthentication();
app.UseAuthorization();
```

```
app.UseEndpoints(endpoints =>
{
    endpoints.MapRazorPages().RequireAuthorization();
});

app.Run();
```

There are quite a few implementation aspects to be seen here, so let's wade through them bit by bit. First of all, the application configures both the authentication in general (cookies for the web app, OIDC for IdentityServer) and the parameters for talking to IdentityServer:

```
builder.Services.AddAuthentication(options =>
{
    options.DefaultScheme = "Cookies";
    options.DefaultChallengeScheme = "oidc";
})
    .AddCookie("Cookies")                                    ⟵── Shows the OpenID
    .AddOpenIdConnect("oidc", options =>                          Connect settings
    {
        options.Authority = "https://localhost:5001";
        options.ClientId = "web";
        options.ClientSecret = "correct horse battery staple";
        options.ResponseType = "code";
        options.ResponseMode = "query";
        options.SaveTokens = true;

        options.Scope.Add("profile");
        options.GetClaimsFromUserInfoEndpoint = true;    │ Accesses user profile
        options.MapInboundClaims = false;
    });
```

Note how the OpenID Connect settings once again use a client ID and client secret. However, the `ResponseType` option is set to `code`, so an authorization code via query string (`ResponseMode` set to `query`) will be used. The last two options make sure that the application gets access to the user's profile and therefore to information such as the username (which will be output in the web application later).

Farther down in the Program.cs file, the call to `app.UseAuthentication()` needs to be added right before `app.UseAuthorization()`. The existing call to `app.MapRazorPages()` will be replaced by a properly configured `UseEndpoints()` call; this allows us to append `.RequireAuthorization()` so that the whole application is accessible only for authenticated and authorized users. The *Index.cshtml* Razor Page can therefore safely assume that a user is present and can output all of its claims. The next listing shows the complete markup and code.

Listing 13.4   **The Razor Page outputs all user claims**

```
@page
@model IndexModel
@{
    ViewData["Title"] = "Claims";
}
```

```
<div class="row">
    <div class="col-md-6">
        <p>
            <ul>
                @{
                    foreach (var claim in User.Claims)
                    {
                        <li>@claim.Type: @claim.Value</li>
                    }
                }
            </ul>
        </p>
    </div>
</div>
```

The web application is ready for action, but IdentityServer still doesn't know about it yet. This is about to change. Using the authorization code grant requires that you can sign into the application that issues the code and later the token. IdentityServer is capable and ready to do that, but you have to scaffold the UI first (similar to scaffolding the UI for ASP.NET Core Identity, as seen in chapter 12). This also allows you to tweak both how that UI looks and how it behaves. Open a command prompt in the root directory of the IdentityServer project, and issue the following command:

```
dotnet new isui
```

This requires that you have previously installed the IdentityServer templates, as described earlier in this chapter. The command adds the IdentityServer UI to the project. When looking in the project folder, you will find the Quickstart and Views folders, which are new.

The remaining configuration will again take place in the Config.cs file by adding information about the new application. In the `Clients` property, add a new entry to the list:

```
public static IEnumerable<Client> Clients =>
    new Client[]
    {
        new Client()
        {
            ClientId = "api-client",
            ClientSecrets =
            {
                new Secret("correct horse battery staple".Sha256())
            },
            AllowedScopes = { "api" },
            AllowedGrantTypes = GrantTypes.ClientCredentials
        },
        new Client()
        {
            ClientId = "web",
            ClientSecrets =
            {
                new Secret("correct horse battery staple".Sha256())
            },
            AllowedScopes = new List<string>
```

Lists the allowed scopes

```
        {
            IdentityServerConstants.StandardScopes.OpenId,
            IdentityServerConstants.StandardScopes.Profile
        },
        AllowedGrantTypes = GrantTypes.Code,
        RedirectUris = { "https://localhost:5021/signin-oidc" },
        PostLogoutRedirectUris = {
          "https://localhost:5021/signout-callback-oidc" }
    }
};
```

Shows the URIs to redirect to after logging out

Uses authorization code grant type

Shows the URIs to redirect to after authenticating in IdentityServer

Apart from setting the usual options (client ID, client secret, grant type), also note the list of redirect URIs. The protocol allows clients to provide a URI to redirect to after authentication, and another one for after logging out. However, this would facilitate open redirects, web applications that allow the forwarding of users users to arbitrary sites, facilitating some phishing and other attacks. Therefore, IdentityServer requires you to specifically provide a list of these URIs. The ones we are setting in the options are those that are automatically enabled in the web application when adding OIDC support. Just make sure that the base URI, including the port number, is correct for your setup.

We are not done yet, though. The `IdentityResources` property in the `Config` class does not support profiles yet, but the application wants to access profile information, such as the user's name. Therefore, add an entry to that property as follows:

```
public static IEnumerable<IdentityResource> IdentityResources =>
    new IdentityResource[]
    {
        new IdentityResources.OpenId(),
        new IdentityResources.Profile()
    };
```

In the last step, we need to make sure that users can actually log in—which means we need users in the first place! Go to the Startup.cs file in the IdentityServer project. As you can see in the `ConfigureServices()` method, the `Config.Identity-Resources` property (as well as `ApiScopes` and `Clients`) are already used to configure IdentityServer. Add a call to the `.AddTestUsers()` method, because that will add two users to the system, `alice` and `bob`. Also, add a call to `AddControllersWith-Views()` so that the login UI of IdentityServer can be shown (the code for that is already there, but as a comment):

```
public void ConfigureServices(IServiceCollection services)
{
    services.AddControllersWithViews();

    var builder = services.AddIdentityServer(options =>
    {
        options.EmitStaticAudienceClaim = true;
    })
        .AddInMemoryIdentityResources(Config.IdentityResources)
        .AddInMemoryApiScopes(Config.ApiScopes)
```

```
        .AddInMemoryClients(Config.Clients)
        .AddTestUsers(TestUsers.Users);
}
```

In the `Configure()` method of the same class, we need to enable a few more things—static files, routing, authorization, and the default controller route. Again, the code is already present, but commented out, since it is only required when the UI is being used. Here is the complete `Configure()` method, with new code in bold:

```
public void Configure(IApplicationBuilder app)
{
    if (Environment.IsDevelopment())
    {
        app.UseDeveloperExceptionPage();
    }

    app.UseStaticFiles();
    app.UseRouting();

    app.UseIdentityServer();

    app.UseAuthorization();
    app.UseEndpoints(endpoints =>
    {
        endpoints.MapDefaultControllerRoute();
    });
}
```

We have reached the end of our journey—at least in terms of getting authorization code to work. Run the Razor Pages project and the IdentityServer project concurrently. First note that the IdentityServer start page at https://localhost:5001 now actually shows a UI (figure 13.12).

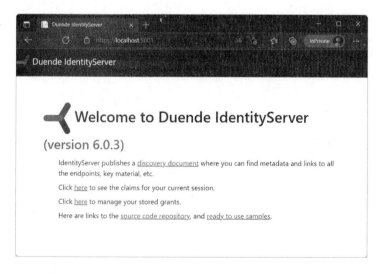

Figure 13.12   The start page of IdentityServer, thanks to scaffolding the UI

The web application, on the other hand, will immediately redirect to IdentityServer, where you are prompted to log in (figure 13.13). Log in as `alice` or `bob`, using the username as the password.

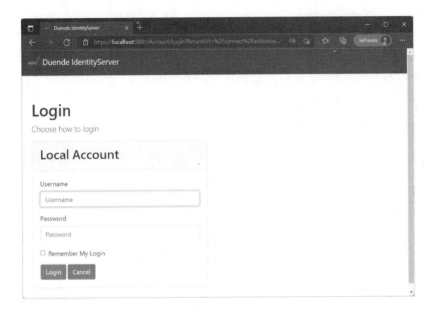

Figure 13.13   IdentityServer's login screen (use `alice/alice` or `bob/bob`)

IdentityServer will automatically redirect the browser back to the Razor Pages web application, and the OIDC middleware will validate the token, grant the user access, and output all the claims (figure 13.14).

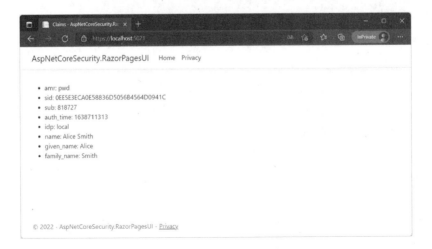

Figure 13.14   The user's claims after authenticating against IdentityServer

A valuable resource for debugging is the IdentityServer console window, which shows debug output, as seen in figure 13.15.

Figure 13.15   Debug output in the IdentityServer console

To add logout functionality to the application, we need to add a logout page to the Razor Pages project. To prevent cross-site request forgery, the logout will happen upon an HTTP POST call; the logout page provides a button for that, as shown in the next listing.

Listing 13.5   The logout page UI

```
@page
@model AspNetCoreSecurity.RazorPagesUI.Pages.LogoutModel
<form method="post">
    <input type="submit" class="btn btn-primary" value="Logout">
</form>
```

The associated page model basically calls the SignOut() method. Its parameters must match the authentication strings from Program.cs (in our case, Cookies and oidc). The next listing contains the complete code.

Listing 13.6   The logout page logic

```
using Microsoft.AspNetCore.Mvc;
using Microsoft.AspNetCore.Mvc.RazorPages;

namespace AspNetCoreSecurity.RazorPagesUI.Pages
{
```

```
[ValidateAntiForgeryToken]                              Validates the
public class LogoutModel : PageModel                    anti-CSRF token
{
    public IActionResult OnPost()
    {
        return SignOut("Cookies", "oidc");              Logs the user out
    }
}
}
```

This logs the user out of the web application (by clearing the authentication cookie) and IdentityServer.

13.3.4 *SPAs and BFF*

We have not covered single-page applications yet. Since they are usually implemented in JavaScript, they are not within the focus of this (ASP.NET Core–centric) book. But Blazor applications count as SPAs, so they are relevant. Not only does IdentityServer offer support for that, but it also comes with an easy-to-use implementation of a pattern that has become increasingly popular: BFF.

According to Merriam-Webster, BFF stands for "best friends forever" and dates back to 1987 (www.merriam-webster.com/dictionary/BFF). The BFF we are referring to here is a bit more recent. In 2015, developer Phil Calçado described an architecture pattern credited to his former coworker, Nick Fisher (if you are interested in the original article, it's at http://mng.bz/VM6X). According to him, BFF stands for "backend for frontend."

APIs (which, in the case of SPAs, serve as their backends) are often very generic and all-purpose. However, different frontends need very specific pieces of information from the backend. In 2015, Calçado was working at SoundCloud and noticed that the profile pages of bands with a reasonably large discography issued more than 150 API calls per page load. He therefore devised a mechanism to implement frontend-specific backends (so that a profile page had to use significantly fewer but more-targeted HTTP requests). BFF was born.

In the SPA world, this approach may have other advantages. We have already discussed the fact that authorization code + PKCE is considered the best OAuth flow for interactive applications such as a website. But still, the web application eventually has to remember a token (to use it in subsequent API calls as a bearer token). If, say, cross-site scripting is possible, the access token may still be stolen. We, of course, covered in chapter 2 how to avoid XSS as much as possible, but there just is no guarantee of protection from all attacks.

With BFF, this risk may be further mitigated. When each frontend has a dedicated backend, that backend could then store the token(s). The backend is therefore also responsible for communicating with the API. The frontend and backend share the same session, so the backend remembers the frontend. As we saw in chapters 3 and 4, protecting sessions works relatively well with modern browsers and various cookie flags such as `secure`, `HttpOnly`, and `SameSite`. Figure 13.16 illustrates the concept.

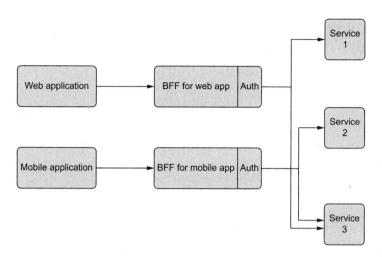

Figure 13.16   BFF: backend for frontend

Back to IdentityServer: the team from Duende Software has implemented the *BFF security framework*, which integrates with IdentityServer. It works well with JavaScript applications and Blazor WebAssembly (Blazor Server requires a different approach that we will briefly cover at the end of this chapter). The BFF framework is also part of the IdentityServer Community Edition, so it is free to use during development and testing and for small companies.

There are several samples available at https://docs.duendesoftware.com/identity-server/v6/samples/bff/ (if, at the time of reading this, there's a newer IdentityServer version out, change the URL appropriately). The following example will use Blazor WebAssembly, but the same principles apply to other SPA technologies as well.

Start by adding a new Blazor WebAssembly app to the current solution, and select the ASP.NET hosting option (or, when using the .NET CLI, the `--hosted` switch). You will end up with three new projects: a client project, a server project, and a shared project. We will need to work on the first two.

In the Properties\launchSettings.json file of the server project, change the Kestrel configuration option so that only HTTPS and the fixed port 5031 are used:

```
"applicationUrl": "https://localhost:5031",
```

As usual, if you have a different setup, feel free to use that, as long as you update the URLs in the IdentityServer configuration accordingly.

Next, install the `Duende.BFF` and `Duende.BFF.Yarp` NuGet packages to the server project. There are a few things that need to be changed or added to the Program.cs file of the Blazor project:

- BFF support needs to be added.
- Authentication needs to be configured similarly to before (cookies and OIDC).

- BFF-specific endpoints need to be registered with the application.
- An extra endpoint is required to call the remote API.

The following listing shows the updated version of Program.cs, with all additions in bold.

Listing 13.7   The `Program` class of the Blazor Server app

```csharp
using Duende.BFF;
using Duende.BFF.Yarp;

var builder = WebApplication.CreateBuilder(args);

builder.Services.AddControllersWithViews();
builder.Services.AddRazorPages();

builder.Services.AddBff().AddRemoteApis();          // Adds the BFF middleware

builder.Services.AddAuthentication(options =>       // Configures authentication
{
    options.DefaultScheme = "cookie";
    options.DefaultChallengeScheme = "oidc";
    options.DefaultSignOutScheme = "oidc";
})
    .AddCookie("cookie", options =>                 // Configures cookie options (with focus on CSRF protection)
    {
        options.Cookie.Name = "__Host-bff";
        options.Cookie.SameSite = SameSiteMode.Strict;
    })
    .AddOpenIdConnect("oidc", options =>            // Configures OpenID Connect
    {
        options.Authority = "https://localhost:5001";
        options.ClientId = "blazorwasm";
        options.ClientSecret = "correct horse battery staple";
        options.ResponseType = "code";
        options.ResponseMode = "query";

        options.GetClaimsFromUserInfoEndpoint = true;
        options.MapInboundClaims = false;
        options.SaveTokens = true;

        options.Scope.Clear();
        options.Scope.Add("openid");
        options.Scope.Add("profile");
        options.Scope.Add("offline_access");
        options.Scope.Add("api");
    });

var app = builder.Build();

if (app.Environment.IsDevelopment())
{
    app.UseWebAssemblyDebugging();
}
```

```
else
{
    app.UseExceptionHandler("/Error");
    app.UseHsts();
}


app.UseHttpsRedirection();

app.UseBlazorFrameworkFiles();
app.UseStaticFiles();

app.UseRouting();

app.UseAuthentication();            Activates authentication,
app.UseBff();                       authorization, and BFF
app.UseAuthorization();

app.UseEndpoints(endpoints =>
{                                              Registers BFF-specific
    endpoints.MapBffManagementEndpoints();  ◁─┘  endpoints
    endpoints.MapRemoteBffApiEndpoint(                              ◁─┐
        "/api/WeatherForecast", "https://localhost:5031/weatherforecast")
        .RequireAccessToken(TokenType.UserOrClient);
    endpoints.MapRazorPages();                         Creates a local endpoint
    endpoints.MapControllers();                           for the remote API
    endpoints.MapFallbackToFile("index.html");
});

app.Run();
```

The `Duende.BFF.Yarp` package deserves some extra explanation: YARP (Yet Another Reverse Proxy) is a very powerful tool for high-performance reverse proxies. With BFF, we want to avoid having the web browser directly call the API (and thus needing to know the user's token); instead, the server issues the HTTP request. YARP allows us to route a call from the Blazor app to the Blazor server directly to the remote API. The Blazor server, however, adds the required bearer token. That's exactly what this part of Program.cs is doing:

```
endpoints.MapRemoteBffApiEndpoint(
    "/api/WeatherForecast", "https://localhost:5031/weatherforecast")
    .RequireAccessToken(TokenType.UserOrClient);
```

The endpoint */api/WeatherForecast* on the Blazor server will issue a call to the remote API. In the Blazor client project, in the FetchData.razor file (in the Pages directory), the [Authorize] attribute prevents unauthorized access to the component.

So far, the forecast service is part of the Blazor server project; we would like to use the functionality from the API project instead. All that needs to be done is to change the URL of the API call to the local endpoint we configured in Program.cs (*/api/WeatherForecast*). The following listing contains the full FetchData.razor file, with all changes and additions in bold.

Listing 13.8   Calling the protected API

```
@page "/fetchdata"
@using AspNetCoreSecurity.BlazorWasmClient.Shared
@using Microsoft.AspNetCore.Authorization
@attribute [Authorize]
@inject HttpClient Http

<PageTitle>Weather forecast</PageTitle>

<h1>Weather forecast</h1>

<p>This component demonstrates fetching data from the server.</p>

@if (forecasts == null)
{
    <p><em>Loading...</em></p>
}
else
{
    <table class="table">
        <thead>
            <tr>
                <th>Date</th>
                <th>Temp. (C)</th>
                <th>Temp. (F)</th>
                <th>Summary</th>
            </tr>
        </thead>
        <tbody>
            @foreach (var forecast in forecasts)
            {
                <tr>
                    <td>@forecast.Date.ToShortDateString()</td>
                    <td>@forecast.TemperatureC</td>
                    <td>@forecast.TemperatureF</td>
                    <td>@forecast.Summary</td>
                </tr>
            }
        </tbody>
    </table>
}

@code {
    private WeatherForecast[]? forecasts;

    protected override async Task OnInitializedAsync()
    {
        forecasts = await Http.GetFromJsonAsync<WeatherForecast[]>
        ➥("api/WeatherForecast");
    }
}
```

The host of the Blazor application is ready for BFF, and the *FetchData* page is ready for BFF, but the Blazor client parts need some more plumbing. Start by installing the

`Microsoft.AspNetCore.Components.WebAssembly.Authentication` NuGet package, as we will need it shortly.

The `AuthorizeView` Blazor component outputs different content for authorized and unauthorized users, so we can actually address users by their names. The following listing shows an accordingly updated Shared\MainLayout.razor file.

Listing 13.9   Showing the user's name, if available

```
@using Microsoft.AspNetCore.Components.Authorization
@inherits LayoutComponentBase

<div class="page">
    <div class="sidebar">
        <NavMenu />
    </div>

    <main>
        <div class="top-row px-4">
            <AuthorizeView>
                <Authorized>
                    <strong>Hello, @context.User?.Identity?.Name!</strong>
                    <a href="@context.User?.FindFirst
                    ➥("bff:logout_url")?.Value">Logout</a>
                </Authorized>
                <NotAuthorized>
                    <a href="bff/login">Login</a>
                </NotAuthorized>
            </AuthorizeView>
        </div>

        <article class="content px-4">
            @Body
        </article>
    </main>
</div>
```

Next, the main App.razor file in the Blazor client project needs to be updated as well. The `AuthorizeRouteView` makes sure that authorized users get access to a resource. If they are not authorized, an error message (in our case, a convenient link to the login page) will be shown. To make this work, we have to wrap the contents of the App component into a `CascadingAuthenticationState` element. The following listing contains the complete code.

Listing 13.10   The updated App component

```
@using Microsoft.AspNetCore.Components.Authorization
<CascadingAuthenticationState>
    <Router AppAssembly="@typeof(App).Assembly">
        <Found Context="routeData">
            <AuthorizeRouteView RouteData="@routeData"
            ➥DefaultLayout="@typeof(MainLayout)">
```

```
                <NotAuthorized>
                    @if (!context.User.Identity.IsAuthenticated)
                    {
                        <p><a href="bff/login">Login</a></p>
                    }
                    else
                    {
                        <p>You are not authorized to access this resource.</p>
                    }
                </NotAuthorized>
            </AuthorizeRouteView>
        </Found>
        <NotFound>
            <PageTitle>Not found</PageTitle>
            <LayoutView Layout="@typeof(MainLayout)">
                <p role="alert">Sorry, there's nothing at this address.</p>
            </LayoutView>
        </NotFound>
    </Router>
</CascadingAuthenticationState>
```

It might not look like it, but that was the easy part. The application needs to determine the authentication state. .NET has the AuthenticationStateProvider for that, but for BFF, some custom implementation is required. The BFF framework sets up an endpoint to retrieve the user information (bff/user), and our custom provider needs to call that. There's a very elaborate implementation for that in the BFF samples (http://mng.bz/rJMg), where the user information is cached and periodically updated, but for our plans, a simpler approach that just calls the BFF user endpoint upon request is good enough. The next listing implements a custom AuthenticationStateProvider.

Listing 13.11   The AuthenticationStateProvider for BFF

```
using Microsoft.AspNetCore.Components.Authorization;
using System.Net;
using System.Net.Http.Json;
using System.Security.Claims;

namespace AspNetCoreSecurity.BlazorWasmClient.Client;

public class BffAuthenticationStateProvider : AuthenticationStateProvider
{
    private readonly HttpClient _client;

    public BffAuthenticationStateProvider(
        HttpClient client)
    {
        _client = client;
    }

    public override async Task<AuthenticationState>
    GetAuthenticationStateAsync()
    {
```

```
        var user = await FetchUser();
        var state = new AuthenticationState(user);

        return state;
    }

    record ClaimRecord(string Type, object Value);

    private async Task<ClaimsPrincipal> FetchUser()
    {
        try
        {
            var response = await _client.GetAsync(        │ Calls the BFF user endpoint
                "bff/user?slide=false");

            if (response.StatusCode == HttpStatusCode.OK)
            {
                var claims = await
                ➥response.Content.ReadFromJsonAsync<List<ClaimRecord>>();

                var identity = new ClaimsIdentity(
                    nameof(BffAuthenticationStateProvider),
                    "name",
                    "role");

                foreach (var claim in claims ??       │ Stores all claims in the ClaimsIdentity
                    new List<ClaimRecord>())
                {
                    identity.AddClaim(new Claim(claim.Type,
                    ➥claim.Value.ToString() ?? string.Empty));
                }

                return new ClaimsPrincipal(identity);
            }
        }
        catch (Exception ex)
        {
        }

        return new ClaimsPrincipal(new ClaimsIdentity());
    }
}
```

We will also need to add yet another class to the Blazor client application. The BFF framework comes with built-in CSRF protection, and the endpoint expects the X-CSRF: 1 HTTP header. The DelegatingHandler from the next listing adds this header:

Listing 13.12 The DelegatingHandler for BFF's CSRF protection

```
namespace AspNetCoreSecurity.BlazorWasmClient.Client;

public class AntiforgeryHandler : DelegatingHandler
{
```

```
    protected override Task<HttpResponseMessage> SendAsync(
        HttpRequestMessage request, CancellationToken cancellationToken)
    {
        request.Headers.Add("X-CSRF", "1");
        return base.SendAsync(request, cancellationToken);
    }
}
```

Finally, both the `AuthenticationStateProvider` and the `DelegatingHandler` need to be configured in the Blazor client project's Program.cs file so that the communication with the BFF endpoint works as expected. The following listing shows what needs to be added.

Listing 13.13   The Program.cs file of the Blazor client project

```
using AspNetCoreSecurity.BlazorWasmClient.Client;
using Microsoft.AspNetCore.Components.Authorization;
using Microsoft.AspNetCore.Components.Web;
using Microsoft.AspNetCore.Components.WebAssembly.Hosting;
using System.Net.Http;

var builder = WebAssemblyHostBuilder.CreateDefault(args);
builder.RootComponents.Add<App>("#app");
builder.RootComponents.Add<HeadOutlet>("head::after");

builder.Services.AddAuthorizationCore();
builder.Services.AddScoped<AuthenticationStateProvider,
➥BffAuthenticationStateProvider>();

builder.Services.AddTransient<AntiforgeryHandler>();
builder.Services.AddHttpClient(
    "backend",
    client => client.BaseAddress =
    ➥new Uri(builder.HostEnvironment.BaseAddress))
    .AddHttpMessageHandler<AntiforgeryHandler>();
builder.Services.AddTransient(sp =>
➥sp.GetRequiredService<IHttpClientFactory>().CreateClient("backend"));

await builder.Build().RunAsync();
```

From a Blazor point of view, the application is done; however, IdentityServer does not know about the new client yet. By now, you should know the drill: go to the Config.cs file and add the configuration options of the new client there. These settings will do in our scenario:

```
public static IEnumerable<Client> Clients =>
    new Client[]
    {
...
        new Client()
        {
            ClientId = "blazorwasm",
            ClientSecrets =
```

```
        {
            new Secret("correct horse battery staple".Sha256())
        },
        AllowedScopes = new List<string>
        {
            IdentityServerConstants.StandardScopes.OpenId,
            IdentityServerConstants.StandardScopes.Profile,
            IdentityServerConstants.StandardScopes.OfflineAccess,
            "api"
        },
        AllowOfflineAccess = true,
        AllowedGrantTypes = GrantTypes.Code,
        RedirectUris = { "https://localhost:5031/signin-oidc" },
        PostLogoutRedirectUris =
   ➥{ "https://localhost:5031/signout-callback-oidc" }
    }
};
```

One minor, yet important piece of the puzzle is missing. The API may not be compatible with BFF yet; it needs to return HTTP 401 instead of a potential redirect to an OIDC provider. This can be done by adding a call to AsBffApiEndpoint() in the API's Program.cs file as follows:

```
app.UseEndpoints(endpoints =>
{
    endpoints.MapControllers()
        .RequireAuthorization("ApiScopePolicy")
        .AsBffApiEndpoint();
});
```

And that's it! When you run the Blazor application in the browser (and launch the API and IdentityServer at the same time), you will be prompted to log in once you access the *Fetch data* page (figure 13.17).

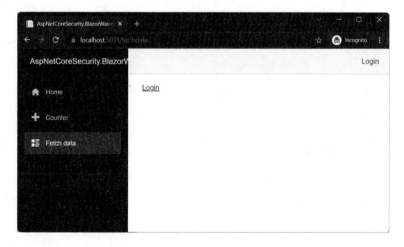

Figure 13.17 Blazor requires the user to log in.

Clicking the login link redirects the browser to IdentityServer; after the user successfully logs in, the browser returns to the Blazor application. The username correctly shows up in the top-right corner. When going to the *Fetch data* page again, the random temperature values are shown after a short delay (figure 13.18).

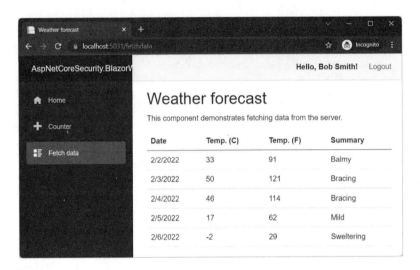

Figure 13.18   Blazor recognizes the user and may call the protected API.

Options for other SPA frameworks

In this chapter we had to make some deliberate choices, including which OAuth and OIDC framework to use (we picked IdentityServer), and which SPA framework to cover (we chose Blazor WebAssembly, since it is closest to the topic of the book). For the latter decision, especially, there were many other options. For the most popular ones, here are a few resources and guidance on what to use:

- *Blazor Server*—Since everything runs on the server, the server itself can issue the call to the protected SPA, so just using IdentityModel is the easiest way. The IdentityServer project provides a sample at http://mng.bz/xnY8.
- *Angular*—The SPA framework that originated from Google is probably the most widely used choice at the moment. There are several OAuth/OIDC libraries written in TypeScript. The two most popular ones are currently `angular-oauth2-oidc` by Manfred Steyer and `angular-auth-oidc-client` by Damien Bod and Fabian Gosebrink.
- *React*—This framework, originally from Facebook, also offers a variety of options. When using IdentityServer and the BFF framework, the good news is that there is already a sample that shows you how to set everything up: http://mng.bz/AyRp.

> • *Other JavaScript frameworks*—When working with a custom-built JavaScript application or using a framework that works with JavaScript (and not Type-Script) such as Vue.js, several IdentityServer samples show possible implementation approaches. Using BFF also allows you to avoid having to handle tokens within JavaScript code. A good starting point is this sample: http://mng.bz/ZA4m.

These are just a few common scenarios where OAuth and OpenID Connect come in handy. There are several more—you could implement these standards in desktop applications, or you could use multifactor authentication to allow users to easily sign into an application on the TV's (hard to remotely control) screen. With frameworks and libraries like OpenIddict, Auth0, IdentityServer, and others, you should be covered. OAuth is hard—so don't attempt to reinvent the wheel; use established solutions and implementations instead.

Summary

Let's review what we have learned so far:

- JWT (JSON Web Token) is a token format that can be signed and optionally encrypted.
- ASP.NET Core Web APIs can be conveniently protected with JWTs from unauthorized access.
- OAuth 2.0 is a framework and protocol for authorization for web (and other) applications.
- OpenID Connect is an authentication layer on top of OAuth 2.0.
- There are several established libraries and frameworks for OAuth 2.0 and OpenID Connect in the .NET ecosystem.
- OAuth's client credentials flow is useful for machine-to-machine communication, whereas the authorization code + PKCE flow is used for interactive applications (usually a web browser is involved).
- The BFF pattern is a fine choice to protect APIs so that they may be called from a variety of clients, including SPAs.
- In this chapter, IdentityServer was used to protect APIs in a variety of scenarios; this would, of course, also have been possible in similar fashion with the other options.

Part 6

Security as a process

No matter how well-versed you are in terms of web application security, if you don't have a process, you cannot use your knowledge to its full potential. This part of the book looks at several security aspects that should be part of your process and that should increase the security of your web application even more.

Chapter 14 talks about dependencies and how to track them and keep them up to date (despite that being an uphill battle). In chapter 15, we briefly discuss several tools for auditing web applications, aiding you in finding potential security risks in your application. Finally, chapter 16 presents the 2021 edition of the popular Top 10 list of the Open Web Application Security Project (OWASP) and how it applies to the contents of this book.

Secure dependencies

The JavaScript package `ua-parser-js` (www.npmjs.com/package/ua-parser-js), available via npm, enjoys quite a bit of popularity. The library provides functionality to detect the browser type the client is using, including information about the operating system; device features such as type, model, and CPU; and much more. The package is pretty useful, especially considering how confusing the user agents in modern browsers can be. Here's one from Microsoft Edge 98 on an iPad:

```
Mozilla/5.0 (Macintosh; Intel Mac OS X 10_14_6) AppleWebKit/605.1.15
(KHTML, like Gecko) EdgiOS/98 Version/13.0.3 Safari/605.1.15
```

On Windows, the same browser has the following identification string:

```
Mozilla/5.0 (Windows NT 10.0; Win64; x64) AppleWebKit/537.36 (KHTML, like
Gecko) Chrome/98.0.4758.80 Safari/537.36 Edg/98.0.1108.50
```

But wait, it gets better—here's Edge 99 on iPad:

```
Mozilla/5.0 (iPad; CPU OS 15_4 like Mac OS X) AppleWebKit/605.1.15 (KHTML,
like Gecko) EdgiOS/99.0.1150.52 Version/15.0 Mobile/15E148 Safari/604.1
```

Those values look similar but different at the same time. Deferring the parsing of this information to a library that has, at the time of this writing, almost 8 million weekly downloads sounds like a good idea. Also, the package seems to be relatively stable. Version 0.7.0 was released in 2014, and 0.7.28 came out in 2021. Over 1,200 packages depend on ua-parser-js. So far, so good.

In October 2021, the US Cybersecurity & Infrastructure Security Agency (CISA) reported that they had discovered malware in version 0.7.29 of ua-parser-js (http://mng.bz/R42j). Someone managed to release this version of the library and included a crypto miner in the code. Every piece of software using ua-parser-js and blindly running npm update (which updates all packages to their latest versions) got the malware.

After the CISA report, the infected version was quickly pulled from npm, and new releases were made. This shows a typical issue when working with dependencies: you are responsible for making sure that not only is your software is secure, but so are all of your dependencies.

There have been more incidents. In early 2022, the maintainer of two popular npm packages, color.js and faker.js, supposedly sabotaged them by releasing broken versions of them, breaking many applications depending on those packages. See http://mng.bz/2nw8 for more details.

The situation is not much better in the .NET world, where NuGet is the dominant package manager (mostly for server-side libraries). An analysis from July 2021 found 51 software components on NuGet with critical, exploitable vulnerabilities. The report at http://mng.bz/1o81 contains all the details. One example they give is the WinSCPHelper library, which includes a vulnerable version of the WinSCP package.

The grass isn't necessarily greener on the other side—it doesn't really matter which technology stack or which package manager you are using. Having outdated dependencies is a general problem, but the remedies depend on the package manager being used. Let's start with npm.

14.1   *Using npm audit*

Many modern JavaScript frameworks suffer from a myriad of dependencies. Maybe "suffer" is not the right term, since all of those extra libraries provide some functionality that the JavaScript framework does not need to implement on its own. But the more dependencies you have, the harder it is to keep control over them. As the ua-parser-js example shows, you can't just blindly update to the latest version whenever there's a new release of a dependency. And sometimes the framework itself requires specific, older package versions.

Let's look at a few examples of how much of an effort may be required to ensure dependencies are up to date. Figure 14.1 shows the console output—as of time of writing—when installing the Angular CLI (https://angular.io/cli), which is routinely used to create new Angular apps and build them.

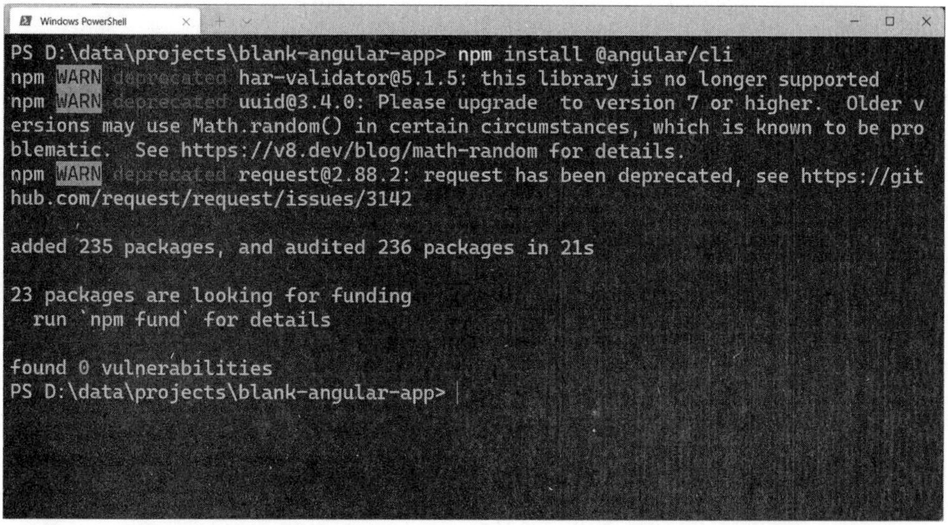

Figure 14.1   Installing the Angular CLI

According to the output, zero vulnerabilities were found, which sounds good at first. However, there are three warnings:

- One of the dependencies is no longer supported.
- For one of the dependencies, there is a much more recent version available (the error message mentions at least 7, but version 8.3 is already out—Angular CLI installs 3.4.0).
- One of the dependencies has been deprecated.

In addition, there are several packages with a version number below 1 (visible as part of the installation process), which historically suggests that they have not reached a final state yet. Angular CLI continues to work just fine, but those messages are at least a bit unsettling, don't you think?

It's even worse when using one of Angular's main competitors, React (https://reactjs.org/). The npx package runner is a common tool used to create a new React app, with the following command:

```
npx create-react-app name-of-app
```

This also installs a bunch of dependencies, not all of them to the liking of security-minded people, as figure 14.2 shows.

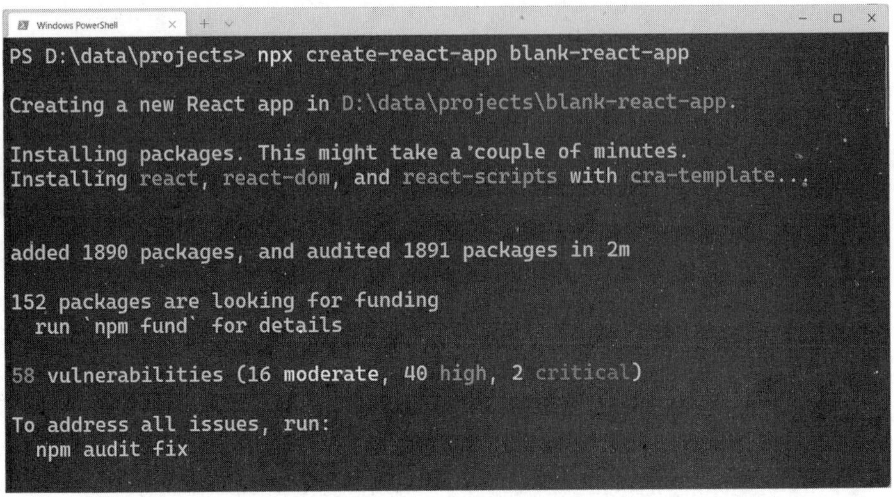

Figure 14.2   Creating a new React app

A stunning number of 58 vulnerabilities are reported by npm, including two critical ones.

> **NOTE** Don't get me wrong—I'm not saying that Angular or React is doing something wrong. There may be many reasons why they are referencing deprecated or potentially vulnerable packages. But this just shows how hard it is to remain in control when having so many dependencies.

In theory, this problem is easy to solve: just verify for each and every package that it is up to date and has no (known) security vulnerabilities and no malware. In practice, this is futile, obviously. Angular CLI, for instance, depends on over 350 packages (including subdependencies: one dependency is the `debug` package, which in turn depends on the `ms` package). This is hard to manage manually. A more realistic approach is to use some kind of automation. In fact, npm already has this built in: the `npm audit` command checks each installed dependency against a database of vulnerable packages. Four vulnerability levels are supported:

- Low
- Moderate
- High
- Critical

You have already seen the output of an `npm audit` call in figures 14.1 and 14.2—the installations ran that command automatically. There are several options for that command, but the most important one tries to fix all vulnerabilities:

```
npm audit fix
```

This tries to update all vulnerable packages that `npm audit` reported to more recent versions. This may often work, but there are cases where this will fail. One common reason: SemVer. This is a set of rules for assigning version numbers, specified by one of the GitHub cofounders, Tom Preston-Werner. The official home page at https://semver.org/ contains a detailed description and many examples, but for explaining `npm audit fix`, a rather concise explanation will do.

Assume that a version number consists of three parts, a major, minor, and patch version. For instance, if a package release is versioned with 1.2.3, then 1 is the major version, 2 is the minor version, and 3 is the patch version. The basic SemVer rules are as follows:

1. Changes that break backward compatibility require a new major version.
2. Adding a new feature that is backward compatible requires a new minor version number.
3. Adding a bug fix that is backward compatible requires a new patch version number.

The package.json file contains a list of all top-level dependencies. Here is an excerpt from the file of a new React app:

```
"dependencies": {
    "@testing-library/jest-dom": "^5.14.1",
    "@testing-library/react": "^11.2.7",
    "@testing-library/user-event": "^12.8.3",
    "react": "^17.0.2",
    "react-dom": "^17.0.2",
    "react-scripts": "^0.9.5",
    "web-vitals": "^1.1.2"
}
```

The `"^0.9.5"` value for the `react-scripts` package means that all version numbers from 0.9.5 (inclusive) to 1.0.0 (exclusive) may be installed—basically, all versions that are backward compatible to 0.9.5. Bummer: the next non-prerelease version after 0.9.5 is 1.0.0, so there is no 0.9.x version that the dependency may be updated to.

If, as is the case here, there are no updates for a vulnerable package version that are backward compatible, `npm audit fix` fails. You can disable the SemVer security mechanism with the following command:

```
npm audit fix --force
```

Of course, there might be a good reason why *package.json* relies on SemVer. There is no guarantee that the application works as before if a package is updated to a version that may not be backward compatible. There is no easy solution to this.

But is vulnerable really vulnerable? I've chosen React as an example for a reason. Dan Abramov, one of the creators of the `create-react-app` script, wrote a very insightful post at https://overreacted.io/npm-audit-broken-by-design/. He gets five vulnerabilities when creating a new React app and running `npm audit`, and goes through them one by one. Long story short: to use Abramov's phrasing, all of those vulnerabilities are "absurd in this context." He goes as far as calling them "false alarms." On a technical level, he may even be right. On the other hand, just the presence of a vulnerability, no matter whether it's exploitable or not, may raise a red flag.

A good compromise may look like this: establish a process to regularly validate whether the packages you are using are up to date. Try to update as early as possible; if you've already established automated testing of your application, you can more easily validate whether everything still works as expected post-upgrade. For every vulnerable package you keep, analyze the security vulnerability and prove that it does not apply to your application.

In the .NET space, npm is still comparably rare (due to its focus on JavaScript packages). For .NET dependencies, NuGet is the default package manager.

14.2   *Keeping NuGet dependencies up-to-date*

When going to the NuGet page of a particular package version number, you will immediately see if that specific version contains a *known* vulnerability. If so, you are told right at the page, as figure 14.3 shows (we are using an old version of the Umbraco CMS package as an example: www.nuget.org/packages/UmbracoCms/8.9.3).

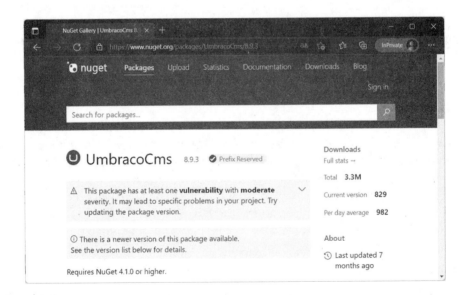

Figure 14.3   This package version is vulnerable.

The warning with the yellow background appears only if NuGet has that information in the system. The data source is the GitHub Advisory Database, located at https://github.com/advisories.

Remember the `WinSCPHelper` example from the beginning of this chapter? The package's NuGet page (www.nuget.org/packages/WinSCPHelper/) does not mention that it contains a vulnerable component (and the last update occurred in 2017). We always depend on that metadata being available.

Visual Studio automatically checks whether there are new versions for NuGet packages used in a project. Figure 14.4 shows the responsible part of the NuGet package manager UI.

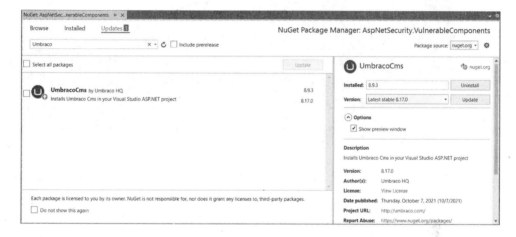

Figure 14.4   Visual Studio shows which packages have newer versions available.

The IDE shows the new versions and offers to update them but does not really mention whether any security vulnerabilities are being closed. Also, it is obviously cumbersome to manually and frequently check whether there is a new, more secure version of a dependency. Luckily, this process may be automated to some degree.

One mechanism is directly built into the `dotnet` command line tool. The `dotnet list package` command shows all packages with the current project. Adding the `--vulnerable` switch also checks whether there are reported vulnerabilities:

```
dotnet list package --vulnerable
```

If you want to check top-level packages and subpackages, too, add the `--include-transitive` switch:

```
dotnet list package --vulnerable --include-transitive
```

Figure 14.5 shows the output when running either of these commands for a project that contains the old Umbraco version from figure 14.3. You can see which packages are vulnerable, and which severity level is reported.

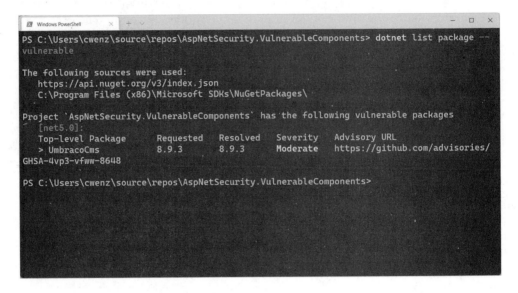

Figure 14.5   The dotnet tool lists vulnerable packages.

NOTE   The `--vulnerable switch` was added in .NET 5. For previous versions, a third-party CLI extension added the `dotnet retire` command, which ran a similar check. Once .NET 5 was released, `dotnet retire` was, well, retired.

Wouldn't it be nice if there was a way to detect vulnerable components at run time? A while ago, OWASP (see chapter 16) provided the `SafeNuGet` project, which can be found at https://github.com/OWASP/SafeNuGet. It implemented an `MSBuildTask` that did exactly that. The only catch: the last update to the project was in early 2015. It would be better to use `NuGetDefense`, a package inspired by `SafeNuGet` but actively maintained. The project home page (https://digitalcoyote.github.io/NuGet Defense/) contains all relevant information. There are two ways to use this package: either as a command-line tool or as a build task. To use the former, first install the tool as follows:

```
dotnet tool install NuGetDefense.Tool -g
```

This will make the command-line tool `nugetdefense` globally available. One way to call it manually is to run it, providing the name of a .sln file.

```
nugetdefense NameOfProject.sln
```

Figure 14.6 shows the output when running this tool for a project referencing an older version of the jQuery JavaScript library that contains a security issue.

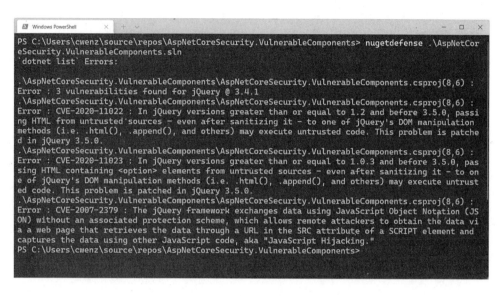

Figure 14.6   The `nugetdefense` tool detects a package with security vulnerabilities.

This tool and its output may be used as part of a continuous integration/continuous delivery process to get an early warning about potential security issues in dependencies.

The second option for using `NuGetDefense` is to install the NuGet package of the same name within your .NET project, either using the NuGet package manager or via the UI in Visual Studio. Then a build task will automatically scan all packages for known security issues (using several vulnerability databases). Figure 14.7 shows that the error window in Visual Studio contains basically the same information that was previously generated by the command-line tool.

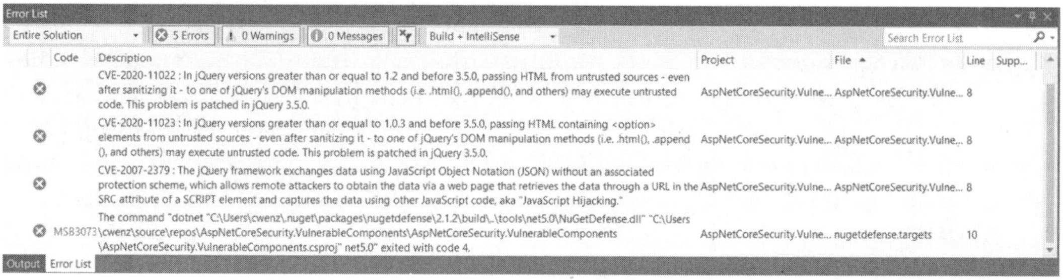

Figure 14.7   The build task makes Visual Studio show errors.

There are other options as well, and a few of them should be mentioned:

- OWASP Dependency-Check (https://owasp.org/www-project-dependency -check/) is an analysis tool from OWASP. It is not tailored to .NET, though.
- Security scanner software Snyk (https://snyk.io/) also offers a CLI version.
- When hosting on GitHub, the Dependabot service (https://github.com/ dependabot) can automatically create pull requests once there is an update for a dependency (independent of whether or not the new version fixes a security issue). Figure 14.8 shows such a pull request. There are more security-related features available at GitHub; see https://github.com/features/security for more information.
- GitLab's Package Hunter (http://mng.bz/PnjY) tries to detect malicious dependencies with run-time monitoring.
- WhiteSource Renovate (http://mng.bz/J2BK) is another popular tool for auto-mating dependency updates and is available as a CLI application and as a GitHub app.

Figure 14.8   A pull request created by Dependabot

It's a challenge to be in control with regards to all dependencies, but at least those packages and libraries are usually scrutinized by many. It's even more important to avoid security issues in your own code. Some software may help with that and will be covered in the next chapter.

Summary

Let's review what we have learned so far:

- If a dependency you use suddenly contains malicious code, this code will be part of your application as well.

- The `npm audit` and `npm audit fix` commands can detect and even update some vulnerable packages, but only to a certain degree.
- .NET comes with a built-in detection feature for vulnerable NuGet packages, `dotnet list package --vulnerable`.
- The `NuGetDefense` package provides both a command-line tool and a `MSBuildTask` to detect vulnerable components used by a .NET project.
- In some cases, using a vulnerable package does not directly pose a security risk—for instance, if the vulnerability may not be exploited due to the way the dependency is being used.

15
Audit tools

This chapter covers

- Finding security vulnerabilities in a web application
- Using OWASP ZAP to automatically scan for vulnerabilities
- Using Security Code Scan and other static code analyzers
- Learning how GitHub Advanced Security helps find security issues

In September 2019, GitHub acquired Semmle, a company providing a code analysis platform for securing software. About a year later, they had integrated and improved the code analysis service and published the results of a 5-month beta phase: 12,000 repositories were scanned, and over 20,000 security issues were identified (see http://mng.bz/woA2).

Not all security issues are visible when just looking at the code, especially for websites. As we have discussed previously in this book—for instance, in chapter 3 (cookie attributes) and chapter 9 (HTTP headers)—even the absence of certain security settings can count as a vulnerability. Therefore, testing an actual, running web application is an important approach as well. The "nine out of ten web applications have security vulnerabilities" study result from chapter 1 (here's the link again: http://mng.bz/qYAJ) was retrieved by doing exactly that: scanning (running) websites for issues.

Wouldn't it be nice to have such a feature available—at the push of a button, any security risks in our application would be found? In theory, that's exactly how those tools work. In practice, however, things are not as easy as they seem. Not everything a tool reports is really a security issue. There might be false positives—vulnerabilities that really aren't vulnerabilities. Also, tools will never be able to reliably find everything security-related in an app. When used correctly, though, code scanners and other software can help in finding (and fixing!) potential issues.

In this chapter, we will look at a few common tools for finding security vulnerabilities and give you a brief introduction to them. We will also discuss gotchas and how to handle the results those tools report. But first, we need to discuss the different approaches to finding security issues in a web application.

15.1 Finding vulnerabilities

When a security audit is conducted, there are usually several processes that help the auditor compile a list of issues and vulnerabilities that are then covered in the report. Tooling can help to a certain degree, and there are two approaches that complement each other well:

- Dynamic analysis is the process that tries to analyze or scan a running application.
- Static analysis analyzes the code itself.

Let's start with dynamic analysis. When talking about web application security, the application that will be scanned is a website. A scanner usually starts by enumerating all the different pages, resources, and APIs that make up the web application. Similar to how search engines like Google index a site, the dynamic scanner tries to determine the structure and components of the target site. Then, each of the pages and endpoints found is scanned. The scanner has a library of potential attack vectors; for instance, sending JavaScript code in different forms, or typical SQL injection payloads. The result from those HTTP requests is scanned to find out whether, for example, the script code sent is now really part of the HTTP response or whether there are any errors on the page once the malicious payload is sent. The scanner also analyzes the HTTP headers that appear in the response to verify the presence of security-related HTTP headers and cookie settings.

> **TIP** The Open Web Application Security Project (OWASP) has compiled a list of dynamic analysis software for web applications, containing both commercial and free tools. You can find it at http://mng.bz/7yRe.

Static code analysis, on the other hand, looks for typical patterns to identify insecure code. In ASP.NET Core web applications, these patterns might include string concatenation for SQL commands or uses of `@Html.Raw()` that potentially allow cross-site scripting. Having access to the source code also allows more complex analysis scenarios, such as determining the source of any data used by the application to verify whether it is (or has originally been) user input or not.

> **TIP** OWASP also curates and maintains a list of static code analysis tools, available at http://mng.bz/mOA4.

Both types of analysis can also be conducted manually, without the aid of specialized software. In practice, both approaches are combined: a tool automatically looks for any incidents. A human then wades through the complete list, throws away the false positives, and manually rechecks the application to find items that are missing. Here, experience and in-depth knowledge can really pay off. For instance, when analyzing a web application based on ASP.NET Framework, there are a few things I am always specifically looking for. For example, is the site using an old version of ASP.NET (prior to 4.5.2, actually), and is the ViewState not secured with a message authentication code? In that case, cross-site scripting is likely. This may be tested in the browser and by looking at the HTML markup sent from the server. However, access to the source code would show us the middlewares being used and the configuration options set, which might also unveil potential issues.

The more information you have about a web application, the more likely you are to uncover security vulnerabilities. There are often situations where the source code will not be made available to the auditor; in those cases, dynamic analysis is the only—but still very powerful—option.

The previous chapters gave you many starting points to look for suspicious application behavior and typical code patterns. With regard to tools, it's hard to recommend just one specific piece of software. Requirements are different, features are different, and the pricing may be very different. In the remaining chapter, we will cover a select number of software products and services that are free to use (and therefore very accessible). Since anything in those tools is subject to change, we limit ourselves to a rather brief introduction to get you started and then point you to further resources. We'll look at a dynamic analysis tool first.

15.2   *OWASP ZAP*

The Open Web Application Security Project, or OWASP, has been mentioned before in this book, including in this chapter. The next chapter will reveal a little bit more about that organization and one of its publications. Now, however, we will focus on one specific software project that OWASP provides for free: the Zed Attack Proxy (ZAP). This is an open source security scanner that conducts a dynamic analysis of web applications. The OWASP website has a section on ZAP, https://owasp.org/www-project-zap/, but due to the popularity of the project, there is also a dedicated website at www.zaproxy .org/.

On that site, you will find in-depth documentation and much more information on ZAP, as well as a download section. At www.zaproxy.org/download/, you can retrieve ZAP for Windows, Linux, and macOS. Even if your operating system is not in the preceding list, if you have Java 11 on your system, the cross-platform package on the download page will enable you to run ZAP.

But before you start using ZAP, you need to find a target to scan. A few important words of caution: don't use an arbitrary web application. ZAP (and other scanning tools) will send many, many HTTP requests to that site. Some applications will consider this a denial-of-service (DoS) attack and temporarily block your IP address, or— even worse—start to malfunction under load. In some jurisdictions, it might even be illegal to do that without the previous consent of the company or person responsible for that site.

There are some publicly available web applications with built-in security holes that purely exist to test scanning tools (and personal hacking skills).

One such web application comes from the team behind the Netsparker application security testing suite. The site at http://aspnet.testsparker.com/, shown in figure 15.1, looks fishy—and it is.

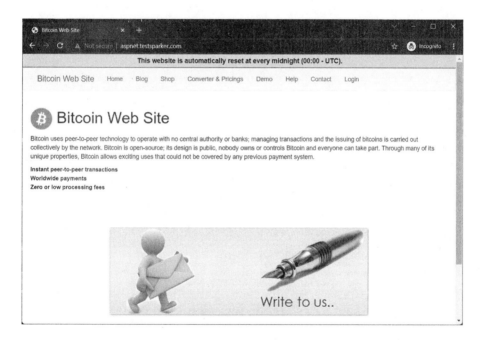

Figure 15.1   An insecure ASP.NET-based web application

As the URL already suggests, this application is implemented using ASP.NET, not ASP.NET Core, but as we have seen so far, the vast majority of attacks work independently of the technology being used. This web application has some well-hidden and some not-so-well-hidden security vulnerabilities, and ZAP might be able to assist in finding them.

Consider using one of those intentionally insecure sites, or even better, your application. Since ZAP runs on your computer, you can also scan web applications in your internal network, not just public ones.

Figure 15.2   Persisting a ZAP session

When you launch ZAP, you are greeted with a modal window asking whether you want to persist the session (figure 15.2).

Keeping a session makes it easier to resume later; either ZAP uses the current timestamp for the session name, or you can specify a specific one (and the location at which to store it). For one-off experiments, there is obviously no need to persist anything, and that option exists as well.

Next up, the actual ZAP application UI appears, including a welcome screen. Click Automated Scan to open a window like the one in figure 15.3, where you can initiate an automated scan (or, as ZAP calls it, launch an "attack").

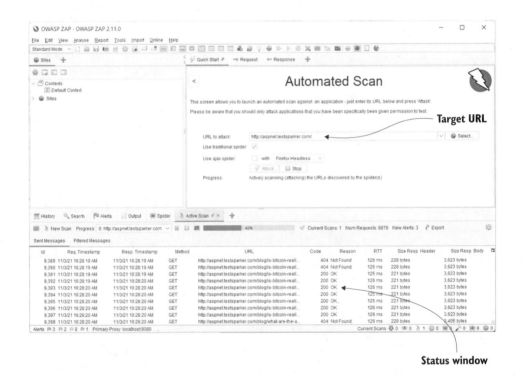

Figure 15.3   The ZAP main screen while a scan is running

You can provide a URL to attack and to use one or two spiders that are responsible for discovering all URLs that the application is using:

- *Traditional spider*—Basically, the application parses the HTML markup on the URL you provide, pulls out all links, and recursively retrieves and parses those.
- *Ajax spider*—JavaScript-based SPAs do not use many regular links, if any. The Ajax (asynchronous JavaScript + XML; an approach used for SPAs in the 2000s) spider launches an invisible browser, loads the application there, and checks which APIs and additional sources are being loaded when simulating user interactions such as mouse clicks.

Afterward, all resources found are now attacked with malicious requests. If you revisit figure 15.3, you will note that in the lower part of the UI, ZAP is running at full steam, having sent almost 9,000 requests, and has found several noteworthy issues (the flags in the lower left corner).

For the Netsparker sample ASP .NET application, figure 15.4 shows the findings after going through the application.

Fifteen alerts don't sound like much, but note that that's just the number of *types* of issues found. For instance, SQL injection was found twice, and something called *cross-domain JavaScript source file inclusion* was found a whopping 471 times.

That was easy—the actual challenge is to find out which of those

Figure 15.4 Findings in the insecure app

items are really worth fixing. For example, including cross-domain JavaScript source files is not an issue per se. The application might intentionally load JavaScript code from a CDN, for instance. It's good that ZAP reports those, since they might also be the result of an XSS attack, but that's also the reason why this issue is marked with a yellow flag.

ZAP provides four categories of issues, or, as they are called in the application, alerts. Here they are in descending order of severity, with one example each:

- *Red*—High (SQL injection)
- *Orange*—Medium (X-FRAME-OPTIONS HTTP header missing)
- *Yellow*—Low (HTTP headers revealing server software)
- *Blue*—Informational (comments found in the HTML markup)

For a complete list of all supported alerts, see www.zaproxy.org/docs/alerts/. Let's look at one of the red-flagged entries. SQL injection certainly deserves a closer look. Figure 15.5 shows the detailed alert information for one of the two SQL injections ZAP supposedly found.

Figure 15.5   Details about a potential SQL injection attack

As you can see from the URL, the `pid` query string parameter is set to 5-2. If you can't see it due to ZAP's tiny font size, here is the full URL: http://aspnet.testsparker.com/ Products.aspx?pid=5-2.

Product IDs in the application are numeric, so this value is certainly invalid. But how does the application react? It turns out that the data returned from the server when requesting that URL is practically identical to that for this URL: http://aspnet .testsparker.com/Products.aspx?pid=3.

It's pretty safe to say that the application interprets 5-2 as 3, and it is highly likely that this happens because the SQL string contains 5-2 (and is then evaluated as 3 by the database). ZAP has successfully detected SQL injection.

OWASP has its own intentionally insecure web application called Juice Shop. Three URLs come in handy here:

- The project home page on the OWASP site is https://owasp.org/www-project -juice-shop/.
- The source code of the app is contained at https://github.com/juice-shop/juice-shop (mostly in TypeScript). Don't copy any of it to one of your own applications, because you copy the security vulnerabilities, too. The code allows you to run the application locally and conveniently do dynamic and static code analysis.
- You can find a running, public instance of the application at https://juice-shop .herokuapp.com/ (figure 15.6). This is the easiest and fastest way to look at the app.

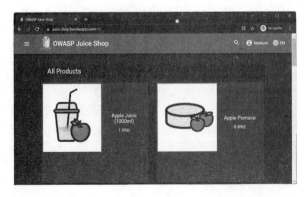

Figure 15.6   The very insecure OWASP Juice Shop

Whether you run ZAP against a local or an online instance of Juice Shop, some (but not all) vulnerabilities will be found. For instance, one of the issues reported is cross-site scripting when calling one of Juice Shop's APIs like this:

https://juice-shop.herokuapp.com/api/Challenges/?sort=<script>alert(1);</script>

Indeed, calling that API in a browser returns content with the `<script>` element intact, as figure 15.7 shows.

Figure 15.7 Looks like cross-site scripting, but isn't

However, as you can also see in the same figure, the `Content-Type` of the resulting page seems to be along the lines of `application/json`, because the browser renders the content as JSON, not as HTML (and therefore does not execute the JavaScript code). This is not a security vulnerability. In the JSON context, a special character that might allow certain injection scenarios would be the double quotes, since they delimit the user-supplied data. Turns out that the Juice Shop implementation does escape double quotes properly (at least within that specific endpoint). To make a long story short, you have to verify and validate each item reported by ZAP and weed out what looks suspicious but in reality, isn't. And that's why an audit is never a fully automated process. Scanning tools are useful but still need human oversight.

This was, of course, just a glimpse of ZAP. The advice given also applies to similar tools: let them run against a web application, and then scrutinize all results, and use additional measures to add more findings to the list.

Authentication for ZAP

ZAP actually missed many of the vulnerabilities in both applications. One of the reasons is that there were issues only visible when the user is logged in, yet we did not provide ZAP with any credentials or with instructions on how and where to use them. There are several approaches to fix that. You might try to log into the application locally and then note the cookies that are created. Most likely, these cookies are used by the application to authenticate the user. If ZAP sends those cookies, it is also logged into the application. It would be even better to specifically tell ZAP how logging into the application works and which username/password combination to use. The ZAP documentation has a dedicated page for this topic at http://mng.bz/5QRa.

You can find much more information on using ZAP in the online documentation at www.zaproxy.org/docs/. A good starting point is the aptly named "Getting Started" section (www.zaproxy.org/docs/desktop/start/), which covers all the basics and dives into many advanced features.

ZAP also supports an add-on system, where you can find those add-ons that are shipped with ZAP by default and can install additional ones using ZAP's own marketplace. There is a tiny Manage Add-ons button in the title navigation bar of the ZAP UI, which opens a dialog to install and update add-ons (figure 15.8).

Figure 15.8   Installing ZAP add-ons

To be honest, the default distribution of ZAP already contains virtually everything you need, but it's still good to know that you might add more features to the application.

ZAP works well independent of which framework is used to create the web application. When doing a static code analysis, it's obviously necessary to have a specialized tool that knows the development stack being used in order to detect insecure code.

15.3   *Security Code Scan*

The open source project Security Code Scan is a static code analyzer for .NET code. It already existed in the .NET Framework days and has been updated to work with .NET and ASP.NET Core as well. The project home page, https://security-code-scan.github .io/, contains installation instructions, a release history, and a pretty thorough documentation. This section will show you how to get started easily.

The first decision to be made is how Security Code Scan should be used, since the project provides three different options:

- A tool integrated in Visual Studio, working globally for all projects
- A NuGet package, working for individual projects
- A standalone command-line application

Let's start with the first option, which can be enabled using the Extensions > Manage Extensions menu entry. Searching for "Security Code Scan" should lead to a result similar to figure 15.9.

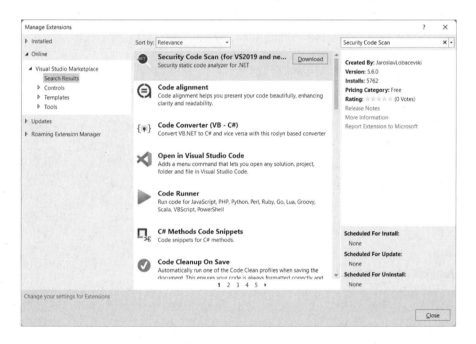

Figure 15.9   Installing Security Code Scan as a Visual Studio extension

If you are seeing an extension just called `Security Code Scan`, resist installing it, since it's an outdated version. There are additional packages specifically for Visual Studio versions 2017 and 2019 (the latter one is also currently the correct one for 2022). After installing the matching extension for your IDE version and restarting Visual Studio, Security Code Scan is activated.

The code is now checked while you are typing it and when compiling. Figure 15.10 shows a typical output listing potential issues.

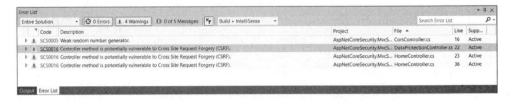

Figure 15.10   The Visual Studio extension found issues in the current project.

Typical findings are MVC controller methods with disabled CSRF protection (as shown in the figure), or potential XSS vulnerabilities or missing configuration options.

Alternatively, you can go the NuGet route, adding Security Code Scan solution-wide, or per project. Once again, don't be tempted to install the package called `Security-CodeScan` (the first option in figure 15.11). Use the version-specific one instead.

Browse	Installed	Updates		NuGet Pac

Security Code Scan   × ▾ ↻ ☐ Include prerelease

SecurityCodeScan by Jaroslav Lobačevski, Philippe Arteau, **3,82M downloads**   ⚠ 3.5.4
Security static code analyzer for .NET
This package version is deprecated. Use SecurityCodeScan.VS2019 instead.

SecurityCodeScan.VS2017 by Jaroslav Lobačevski, Philippe Arteau, **896K downloads**   ⚠ 3.5.4
Security static code analyzer for .NET
This package version is deprecated. Use SecurityCodeScan.VS2019 instead.

SecurityCodeScan.VS2019 by Jaroslav Lobačevski, **650K downloads**   5.6.0
Security static code analyzer for .NET

Figure 15.11   Installing Security Code Scan as a NuGet package

Once the package is installed and active, you might see warning messages in the output window of Visual Studio (figure 15.12). As you can easily see, the messages are the same as the one from the Visual Studio extension.

```
Controllers\DataProtectionController.cs(22,30,22,35): warning SCS0016: Controller method is potentially vulnerable to Cross Site Request Forgery (CSRF).
Controllers\HomeController.cs(23,30,23,39): warning SCS0016: Controller method is potentially vulnerable to Cross Site Request Forgery (CSRF).
Controllers\HomeController.cs(36,30,36,39): warning SCS0016: Controller method is potentially vulnerable to Cross Site Request Forgery (CSRF).
Controllers\CorsController.cs(16,20,16,37): warning SCS0005: Weak random number generator.
```

Figure 15.12   The NuGet package found issues in the current project.

The third option for using Security Code Scanner is a command-line tool, which can be installed globally using the `dotnet tool` command. Here is the complete call required to get it onto your system:

```
dotnet tool install --global security-scan
```

Afterward, you will have the `security-scan` command at your disposal. The easiest way to run it is to provide the .sln file of the Visual Studio solution to scan as an argument:

```
security-scan MyProject.sln
```

Figure 15.13 shows both the installation and the output of running the tool against the same application that was previously used for the NuGet and Visual Studio extension versions.

Figure 15.13 Security Code Scan as a standalone application

The warnings created are the same, but this time, you have more options at your disposal due to the command-line arguments supported (`security-scan -?` gives you a complete list, including options to exclude certain projects and to run scans in parallel). The standalone tool also allows you to explicitly execute the scan, whereas the options integrated in Visual Studio basically scan the application all the time.

As usual, the quality of the results depends on the quality of the rules included in the code scanner. Security Code Scanner comes with more than 30 rules (https://security-code-scan.github.io/#Rules provides a complete list). It cannot detect everything, but it is still helpful. Remember: defense in-depth is key in security.

More often than not, an application's source code is checked into a repository. If GitHub is being used, we have an additional scanning opportunity at our disposal.

15.4   *GitHub Advanced Security*

Remember GitHub's 2019 purchase of the Semmle company we mentioned at the beginning of this chapter? The technology GitHub was probably most interested in was CodeQL, a code-analysis engine. In the meantime, it is now an integral part of the distributed code-hosting service. GitHub calls this *GitHub Advanced Security*. For public repositories, you can currently activate scanning at no cost. For private repositories and enterprise accounts, a license is required.

The service is very easy to use: just configure a workflow that essentially triggers CodeQL. The engine currently supports the following languages:

- C++
- C#
- Go
- Java
- JavaScript
- Python
- Ruby
- TypeScript

C# and JavaScript, possibly the two languages the audience of this book primarily uses, are included, so we should be ready to go. First, we need to create a YAML file that configures CodeQL and sets up a workflow. Go to the settings page of any of your applicable (i.e., public, unless you have a license) repositories, and select the Security & Analysis tab. The result may look similar to figure 15.14.

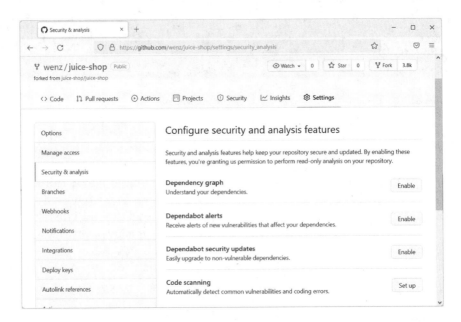

Figure 15.14   GitHub's security and analysis features

You are provided with several choices, including the option to use Dependabot (see chapter 14), and, as the final item, setting up code-scanning services. Click the appropriate Set Up button to load a URL with this pattern: https://github.com/<GitHub user name>/<repository name>/security/code-scanning.

The resulting page provides a list of all available code-scanning services, as shown in figure 15.15.

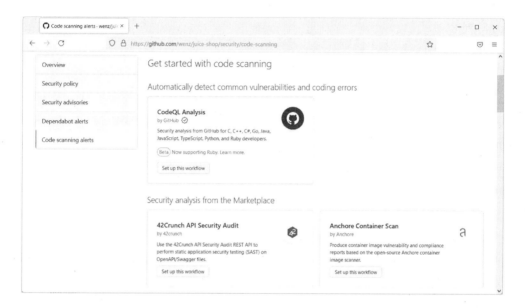

Figure 15.15   GitHub's code-scanning services

At the time of this writing, the first entry is GitHub's CodeQL Analysis service, but there's also a marketplace with three dozen third-party alternatives. When selecting CodeQL, you are prompted to create a file called codeql-analysis.yml in the .github/workflows folder of your repository. GitHub uses the contents in this folder to find, configure, and execute workflows.

GitHub already suggests content for the new YAML file, including configuring it for the languages supposedly used in your code. Some projects already come with such a file (in that case, you may skip creating the new file). The contents of the file, of course, depend on the mechanism and structure of your repository and code, but the following listing shows a good starting point with reasonable settings for most projects.

Listing 15.1   Configuring a CodeQL workflow

```
name: "CodeQL"

on:
  push:
```

```
    branches: [ main ]                                                  Starts analysis
  pull_request:                                                         when a push
    # The branches below must be a subset of the branches above         happens to these
    branches: [ main ]              Starts analysis when a              branch(es)
  schedule:                         pull request for this/these
    - cron: '44 5 * * 1'            branch(es) is created

jobs:
  analyze:
    name: Analyze
    runs-on: ubuntu-latest
    permissions:
      actions: read
      contents: read
      security-events: write

    strategy:
      fail-fast: false
      matrix:                                             Shows languages used
        language: [ 'javascript', 'csharp' ]              in the code to be scanned

    steps:
    - name: Checkout repository        Does checkout
      uses: actions/checkout@v2        prior to scanning

    # Initializes the CodeQL tools for scanning.
    - name: Initialize CodeQL
      uses: github/codeql-action/init@v1      Initializes CodeQL for the
      with:                                   language(s) selected
        languages: ${{ matrix.language }}

    - name: Autobuild                              Automatically builds the
      uses: github/codeql-action/autobuild@v1      application prior to analysis

    - name: Perform CodeQL Analysis
      uses: github/codeql-action/analyze@v1      Performs the analysis
```

Basically, you define when to run code analysis (e.g., after pushing code or receiving a pull request), which languages to scan, and what to do prior to the analysis (checking out the repository, building the solution, and so on).

Once that file has been added to your repository, it won't take long for GitHub to pick it up and process it. If you go to the *Actions* page of your repository (https://github.com/<user name>/<repository name>/actions), you will see your workflow. It could still be in the queue, waiting for a slot to run, or already in progress (figure 15.16 shows the latter).

Any issues the code-scanning process finds are reported in the Security tab of the repository, under Code Scanning Alerts. Figure 15.17 shows the results when running such an analysis over a forked version of the Juice Shop source code.

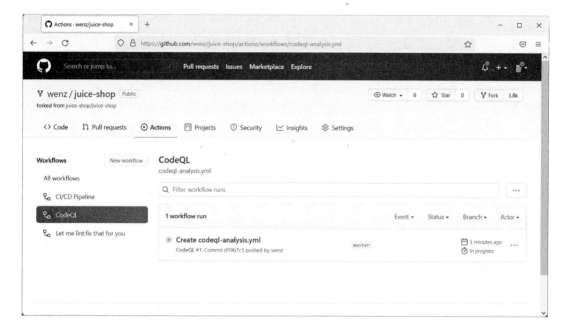

Figure 15.16   The code-analysis workflow is running.

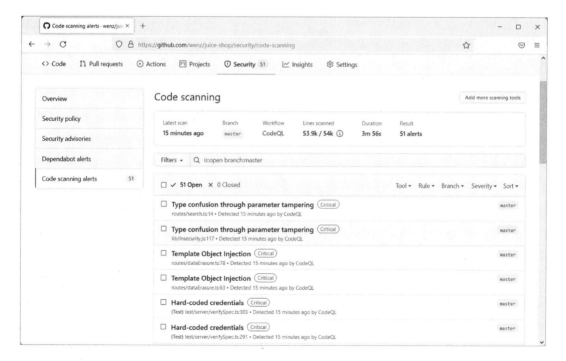

Figure 15.17   The issues found by the CodeQL code-scanning service

Fifty-one alerts—that's quite a lot. All potential finds have been converted into issues ready to be verified and resolved by the development team. The same caveat applies as for the other automated tools: not everything they find is necessarily a security vulnerability, and they also won't find 100% of the issues all of the time. But with minimal configuration, applications have yet another extra safeguard against insecure code.

Summary

Let's review what you have learned so far:

- Static code analysis looks at the source code, searching for patterns known to be insecure.
- Dynamic code analysis tries to attack a running (web) application, finding exploitable vulnerabilities.
- During a security audit of a web application, static and dynamic code analysis are routinely used, utilizing tools and manual analysis.
- OWASP ZAP is an open source dynamic code-analysis tool that can help find security issues in a web application.
- Security Code Scan is a static code-analysis tool, available as a Visual Studio extension, a NuGet package, and a standalone command-line tool.
- GitHub Advanced Security provides free static code scanning to public GitHub repositories, using the CodeQL technology acquired in 2019.

OWASP Top 10

OWASP (https://owasp.org) is a nonprofit organization that advocates web application security. It was founded in September 2001 and has since created a lot of content and offerings:

- Events, local and global
- Cheat sheets for various kinds of attacks, with technology-specific advice
- Checklists and guidelines for security testing
- Software such as the OWASP Zed Attack Proxy, ZAP (see chapter 15)
- Training material such as the Juice Shop, an application with many (intentional) security vulnerabilities
- And much more

The best-known OWASP project, however, is the OWASP Top 10 list, which we will cover in this chapter, along with other top 10 lists. Not surprisingly, we have covered all aspects of these lists in previous chapters (or, at least, have good reasons why we didn't). This chapter serves as a refresher on many things we discussed earlier in this book and reiterates how the threats from the list items may be mitigated with ASP.NET Core.

16.1 OWASP Top 10

The first edition of the OWASP Top 10 was created in 2003. The next release came one year later, in 2004. Then OWASP decided to use a three-year cadence, so subsequent editions of the list were released in 2007, 2010, and 2013. For the last two editions, the planned three years turned into four. The 2016 list was delayed until 2017, and the 2020 list was released in September 2021, conveniently coinciding with the OWASP 20-year celebration. This chapter is based on the 2021 list but will reference the 2017 edition a few times to describe the evolution of the list.

The OWASP Top 10 is *not* a list of the top 10 security vulnerabilities for web applications. Instead, it's a list of the top 10 security risks. Therefore, the list contains both specific attacks and more general threats. The OWASP Top 10 is an awareness document, so its major aim is to help developers manage security of their web applications by having a "standard" to adhere to. The word "standard" is in quotes here because the list is a rather de facto standard. Still, in creating the list, the OWASP team tried to use a data-driven process as much as possible (even though there are some subjective elements in it).

16.1.1 Top 10 creation process

Whenever it's time for a new OWASP Top 10 list, a community survey is created. Web application security practitioners—for instance, companies and individuals doing security audits—basically provide the results of their findings, specifically their numbers: security vulnerability *X* was found *Y* times. As a basis for the categories to report, OWASP uses the CWE (Common Weakness Enumeration) category system, which is sponsored by MITRE (www.mitre.org). The CWE standard is continuously updated and is approaching 1,000 entries. Looking at the number of a list entry, you can (to some degree) deduce the age. For instance, cross-site scripting (XSS) is item number 79, whereas missing or insecure `SameSite` cookie values is at number 1,275. (Yes, that's more than 1,000, but there are also meta categories in the CWE list that I do not count as individual weaknesses.) Figure 16.1 shows the CWE entry for XSS (https://cwe.mitre.org/data/definitions/79.html).

Previous editions of the OWASP Top 10 picked about 30 CWEs for the community survey and asked participants to report only numbers for those. For the 2021 list, no such restriction was given. This led to a greater variety of data, but also meant more work for the OWASP Top 10 team. Putting values for 30 CWEs into ten categories is

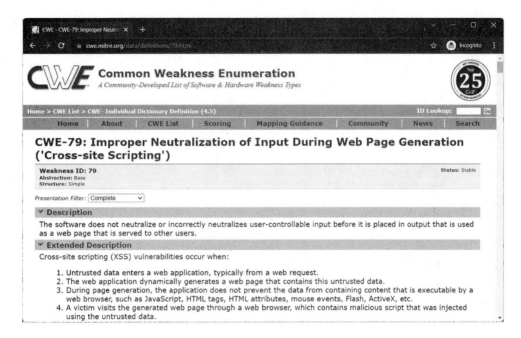

Figure 16.1   XSS in the CWE from MITRE

certainly easier and less time-consuming than having potentially hundreds of CWEs (actually, almost 400 CWEs were turned in during the survey).

It therefore took several months to group those CWEs into eight categories that make up the OWASP Top 10. Some categories hold a few dozen CWEs, whereas others contain only a few. The OWASP team started with the incidence rate of a CWE and then looked at the exploitability (how easy is it to exploit such a weakness if found), and also the technical impact (how bad it is if someone exploits the weakness). Although there are a few aspects that may be nondeterministic—for instance, which categories should be used and which CWEs will be put into them—the end result is as data-driven as possible.

But wait—why eight items on a "top 10" list? Because there was also a second community survey. In that survey, practitioners were asked what their personal top 10 list would look like. The two highest-ranking entries on that list that were not among the top eight determined by the data analysis were then added to the list, resulting in ten items in total.

The OWASP Top 10 is such a flagship project that it is the top item in the Projects navigation menu on the OWASP home page (figure 16.2; note that it's written "Top Ten" there and "Top 10" almost anywhere else). There is much more information about the OWASP Top 10 list and the methodology used at the dedicated subsite, https://owasp.org/Top10/. And with that, let's look at all items on the 2021 Top 10 list.

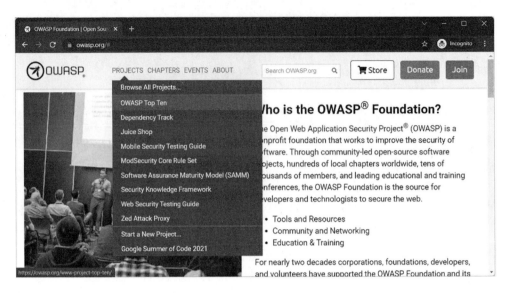

Figure 16.2   The OWASP Top 10 is prominently featured on the OWASP site.

16.1.2 *#1: Broken access control*

The most common security risk for web applications, at least according to the 2021 OWASP Top 10, is a broken access control. In the previous edition of the list, this item had the #5 spot, but it moved to the top in 2021. One of the reasons may be that it encompasses 34 CWEs, covering a large variety of vulnerabilities.

The name of the category is pretty self-descriptive; anything going wrong related to authentication and authorization is part of it. We covered those topics in great detail in part 5 of this book (chapters 12 and 13). Often, broken access control is caused by improper input validation, which was the topic of chapter 5.

A rather surprising addition to the "broken access control" list item is cross-site request forgery (CSRF), the topic of chapter 4. In the 2017 list, CSRF fell off of the Top 10; in 2021, it reappears as part of the #1 category.

16.1.3 *#2: Cryptographic failures*

"Only" 29 CWEs are mapped to the #2 item of the 2021 Top 10 List, "cryptographic failures." The high position on the list may sound surprising at first, since cryptography is something all modern frameworks provide in the form of a proven and tested reference implementation. Cryptographic algorithms should not be implemented by us from scratch. Things get a bit clearer when we look at what this item was called in the 2017 list (then at the #3 spot): "sensitive data exposure." Data transmitted in cleartext is one of the main risks for this category. Using HTTPS throughout is a quick and effective remedy for many aspects of this list item.

Chapter 3 covered the `secure` attribute for HTTP cookies, which makes sure they are not transmitted via plain HTTP. The chapter also described several approaches to make sure HTTPS is used throughout, including HTTP Strict Transport Security (HSTS).

A specialized vulnerability in this category is the use of hashes without salting, or using a predictable salt. This is especially relevant when hashing passwords, and chapter 8 demonstrated how to do that in a secure manner.

16.1.4 #3: Injection

Since the very first OWASP Top 10, "injection" has held the number one spot. There are several kinds of injections—the major ones are covered in chapter 6—but SQL injection is the most common one by far. The high position in previous lists was a bit of a surprise to me, since defending against SQL injection is relatively easy, especially when using a modern framework. Also, in audits that I conduct, I very rarely encounter this kind of vulnerability these days.

Therefore, it was a great relief to see injection drop to the #3 spot in 2021. According to the sheer numbers, the risk would have barely made the list, clocking in at #9 or #10. However, OWASP decided that XSS, which was covered in great detail in chapter 2, now also belongs in this category. Technically, that's not completely incorrect, since XSS usually means injecting JavaScript or HTML content. Still, blending these two attacks into one category comes as a surprise. XSS attacks are much more varied than SQL injections, and countermeasures are also pretty different; just remember how defense-in-depth techniques such as Content Security Policy (CSP) help mitigate this risk.

On the other hand, XSS alone should earn a high position in the list. In 2017, the attack fell to the #7 spot. The new #3 position gives XSS (and SQL injection) a visibility that is justified. Who knows, maybe the next edition of the list will have XSS as its own category again, and SQL injection will be dropped completely.

16.1.5 #4: Insecure design

The first of the two community additions to the Top 10 list can be found at the #4 spot: "insecure design." This may mean that a web application is missing a few important aspects that are more closely related to architecture and process than to code:

- Threat modeling
- Security-focused user stories
- Plausibility checks everywhere
- A secure development life cycle, such as Microsoft's aptly named Secure Development Lifecycle (SDL)
- And more

Since this book puts its focus on writing secure applications, there are no chapters dedicated to this category. Also, the risks included in this item are not very tangible (one main point of criticism raised when the 2021 list was released). However, chapter 5 covered ASP.NET Core's approach to data validation, which is helpful. And chapter 15 introduced some ways to audit an application for security vulnerabilities. The

OWASP Top 10, as covered in this chapter, may serve as a to-do list for security assessments.

16.1.6   *#5: Security misconfiguration*

The #5 entry of the 2021 Top 10 list is 2017's #6 item: "security misconfiguration." To some degree, this relates to administrative aspects of the web application, like hardening the server (which is not part of this book). Yet, there are many security-related configuration options for ASP.NET Core that can be set within the application and should therefore be the developer's responsibility. These settings are sprinkled over many chapters, including cookie flags in chapters 2, 3, and 4. Chapter 9 focused on security-related HTTP headers, mitigating several kinds of risks. Properly handling secrets in configuration files was covered in chapter 8, and correct error handling (including a custom error page) was the topic of chapter 10.

Somewhat surprisingly, XML external entities (XXE) are now also part of this category. In the 2017 list, XXE had its own list entry (which a few people did not understand), and even got the #4 spot (which many people did not understand). Nevertheless, chapter 6 covers XXE and also explains why ASP.NET Core is protected by default.

16.1.7   *#6: Vulnerable and outdated components*

The #6 item on the list covers the risk of using components that are outdated and/or vulnerable. CWE item 1,104 is mapped to this category: "use of unmaintained third-party components." Chapter 14 discussed keeping dependencies up to date in great detail. Keeping control over the long list of explicit and implicit dependencies can be a major challenge, especially with some complex frontend frameworks.

16.1.8   *#7: Identification and authentication failures*

The #7 item on the list, and the two following ones, all have "failures" in their names. That has not always been the case; previously, this category was called "broken authentication" (mirroring #1, "broken access control"). No matter whether something is broken or a failure, it's a risk that needs to be mitigated. In this category, everything that can go wrong with authentication is covered, obviously overlapping a bit with the top item on the 2021 Top 10 list. Among the risks included are certain kinds of session attacks, such as session fixation and insufficient session expiration (covered in chapter 3) and weakly hashed passwords (covered in chapter 8 and overlapping with list item #2, "cryptographic failures," one more category name with "failures"). Authentication and authorization were also covered in great detail in chapters 12 and 13.

16.1.9   *#8: Software and data integrity failures*

The "software and data integrity failures" category is new to the 2021 OWASP Top 10, and kind of replaces "insecure deserialization," which also held the #8 spot on the list in 2017. The new category name is more general and therefore covers more CWEs (ten in total). The main idea of this new list item is that an application makes assumptions about other parts such as plugins or libraries, or about the build process (continuous delivery/continuous integration). Attacking the build pipeline, for instance, can inject code into the application even though the app's code is secure.

Chapter 5 covered secure deserialization of data, as well as mitigating mass assignment, which also falls into the "software and data integrity failures" category. A special kind of integrity check for JavaScript code was mentioned in chapter 2: Subresource Integrity, validating whether JavaScript (and CSS) files loaded from a page match a hash of the expected files.

> **NOTE** In case you are checking the CWE on the OWASP website and don't find "mass assignment" right away, it's CWE 915, hidden under the name of "improperly controlled modification of dynamically determined object attributes."

16.1.10 #9: Security logging and monitoring failures

The penultimate list entry was called "insufficient logging & monitoring" in the list of 2017 but was renamed to "something with failures" in 2021 (and also climbed up one position). As with the #4 item, "insecure design," this category is not as tangible as some of the others, since the obvious remedies—do log, do monitor—are not very specific. Still, chapter 11 introduced the ASP.NET Core options for logging and for health checks (which can contribute to a monitoring strategy).

16.1.11 #10: Server-side request forgery

The last item on the 2021 OWASP Top 10 List is server-side request forgery (SSRF). This attack is related to CSRF, but this time, the server is tricked into sending an unwanted HTTP request or accessing a resource via a URI. We have covered SSRF together with XXE in chapter 6.

This list item came from the community survey; it is the second list entry (after #4—"insecure design") that was not in the top eight derived from the data-driven approach. Based on the numbers alone, this risk would have never made the top ten, but it did reach the top spot in the survey, so it was added to the list. I personally doubt that it will stay: the attack is rare and hard to pull off, and there is only one CWE mapped. If all goes to plan, the next edition of the OWASP Top 10 will be released in 2024 (or 2025, judging by the last two lists), and I am already curious as to which changes will be seen then.

Further risks

The 2021 OWASP Top 10 also comes with a pseudoitem, #11—"next steps." This contains risks that just did not make the cut. The following three issues were identified:

- *Code quality issues*—Use of a static code analysis tool might help identify many of these.
- *Denial of service*—Hard to protect against, but it's vital to have monitoring in place.
- *Memory management errors*—Not as much of an issue in the ASP.NET Core world.

Table 16.1 provides a cross-reference between OWASP Top 10 items and the chapters that covered at least some aspects of each category.

Table 16.1   2021 OWASP Top 10 categories and book chapters

Category #	Name	Associated book chapters
1	Broken access control	4, 5, 12, 13
2	Cryptographic failures	3, 8
3	Injection	2, 6
4	Insecure design	5, 15, 16
5	Security misconfiguration	2, 3, 4, 6, 8, 9, 10
6	Vulnerable and outdated components	14
7	Identification and authentication failures	3, 8, 12, 13
8	Software and data integrity failures	2, 5
9	Security logging and monitoring failures	11
10	Server-side request forgery (SSRF)	6

Apart from the OWASP Top 10 for web applications, there are other Top 10 projects at OWASP, including one for APIs.

16.2   *OWASP API Top 10*

The release candidate for the 2017 OWASP Top 10 contained an item called "under-protected APIs." I did not find the adjective in Merriam-Webster's dictionary, although we all know what it means. Still, that category was dropped from the final version of the Top 10 in that year. The intention of adding the item was clear: not only the web applications per se should be protected, but also all of the APIs. There is certainly some overlap risk-wise, but there were enough differences for the OWASP to decide to create a new initiative: the OWASP API Security Project.

The project, located at https://owasp.org/www-project-api-security/, has so far issued one list of top 10 security risks for APIs—the OWASP API Security Top 10 of 2019. Looking at the list, we find many items that are also in the OWASP Top 10, or that at least exist there in a similar fashion. Without further ado, here is the list:

1 *Broken object level authorization*—This item is one half of "broken access control," the #1 item in the "regular" Top 10.

2 *Broken user authentication*—This category corresponds to #7, "identification and authentication failures," in the OWASP Top 10.

3 *Excessive data exposure*—APIs may return more data than expected, especially when query parameters are not property validated (see chapter 5).

4 *Lack of resources and rate limiting*—When providing an API, you need to monitor (and limit) resource usage (in part covered in chapter 11), and you may limit

the number of calls per time unit. When using Azure, for instance, the API Management platform can help with that (other clouds have similar offerings).

5 *Broken function level authorization*—The other half of "broken access control," together with "broken object level authorization."

6 *Mass assignment*—This attack is hidden in the #8 item of the OWASP Top 10, "software and data integrity failures," but got a category of its own in the API list.

7 *Security misconfiguration*—Configuration issues are prevalent in APIs and web applications, so this category shows up in both lists.

8 *Injection*—In the 2019 API list, this item does not include XSS (unlike the 2021 OWASP Top 10), which explains the relatively low position.

9 *Improper assets management*—This category includes old, deprecated API versions still available, or different API versions not being properly maintained and documented. This item is somewhat related to the OWASP Top 10's "vulnerable and outdated components" category.

10 *Insufficient logging and monitoring*—The final item in the API Top 10 is the penultimate one from the "regular" Top 10.

Just like the OWASP Top 10, the OWASP API Top 10 is an awareness document, so it may be used as part of a security strategy, but it does not provide (or claim to have) scientific scrutiny. The same thing also holds true for other lists available.

16.3 Other lists

The SANS Institute (www.sans.org/) is a company that provides various security services. Together with MITRE (remember—creators of CWE), they have created the CWE/SANS Top 25, currently also called the CWE/SANS TOP 25 Most Dangerous Software Errors. The list starts with the data found in the NIST National Vulnerability Database (NVD), maps it to MITRE's Common Vulnerability and Exposures (CVE; we briefly covered that in chapter 9), and then scores it with regard to prevalence and severity. The dedicated website at https://cwe.mitre.org/top25/index.html explains the methodology in much greater detail.

> **WARNING** There is also a Top 25 page on SANS' website, www.sans.org/ top25-software-errors/. However, at the time of this writing, this site still shows the list from 2019, so it would be better to refer to the MITRE page for up-to-date information.

The CWE/SANS Top 25 is much more generic than the OWASP Top 10 since it is not limited to web applications. Still, when you look at the categories in that list, as shown in the following 2021 edition, you'll see many items that are also part of the OWASP lists. For instance, XSS is at the #2 spot and CSRF is at #9:

1 Out-of-bounds write

2 Improper neutralization of input during web page generation (cross-site scripting)

3 Out-of-bounds read

4   Improper input validation

5   Improper neutralization of special elements used in an OS command (OS command injection)

6   Improper neutralization of special elements used in an SQL command (SQL injection)

7   Use after free

8   Improper limitation of a pathname to a restricted directory (path traversal)

9   Cross-site request forgery (CSRF)

10   Unrestricted upload of file with dangerous type

11   Missing authentication for critical function

12   Integer overflow or wraparound

13   Deserialization of untrusted data

14   Improper authentication

15   NULL pointer dereference

16   Use of hard-coded credentials

17   Improper restriction of operations within the bounds of a memory buffer

18   Missing authorization

19   Incorrect default permissions

20   Exposure of sensitive information to an unauthorized actor

21   Insufficiently protected credentials

22   Incorrect permission assignment for critical resource

23   Improper restriction of XML external entity reference

24   Server-side request forgery (SSRF)

25   Improper neutralization of special elements used in a command (command injection)

OWASP has yet another list project, this time for mobile applications. Its home page is at https://owasp.org/www-project-mobile-top-10/. Unfortunately, the last (and first) edition of the list came out in 2016, and there is currently no public schedule for the next release. OWASP provides two major offerings for mobile applications:

- *MSTG*—The OWASP Mobile Security Testing Guide
- MASVS—The OWASP Mobile Application Security Verification Standard (which can be tested against using MSTG)

It can therefore be expected that the OWASP Mobile Top 10 project will eventually be continued. Here is the 2016 list:

1   Improper platform usage

2   Insecure data storage

3   Insecure communication

4   Insecure authentication

5   Insufficient cryptography

6 Insecure authorization

7 Client code quality

8 Code tampering

9 Reverse engineering

10 Extraneous functionality

All of the preceding lists focus on risks rather than on actionable items. For a more checklist-like approach, the OWASP Application Security Verification Standard (ASVS) is a commonly used option. This project defines requirements that a web application needs to meet to be considered secure. ASVS defines three levels:

- *Level 1*—First steps
- *Level 2*—Applicable to most applications
- *Level 3*—High security

More information on ASVS can be found on the OWASP site at http://mng.bz/6XRA.

No matter which list(s) you use to create awareness for web application security, it is crucial that you know about risks and attacks and that you understand and implement countermeasures. With ASP.NET Core (and, forgive me for the self-praise, this book), you have all the tools required to mitigate those and other risks, no matter which list position they may have.

Summary

Let's review what we have learned so far:

- The Open Web Application Security Project provides heaps of offerings on web application security, from documentation over tools to events.
- The OWASP Top 10 is the de facto standard when it comes to listing web application security risks.
- The OWASP Top 10 is generated by compiling the results of security audits with feedback from a community survey.
- Each item on the OWASP Top 10 maps to at least one CWE item.
- Every chapter of this book touched upon at least one item on the 2021 OWASP Top 10.
- The OWASP API Top 10 project lists the top security risks for APIs.
- Other relevant lists in that space are the CWE/SANS Top 25 Most Dangerous Software Errors and the OWASP Mobile Top 10.
- The OWASP Application Security Verification Standard (ASVS) defines security requirements, in contrast to the other lists that collect risks.
- This is the end of the book. Thank you for buying it and reading along!

index